Worker Capitalism
The New Industrial Relations

Worker Capitalism
The New Industrial Relations

Keith Bradley and Alan Gelb

The MIT Press
Cambridge, Massachusetts

First MIT Press edition, 1983
First published by Heinemann Educational Books Ltd, 1983

Library of Congress catalog card number: 83-42521

ISBN 0-262-02191-0

Printed and bound in Great Britain

Contents

Preface

This book grew out of interdisciplinary research into plants bought by their workers to stave off closure and redundancy. Out of such studies emerged a common pattern suggesting an alternative form of industrial policy aimed at saving jobs (or at least slowing redundancy) and possibly regenerating firms. In some circumstances a state-assisted worker takeover strategy promised quite significant advantages over more conventional support measures directed at similar ends. It also seems well suited to the combination of (a) an uncertain economic environment so characteristic after the mid-1970s and (b) electoral pressures on representative-democratic governments to save jobs coupled with (c) the growing realisation that government cannot be expected to assume unlimited responsibility without longer-run consequences. A narrowly economic or political perspective, or one concerned exclusively with labor relations under employee ownership, seemed inadequate in attempting to assess worker buyouts as part of industrial policy. Accordingly, we have tried to synthesise these perspectives, perhaps at the cost of sometimes straying into less well charted territory or missing some signposts in our hurry. But it seemed best to sacrifice elegance for timeliness.

Some of the many to whom we are indebted would perhaps prefer to remain anonymous. However, we cannot avoid mentioning Michael Mann, David Lockwood, Robert Oakeshott, Meghnad Desai, Patrick Laurent, Serge Lord, Allister Blair and Tony King. All these have contributed materially to the present work, although we would not wish to burden them with responsibility for its inadequacies. Several gifted referees and participants at seminars in Britain, Canada and the United States have also made useful suggestions. We are indebted to a number of friends including Mary Braithwaite and Barbara Bruns for assistance in obtaining documents. And special thanks are due to Caroline and Nuria for their tolerance and encouragement during the writing of this book.

Finally, we wish to make it quite clear that the views expressed in this book are those of the authors and do not necessarily reflect those of the London School of Economics, the Wharton School or the World Bank.

March 1982

1 Introduction and Overview

Through the decade of the 1980s – and possibly beyond – industrial policy in the major western economies will almost surely confront greater and more subtle demands. The general trend since the early 1930s, and one especially noticeable since the end of World War II, has been for governments to respond to increasingly complex economic problems and to accept responsibility for an ever greater range of social objectives. In many respects this trend is unobjectionable; indeed, an increased emphasis on social factors may appear to be a laudable and natural evolution of the mixed economy-representative democracy model. Yet within such systems policy makers have found themselves attempting to reconcile progressively more diverse, but interrelated goals. Some objectives may reasonably be labelled as 'economic': growth rates of aggregate output, productive efficiency, and the alignment of economic structures with patterns of comparative advantage. Others are social by nature, reflecting the need to cushion the impact upon different regions, occupational and ethnic groups or classes, of rapid structural change.

At the intersection of economic imperatives and social claims lies the third set of goals – or perhaps constraints – those relating to the political process. While recent electoral swings towards a more conservative stance in the USA and Great Britain suggest dissatisfaction at attempts by 'interventionist' government to reconcile conflicting objectives over the 1970s, there are no panaceas in sight. Electoral pendula might swing the other way should voters become disillusioned. Rapid growth might help to lubricate the wheels of adjustment to shifting patterns of comparative advantage and technical change. But relative to the last decade the global economic outlook is gloomy. Social objectives remain, and are complemented by newly aroused environmental concerns. These considerations suggest a sequence of ever more acute dilemmas facing successive elected governments, whether of conservative or reformist bent.

To face the challenge, new forms of industrial policy are called for. These need to be directed particularly towards two objectives – the stimulation of employment and the furthering of productive efficiency. A fairly broad consensus appears to be emerging that simple repetition and extension of the measures of the 1950s, '60s and '70s will not suffice, although many past and current features of industrial policies will undoubtedly continue. But especially required seem policies to slow down the rate of loss of the industrial base in a number of traditionally industrialised countries and regions, and simultaneously to encourage a period of industrial 'regeneration'.

This book describes and analyses one alternative form of industrial intervention directed towards problems created by the shutdown of industrial plants. Besides steady erosion of national or regional manufacturing bases these problems include long-term worker redundancy and community decay. The policy alternative emphasises the potential contribution of changes in the structure of asset ownership in reconciling political, economic and social objectives. Certain declining firms convert, with state assistance, into wholly or partially employee-owned enterprises, or possibly to enterprises owned jointly by their workforces and local communities. Such a policy is seen as a potentially superior alternative, in certain cases, to more usual subsidisation or protective measures, and as a useful component, in some circumstances, of a program of 'reindustrialisation'.

Naturally, it is not intended to put forward changes in ownership structure as the sole cure for all industrial ills. In many cases nothing useful is likely to result from such a step, which anyway cannot deal with redundancy arising out of continuing operation of successful firms. Rather, asset restructuring is seen as a potentially useful measure when judiciously applied to problems of a specific nature.

It should be stressed that the rationale behind such a seemingly radical suggestion need not be primarily ideological. Neither need it hinge on any assumed long-term superiority of the cooperative form, nor of employee ownership over more conventional ownership/management structures in terms of productive efficiency. On these important issues, the stance adopted is only mildly positive – at least in intent. It is accepted that over the long term employee ownership may not be a stable organisational form for manufacturing industry. However, it is argued that within the mixed economy-representative democratic systems now prevailing in many mature industrialised countries, complete or partial worker takeovers of certain declining firms are not an unnatural response to threatened closure. If appropriately aided by government, these spontaneous responses may provide a useful supplement to methods of industrial support currently employed. Relative to conventional policies, the impact on efficiency of judicious industrial policy structured on such lines is likely to be favorable regardless of whether the firms assisted by such policy prove eventually to be viable. Employee ownership might be a transient, but useful, phase of reorganisation for ailing enterprises. And, by relieving social and political pressures for conventional measures which, in the long run, prove more damaging to a substantially free-enterprise economy, the strategy can assist to reconcile the institutions of free enterprise with those of representative democracy.

A generally 'preservationist' industrial policy is also not advocated. In the longer run, adjustment should proceed in the directions indicated by comparative advantage and technological change. Where would we be now had the steam engine been proscribed by mule-owners, or Luddite candlemakers succeeded in outlawing electric generating plants? From a narrowly economic viewpoint, policies to assist adjustment are to be preferred over those designed to preserve outmoded, archaic, industrial structures and 'lame duck' enterprises indefinitely. Representative-democratic political systems are seen, however, inevitably to evoke powerful conservationist sentiments and pressures to keep uncompetitive firms or industries alive. Such pressures are here taken as given. So is the observation that rapid shifts in comparative advantage or technology sometimes impose unduly harsh costs of adjustment on individual communities or regions. The problem facing mature industrial democracies may then be interpreted as that of accommodating social factors at minimal long-run economic cost given the mode of political representation.

Worker capitalism arouses strong emotions over much of the political spectrum. To prevent misunderstanding, it is as well to delineate the subject of this book at an early stage. Its central theme is not the establishment of new employee-owned firms (or cooperatives as they tend to be termed in Britain), or the analysis of specific organisational rules. Neither is it the performance of cooperative economy, such as the Yugoslav. The pros and cons of workplace democracy are not central to the subject either, although the prospects for cooperative type firms, and the view of the worker management held by broader society, are important. Rather, the central theme is industrial policy working through a particular route – that of worker-management buy-outs – to employee ownership. Worker ownership and control have many possible dimensions, some of which are virtually unrelated to each other. Employee ownership may be complete or partial. Worker shareholding can be direct or beneficial, concentrated or dispersed over the workforce. Employee ownership might spread over a spectrum of assets from ordinary shares to preferential shares or bonds or other liabilities of the enterprise. Joint ownership with a local community is an alternative to teaming-up with a capitalist. There is also a fine and uncertain line between employee-owned firms and worker co-operatives. Ownership patterns may not be directly reflected either in job control or in influence over broad decisions of the firm. Substantial worker influence may not, either, be mirrored in substantial employee equity as commonly defined. In practice, a wide variety of institutional arrangements is possible and has been observed – yet certain features general to industrial policy operating through worker (or employee-community) ownership emerge as common to such a broad set of institutional arrangements.

In this book, the terms 'employee-owned firm' and 'worker co-operative' are used rather loosely, for want of a better alternative. By theoretical standards some of the case studies analyzed below are not worker-owned firms. Few can be considered to be (or to have been) enterprises whose nonmanagerial workers actually exert a determining influence on important decisions. However, in a number of respects including the rhetorical, the examples have considerable commonality. Further, the transitions from conventional firm to some form of worker ownership as analyzed in this book exhibit a common trend, which for present purposes is more important than the precise pattern of owner-ship and control after the transition. Here what is intended by 'worker ownership' is a form of industrial organisation where, generally speak-ing, at least a part of the equity is owned by members of its workforce who also assume a considerable degree of responsibility for the com-mercial survival of 'their' enterprise, although they may have little formal control. This terminology should not be permitted to obscure the large differences in ownership and control structures among the various examples, and between these and 'true' cooperatives or em-ployee-owned enterprises. The organisational structure after the tran-sition might well influence the commercial success of the enterprise through its effect on labor relations. It certainly influences the sub-sequent evolution of ownership patterns assuming a successful enter-prise.

To date, conversion of declining enterprises to employee ownership is not included in the arsenal of industrial policy measures routinely employed by any major Western economy. The ideologically conser-vative United States has probably come closest to introducing a policy resembling that advocated here. Although this may seem surprising, any paradox vanishes once it is realised that a major obstacle to assessing the 'pragmatic' potential of worker takeovers is the ideol-ogical controversy surrounding worker control. This, understandably, is more acute in Britain than in the US because ideological polarisation is stronger there. But at the other extreme, in terms of size, the tiny economy of Malta has seen imaginative application of employee-par-ticipation strategies, admittedly in rather unusual circumstances.

Paralleling the absence of institutionalisation, there appears not to have been an assessment of the potential of such policies from a national perspective, although cost-benefit analyses from the viewpoint of local communities have been carried out in the USA for several cases. Any national assessment of a form of industrial policy cannot actually proceed straightforwardly from a formal economic cost-benefit anal-ysis, in view of the importance of the political dimension. Suppose we take as given electoral pressure to slow the rate of industrial collapse or limit the speed of economic restructuring. The issue, then, is not always whether encouraging a worker takeover is socially or economically preferable to the policy alternative of doing nothing. The latter may not be a realistic action given the political environment. A more appropriate comparison would include the costs of other policies likely to be invoked through the political process in the event that an employee takeover is not permitted to fulfil this role.

Appreciable numbers of *ad hoc* examples of employee takeover conversions have been documented in several countries. Undetermined but large numbers have occurred in the US, France and Italy. Several Canadian and British cases are known, and at least one in Australia. In the broad circumstances surrounding such takeovers, there is a surprising degree of similarity, although a more detailed look reveals significant differences in the profitability and prospects of the converted enterprises, in institutional arrangements for assisting the conversion, in the eventual configurations of ownership and control and in the commercial success of the reconstituted firms with their new ownership structures. As is argued here, the parallelism of cases across countries is not coincidental. It reflects rational accommodation, within existing socioeconomic systems, to widespread and common economic imperatives. Worker takeovers of declining firms have not aimed at undermining existing political and economic arrangements, but represent a quite conservative response. Current institutional arrangements are not now sympathetic to this form of accommodation in any major country. In the UK at least, the ideological reaction to worker control similarly inhibits a sympathetic response.

Might there not be advantages, nationally as well as locally, in facilitating spontaneous impulses towards employee ownership rather than hindering them? This argument is developed in the remainder of this book; in the rest of the present chapter some central points are briefly summarised.

Structural problems facing major developed economies have recently received increasing attention. Particularly troublesome appear to be the rate of loss of manufacturing jobs, and regional stresses caused by industrial relocation. In the United States, Britain and certain European countries, the need for 'reindustrialisation' receives ever growing attention and publicity. In the long run, structural change in the manufacturing sector is not merely desirable, but vital to ensure sustained competitiveness, especially with industry in Japan and the newly industrialising countries. Traditional industrial centers must accommodate the growth of new industrial powers, new products and changing technology. But the short to medium run sees increasing resistance to structural change. High costs inflicted on politically powerful social groups by adjustment are reflected, through the political process, in regulations aiming to limit the speed of change in general, and rates of industrial closure in particular. Such measures may not encourage the regeneration of industries over a rather broad spectrum – the ultimate objective of the new reindustrialisation thrust – but are likely to lower efficiency, leading to renewed need for assistance.

Policies to slow and prevent industrial collapse are hardly in short supply. In all major economies 'conventional' policies operating at the level of the firm, the industrial sectors or on individuals, include all or most of the following: protection by tariffs, quotas or other restrictions on foreign competition, sector, firm and region-specific subsidisation, investment incentives and subsidisation of specified factors of production. Such 'conservative' measures are complemented by policies designed to facilitate adjustment: relocation allowances, retraining schemes and advance notice of major redundancy, to name but three. Their total impact, while welcome, is small relative to the need for adjustment.

It is analytically convenient to distinguish two categories of closures. Firstly, the potential competitive position of a firm may be sufficiently strong, given certain theoretically attainable internal changes, for a serious rescue attempt to be desirable. The issue, then, is how to structure intervention to promote such changes. These frequently will require improving labor relations or surmounting institutional constraints to internal factor allocation which have hampered efficient operation. Bankruptcy, or threat thereof, may be insufficient to induce these changes. Secondly, market forces may be such that from an economic viewpoint the firm should clearly close. But the political power of groups adversely affected by closure may render it difficult for government to avoid some measure of assistance.

In both circumstances industrial policy operating through employee buyouts can offer advantages. In the first instance, it can promote reorganisation and lead to improved efficiency. This is valuable, too, in the second case, particularly since it is not always easy to classify cases, *ex ante*, into one of these two categories given an uncertain economic environment. But additionally, in the second case, providing employees with 'one last chance', conditional upon their accepting a certain measure of responsibility, gives government a later opportunity to say that 'not much more can be done', alleviating the cumulation of pressure for support over time.

More specifically, when compared to conventional 'conservative' measures, the suggested policy of employee takeover offers three advantages. Conventional policies, firstly, are apt to become permanent and institutionalised, although in many cases they are initially conceived and promoted as temporary palliatives. The policy described here has powerful built-in, self-liquidating characteristics, making it more difficult for successive rounds of subsidisation to cumulate across the economy. A useful 'cooling-out' period is provided to government on the collapse of major, or at least locally important, firms. During this stressful period a constructive resolution of the basic imperative – the need to slow or avoid redundancy – may proceed without committing the state to interventions liable to become open-ended.

Secondly, a policy operating through employee takeovers relies on the generation of consensus for its successful implementation. Indeed, the execution of industrial policy may itself represent a powerful consensus-creating mechanism. The importance of consensus in facilitating efficient operation and its potential impact on production performance is strongly suggested by the spurt of Japanese and West German industry following the Second World War. Divided, alienated elements of an industrial enterprise cannot hope to match the performance of internally cohesive units in full agreement over enterprise goals. This element of the policy is therefore especially relevant to the need to 'reindustrialise'. Such a task is made far easier by an improvement in the climate of labor relations. This renders such major declining industrial regions as the UK and the Northeast 'graybelt' of the US more attractive to investment.

Thirdly, an important and distinctive feature of industrial policy of the present kind is a shift of responsibility away from central government, and towards those parties most directly and seriously affected by the collapse. Decentralisation of responsibility and of the details of decision-making proceeds to employees and local authorities concerned for the loss of their tax bases. These groups may be augmented by creditors, suppliers, dealers and merchants dependent for trade on the survival of the economy local to the collapsing firm. Nevertheless, central government does not abdicate overall control of the conversion to worker ownership. The degree of influence needed to maintain a continued public presence is ensured through the financial weakness of such enterprises during their transitions. This renders the government role a vital one.

Despite decentralisation government does not disclaim ultimate social responsibility for sections of the population adversely affected by the winds of economic change. On the contrary, industrial policy of the kind explored in this book is motivated by a perception that the state will increasingly be called on to live up to such responsibility. Rather, the details of *how* accommodation to change is to proceed – whether through the closure of an industrial plant and the reallocation of labor and capital to other uses and locations, partial redundancy, a reduction in payments across the workforce or reorganisation and improved efficiency – is left outside direct central government decision-making.

Government may often need to provide specialised services to assist in the drawing-up and assessment of the spectrum of alternatives facing a workforce about to be made redundant. In this respect, the role of public agencies may not be too different from that conventionally played at present. But decentralised decision-making replaces remote administrative control by pseudomarket interaction between individuals and groups affected by closure. This promotes efficient operation of assisted enterprises. It also contributes to the appropriate self-selection of employees to be kept in jobs by government.

In one important respect the resource-allocating potential of the policy may actually *exceed* that of the market. Firm closure frequently has adverse consequence for suppliers, merchants producing 'local' goods and services for sale to its workforce, distributors, municipalities dependent on the firm for revenues, and so forth. When, as is not infrequent, an element of commercial failure can be attributed to poor labor relations, disputes between groups A and B in the firm diminish not only their own job prospects but also those of group C outside it. Many instances of closure might not have occurred were these 'local pecuniary externalities' institutionally able to influence firm and employee behavior patterns. But the policy of conversion to worker ownership internalises such externalities to a considerable extent.

Case studies show that the extent and form of government involvement may vary considerably among cases of employee takeover. Such differences are not random. Government involvement, in the form of equity participation loans, or loan guarantees, is likely to be larger the more urgent are the social imperatives and immediate political pressures to avoid redundancy and the weaker is the underlying position of the affected firm. These differences account, in good part, for the greater degree of central government involvement in worker takeovers in Britain relative to the US. Not all industrial collapses involve clearly unprofitable enterprises. Many plant closures in smaller industrial centers of the northeastern US have occurred through corporate divestiture of apparently moderately profitable subsidiaries unable to meet high target rates of return, rather than clearly 'dead end' firms. A notable exception to the pattern (since it involved the entire corporation) was the rescue operation mounted for the ailing auto-giant Chrysler. The 'Chrysler Corporation Loan-Guarantee Act of 1979' and the process of negotiation leading up to it bear a considerable resemblance to the alternative policy elaborated below. Although heavily criticised the Chrysler strategy may offer substantial advantages over forms of assistance routinely conceded to other American and British industries.

In marked contrast to the majority of US cases, the most prominent examples of employee takeover in the UK have involved exceptionally weak firms which received limited support from the 1974 Labour government during a period of extreme political stress. This difference in the structural characteristics of firms undergoing conversion to cooperatives in the two countries is mirrored in the greater involvement of central government in the UK and in the dismal survival record of the British 'cooperatives' relative to that of their American counterparts. Yet commercial failure of enterprises assisted by government does not necessarily imply errors in industrial policy. As observed below, an appreciable probability of failure of the assisted enterprises is almost inevitable. Indeed, a one hundred percent success rate would suggest that the markets for financial capital and management expertise were seriously defective, unless the efficiency gains from cooperative organisation were truly immense. And, in this case, employee ownership would be expected to have become a dominant mode of industrial organisation rather than remaining a curiosity.

The probability of failure attached to government-assisted worker takeover may be viewed as an indicator of the social benefit/cost ratio of intervention as perceived by government through the political process relative to the private benefit/cost ratio. The latter ratio measures the intrinsic commercial appeal of the assisted enterprise as measured by private capital. The British examples merely point to one end of a spectrum – high political relative to market imperatives – whereas many US cases highlight the other extreme. At all points on such a spectrum, the employee takeover strategy may, however, prove to be a cost-effective tool for reconciling economic, political and social goals.

Corresponding to this difference in position on the political versus market-imperative spectrum, and to greater ideological conflict in the UK relative to the US, is a marked divergence in the way in which the conversion to cooperatives is viewed. The US perspective is essentially pragmatic. Here, 'pragmatic' is used in a specific sense: it indicates a response or action undertaken within the accepted constraints of the existing economic system, generally for direct financial or managerial advantage. Pragmatic employee takeovers aim to prevent or slow redundancy and to preserve dependent communities. Ideological questions related to worker control barely figure in US legislative debate, which centers instead on the desirability of the state becoming involved in the free-enterprise system at all. Employee takeovers are emphasised for their role in correcting failures in capital and managerial markets. An undue emphasis on this function, however, necessarily assigns them a peripheral role in industrial policy. In Britain, on the other hand, the ideological debate surrounding worker takeovers has obscured their origin as an accommodative response to stress within the established social, political and economic system, and their managerial potential. In assessing the strategy from a national perspective, partial views, whether American or British, should be avoided.

The present work aims to analyze political and economic facets of the worker takeover strategy and to relate it to labor relations and the situation of affected individuals. The approach adopted is a blend of theoretical inference and empirical study with the objective of isolating commonality and drawing out its relevance for policy. Although cases are described, this is *not* a compendium of case studies or a detailed 'how to do it' manual. Descriptive material is deliberately kept concise. The specific institutions to effect transitions and the precise form of asset restructuring will be molded by (a) national and local characteristics, (b) the particular case under consideration and (c) the political situation prevailing at the time of conversion. Every case is likely to differ in important respects. For this reason some abstraction is required from the details of individual cases to express the phenomenon in general terms. The modest attempt here is to describe a suggested strategy and to investigate its conceptual underpinning.

To demonstrate the need for new and innovative strategies a review of present difficulties facing those responsible for shaping industrial policy is presented in Chapter 2. The chapter outlines constraints seen to be central in limiting the scope of feasible policy alternatives and the limits to resolving problems. The following chapter develops a theory to explain the source of spontaneous pressures towards employee takeovers as observed in a wide variety of circumstances across several countries. A formal model of this process is presented in the Annex. A number of conversions to employee ownership is presented in Chapter 4, where the main features of the process leading to worker ownership are outlined. This synthesis is necessary to understand the extent to which individual cases conform to a general pattern consistent with the theory advanced in the previous chapter despite their significant divergences.

Although cases display considerable commonality across countries, the general view of workers taking over their closing plants differs considerably between Britain and the US, with a more sympathetic, less ideologically polarised view prevailing in the latter country. This has had important repercussions for legislative developments. Chapter 5 attempts to explain the different perspectives with a view to clarifying the potential policy role of state-assisted worker buyouts, and reviews comparative legislation. In overall assessment, the general principles of implementing the worker takeover strategy as industrial policy, and the criteria by which it may be judged, are addressed in Chapter 6. Relative to present policies, the strategy is seen to represent a form of social compromise. This has advantages and drawbacks for various social groups and organisations. These are weighed from the perspectives of workers, capitalists, trade unions, the government and 'society.' Government, it could be noted at the outset, is here assumed to possess a broadly similar set of interests and objectives to 'society', but at particular conjunctures these diverge quite markedly. At critical times government becomes more partial to certain interests and lays greater stress on outcomes in the near future than would be appropriate as judged by true social criteria.

The final two chapters offer descriptive and analytical case studies to ground the theory in empirical reality. Chapter 7 describes briefly a number of employee takeover case studies in the US, Canada and France which can be considered to have been commercially successful, although not generally leading to true worker control. These have been selected to display the diversity of circumstances, outcomes and institutional arrangements, as well as to illustrate parallelism across the cases. Chapter 8 presents a more extensive analysis of a takeover that ended in dismal commercial failure. Such an example permits advantages of the intervention method to be illustrated despite an unfavorable context, and therefore provides a more rigorous testing ground.

Philadelphia has lost at least 40,000 manufacturing jobs in the last ten years, and Pittsburgh and other cities in Pennsylvania have suffered similar losses. New England's manufacturing employment has declined nine percent in the last ten years and that of the Mid-West declined 14 percent between 1960 and 1965. New Jersey has lost 115,000 factory jobs since 1969 and heavily industrialized regions like Michigan and Ohio lost nearly 200,000 each in plant shutdowns in relatively the same period.[1]

Employment Protection in the 1980s

The policy spectrum

Production is too politically important an activity to be left solely to the private sector. National public intervention into commodity-producing activities dates back at least to the emergence of the modern nation state. Before Adam Smith this may not have been surprising. But in most developed Western economies, mercantilist doctrines have long been superseded by economic theories emphasising the general superiority of the market over alternative forms of economic organisation. The web of regulation in most industrialised societies has nevertheless tended to increase in scope and intricacy. To attempt to fully document the ways in which industrial policy is effected, to account for their evolution and assess the consequences would be a task far beyond the scope and intent of this book and the competence of its authors. Yet, a brief discussion of certain features of conventional industrial policies is necessary to establish a perspective from which the policy of cooperation, described in this book, may be judged. Also relevant is the relationship between closures of industrial units and possible elements of organisational failure in conventionally-owned enterprises.

The set of actions conventionally included under the heading of 'industrial policy' is truly an extensive one. A partial list would include[2] (a) antitrust and competition policy, which generally has the goal of controlling restrictive business practices; (b) technological policy, to promote research and development activity nationally; (c) regional policy, aimed at reducing spatial imbalances in economic activity; (d) adjustment policy, whose goal is to facilitate the adjustment of industrial structures to changes impelled by the forces of demand, changing technology and those of foreign competition; (e) environmental and associated policies aiming to protect the quality of life and work, and consumer safety; (f) interventions connected with national security, public goods and large-scale risky projects for which private capital and entrepreneurial markets may not function adequately; and (g) regulation directed towards other, generally social, objectives. This last class of regulation, in particular, has come to include increasingly detailed legislation which substantially influences the pace and pattern of change in industry and agriculture. The broad objective of a great deal of such intervention is to insulate adversely affected individuals and societal groups from the vicissitudes of market forces. Measures specifically or indirectly designed to support failing industries and collapsing firms are one class of such policies of special interest in the present context.

Mounting controversy: a search for alternatives

In most respects the ultimate goals of industrial policies are both morally defensible and realised through political mechanisms which for present purposes are taken as legitimate. The objective, then, is not to argue against industrial policy *per se*. Yet, the well-intentioned policy framework has increasingly become a source of concern and controversy. Pagoulatos and Sorenson (1980) suggest that this can ultimately be traced to the combination of three factors. Firstly, the theoretical basis underlying the desire for intervention and selection of appropriate techniques is of limited operational value. Secondly, information on the favorable effects of specific policy measures is scarce. Thirdly, there is evidence in some cases of significant policy-induced distortions. The various consequences of intervention are indeed difficult to measure under the best circumstances. More commonly, it is almost impossible to assess whether industrial policies fulfil their objectives, in no small measure because of the general lack of coherence which is seen to characterise their formulation and execution.

This tendency for policies to conflict with each other, in turn, stems partly from the origin of much industrial legislation in compromise and partly from the sequential nature of policy evolution. It is easier to introduce new measures in response to political pressures than to systematically alter a wide range of past legislation. In this way successive rounds of policy are introduced to counteract side effects of preceding regulation. Because policy also has symbolic value in demonstrating the willingness of government to do something, when in reality little constructive action is envisaged, the *real* objectives of much conflicting legislation are not apparent. Consequently, despite the fact that in a number of countries public documents lay out in a clear and relatively coherent manner the goals and framework within which policy should proceed,[3] in many instances what actually occurs is closer to a sequence of *ad hoc* interventions, sometimes working at cross-purposes.

In such institutional circumstances, it is not surprising that many observers consider attempts by government to intervene into industry to be self-defeating and contradictory. The search for realistic alternatives must, however, depart from the concerns of present policy and the institutional circumstances of policy-making, unless the real objective is to argue for fundamental political and social change. This chapter contends that present forms of industrial intervention are ill-suited to the particular postwar combination of (a) post-Keynesian concern with equalising *ex post* incomes, (b) a stochastic economic environment and (c) volatile political pressures sometimes provoked by industrial crises. It is relative to these concerns and institutional constraints that the advantages, in some circumstances, of the cooperative policy form over more conventional policies are developed in subsequent chapters.

Post-Keynesian Industrial Policy

Growth, structural change and the conservative social welfare function
Employment maintenance is naturally a prime instrumental variable through which efforts are made to maintain income levels. In principle, political pressure directed towards preserving jobs could act in two ways. On the one hand, pressures could point in the direction of encouraging new industries and opportunities. On the other, they could assume a 'preservationist' stance opposing plant shutdowns, relocations and redundancy. Simple economic theory provides no reason for the latter thrust to dominate. But, in practice, the power asymmetry between actually and potentially organised employee groups and firms, and between present versus hypothetical communities, lends a strongly conservative bias to attempts to preserve jobs. This bias then effectively translates into the preservation of *existing* jobs. As employment has become a more pressing problem in most industrial countries since 1974, it is not surprising that a tendency to greater intervention dates from this time.[4] It seems appropriate, however, to see in this a confirmation of an underlying trend over the entire postwar period rather than a fundamental about-face away from laissez-faire policy.

The trend appears to have involved increasing resistance to structural change. By the mid-1960s the outlook seemed assured for the Western market economy model. General prosperity and a perception that growth was capable of substantially resolving the contradictions of capitalism were reflected in the orientation of much debate in the social sciences. Emphasis in Britain, for example, shifted away from the 'class struggle' and towards 'pragmatic acceptance' of the existing socio-economic order, as described in Chapter 5. But even during its heyday the rapid growth of the 1950s and 1960s was not uncontroversial, as market economies were forced to accommodate to significant changes. In all countries, growth required rapid structural shifts in the allocation of investment and labor. The components of structural change may be considered as demand-driven, technological and regional.

Responding to Engel's law – the effect of growing incomes and demographic change in shifting demand patterns, the composition of output shifted from agriculture towards services. Over 1950–76, the former saw its share of GDP decrease from 16 to 6 percent in the major industrial countries while the latter expanded its share from 43 to 53 percent. Industry's share held firm at about 41 percent.

Meanwhile, in response to differential rates of technological change, labor productivity increased most rapidly in agriculture and least in services. This amplified the sectoral shift of labor relative to output. In Austria, Belgium, West Germany, the Netherlands, Sweden, Switzerland and the United Kingdom, industrial employment peaked in the mid-1960s.[5] It declined in almost all industrialised countries over the 1970s, even as, within individual sectors, the profile of job composition swung from largely blue- to substantially white-collar occupations. Over 1965–74, the number of men employed in British industry fell by 14 percent, despite, or perhaps because of, higher labor productivity growth than in the previous decade.[6]

Regional employment shifts towards the West and the Sun Belt were especially marked in the US. Between 1970 and 1977, for example, the number of jobs in New York State fell by 6.4 percent whereas employment grew by 37 percent in the Mountain States.[7] Various reasons have been advanced to account for the magnitude of these shifts, including a desire to escape unionisation, spatial congestion and high rents in traditional urban areas, and tax incentives offered by industry-hungry states. The decline of the industrial base in the UK, and a perception in the US of a manufacturing sector steadily falling behind those of international competitors, led, from the mid-1970s onwards, to concern in both countries with 'deindustrialisation' and the associated need for policy to encourage 'reindustrialisation'.[8]

Despite the apparent flexibility, the postwar period saw the steady introduction of policies and institutions to attenuate free market forces into the more developed market economies. The process proceeded in parallel with increasing shares of government in national expenditures. Between 1955 and 1980, for example, the US federal government budget increased from 20 to 35 percent of GDP. In the UK central government raised its share of GDP from 35 to 50 percent over 1955–76. Transfer payments, in particular, expanded spectacularly. In the US, for example, shifting of income from the active to the non-active population was evidenced by a dramatic increase in the ratio of transfers to wages, and salaries from 8 percent in 1970 to 20 percent in 1980.

Similar trends are observable in most industrialised economies. They can be interpreted as signifying a fairly general shift in political and social preferences towards a greater degree of insulation from the market. Government in the 1970s was *expected* to play a larger role in this respect than in the 1950s. 'Social' factors thus provided an increasingly strong source of legitimation for the consolidation of special interest groups and signalled a trend towards pressure group politics.

The growth of regulation

In the process of shifting responsibility for the maintenance of income levels from private individuals and institutions to government, a complex overlapping network of programs, regulations, services and institutions has been created in most industrialised economies. Certain European countries, notably Italy and the UK, lead the US by a considerable margin in the extent and coverage of such programs. Restrictive manpower legislation, subsidisation of ailing industries or outright nationalisation is considerably more advanced in the former countries. In the policy environment of the 1970s, it was indeed difficult to fire an Italian worker, even for absenteeism or incompetence. Workers able to prove unlawful dismissal (which, apparently, is not too difficult) stood to collect substantial compensation from their former employer. Across countries, the emphasis of policy seems to relate somewhat systematically to the preferences of policy 'consumers'. West Germany, for example, with a higher tolerance of structural change, has, so far, accepted more readily the maintenance of market discipline in the pattern of its industrial interventions. British policy, on the other hand, while maintaining *formally* an overriding concern for the 'viability' of enterprises assisted by government, has placed much emphasis on social considerations in practice, and limited the speed with which economic restructuring should occur.[9] Recent leftward swings in Europe make it difficult to judge whether Thatcherite policy experiments and Reaganomics represent a break with postwar trends or a temporary aberration to be scotched at the polls.

Britain relies heavily on industrial subsidies, redundancy payments and unemployment compensation to cushion closures and partially insulate affected individuals from the consequences. Relative to the US, government rescue of failing firms has been quite common: at the other end of the spectrum, in Italy rescue might be viewed as standard practice. Over 1975–79 the number of British jobs protected by selective subsidisation could have averaged one million,[10] although this may be an overestimate. Relatively generous notice and redundancy allowances did not noticeably diminish resistance to structural change

or prevent the Trades Union Congress from advocating that all redundancies need have the approval of the Department of Employment.
So far this initiative has not succeeded.

Relative to most European countries, the US currently boasts little
legislation dealing with plant shutdowns. In this field, policy formulation has been noticeably *ad hoc*, with special emphasis on the impact
of freer trade on domestic employment: only the Trade Adjustment
Assistance Programs have been of any real magnitude, as is shown in
Table 2.1.

Table 2.1   Major US employee protection programs: selected program data[11]

Program	Period	Number of persons served	Cumulative expenditures
Trade Adjustment Assistance (1974)	thru 7/79	481,476	$765.4M
Redwoods (1978)	thru 10/79	2,197	12.2M
Urban Mass Transit	1964 thru 12/74	n/a	1.3M
AMTRACK (1970)	thru 1977	19,890	42.5M
CONRAIL (1973)	thru 11/79	40,379	187.3M

Legislation proposed at federal and state levels plus the rise in
transfer payments, does, however, suggest a long-term trend towards
'Europeanisation' – a perception that uncompensated job loss is below
the 'social minimum' to which employees are entitled.[12] As in Europe,
responsibility for the adverse effects stemming from economic dislocation has over the long term increasingly been seen to lie with government.

At the same time, such developments have not obscured fairly
general recognition of the danger of reducing the capacity of major
industrial economies to respond to market forces. Lip service to a
'competitive ideal' has managed to coexist with the trend towards
regulation. The tension between system ideology and reality has itself
caused a variety of inconsistencies. Governments, for example, are apt
to accept the strictures of Common Market or Tokyo Round negotiations, and then introduce less transparent (therefore frequently more
intricate) legislation to substitute for forms of intervention newly
outlawed. The lack of transparency then complicates further the task of
assessing the impact of regulation.

Government: The Social Insurer

The increased post-Keynesian public responsibility briefly outlined above as evolving over the last three decades – comprehensive and specific in terms of industries, regions and even individuals – differs significantly in nature from that theoretically assumed by the state during the 'Keynesian revolution'. The classic role of Keynesian government was to maintain *aggregate* effective demand and, by promoting an environment conducive to economic activity, at least assure widespread access, *ex ante*, to employment. The shift of emphasis towards equalising *ex post* incomes and working conditions has increasingly cast central government in a different role: that of social insurer. This has increasingly forced the state to provide insurance of a kind not generally available from private sources.

Dreze (1979) notes the paramount limitations to the extension of private insurance markets to be transactions costs (the resources required to effect trade in the relevant risks), adverse selection (the tendency for only self-admitting bad risks to take out policies) and moral hazard. Although the administrative costs of government are hardly trivial, the first two factors are probably less significant in the present context than the third, which applies to cases where the degree of risk is, to some extent, affected by behavior which, in turn, may change if insurance is offered. Arrow's 1965 observation is equally applicable to organisations as to individuals:

> The insurance policy might itself change incentives and therefore the probabilities upon which the insurance company has relied. Thus, a fire insurance policy for more than the value of the premises might be an inducement to arson or at least to carelessness.[13]

Insurance companies therefore do not protect students against inadequate grades, employees against lack of promotion or, in general, companies against bankruptcy. For, except when overall macroeconomic conditions are truly exceptional, it is almost impossible to separate out the exogenous component of failure from internal, endogenous causes. Insurance companies – and here the government is included as a potential insurer – cannot reasonably be expected to have the intimate knowledge of each enterprise, of market conditions, the behavior of competitors, missed opportunities, production techniques and so forth, to separate the deserving cases from the less deserving.

This problem is especially intractable given the strong incentive to management and other employees not to provide accurate information to the agents of an insurer. It should be recalled that one of the principal reasons advanced for the very existence of firms – as opposed merely to market relationships between individuals – is the richness of internal information flows relative to external communications.[14] Thus, failure to graft the objectives of government onto the internal goals set by firm-level decision makers has been seen as a major source of the failure of industrial policy in the UK.[15]

Factors limiting the expansion of private insurance to cover bankruptcy or closure and consequent job loss may, alternatively, be described in terms of leakage, monitoring constraints and X-inefficiency. Leakage refers to the appropriation of a portion of subsidy by firms or individuals not genuinely in need, and results from the difficulty of monitoring and distinguishing exogenous influences from endogenous behavior. The consequences of subsidisation may consequently be perverse. By relaxing the market constraint on firm behavior, public assistance may also remove the only barrier to cumulating X-inefficiency. Cost curves of assisted firms may rise far above their potential levels in the absence of actual or potential support.[16] Public assistance then is converted into firm-specific rent, possibly in the form of greater monetary rewards, possibly in the form of leisure. That levels of industrial efficiency can, indeed, vary widely between almost identical plants is attested by much empirical study.[17]

It should be noted that the *sequential process* associated with a particular form of industrial intervention is central to its adverse effects on X-efficiency. As observed by Corden (1974) and Martin (1978), in a timeless framework involving all economic feedbacks (the static general equilibrium model) subsidisation of one sector necessarily implies taxation of another. Unless the response is presumed to be asymmetric between taxed and subsidised groups, there is no presumption that overall X-efficiency will rise or fall, even if subsidisation is perceived as affecting management incentive, and hence efficiency. Static analyses, however, obscure the fact that subsidies motivated by a conservative social welfare function in an uncertain environment are normally granted *ex post* on the basis of perceived necessity rather than *ex ante*, so that observed behavior becomes crucial in determining eligibility. X-efficiency then is reduced through the moral hazard effect.

Casting industrial policy increasingly in the role of social insurance serves to illuminate the dilemma faced by policy makers in the 1980s. Traditional policies directed towards industrial job preservation run into two sets of difficulties depending on their degree of selectivity. On the one hand, aggregate macroeconomic policies, generally involving increased deficit spending or accommodating monetary policy, are inappropriate to the new selective social welfare function. As the problem faced by specific regions, sectors and firms may not be primarily due to a deficiency of aggregate demand, such measures, if combined with a less flexible economy, are likely to result in accelerating inflation, little easing of 'structural' unemployment and failure to appease political pressure groups. On the other hand, more selective policies run into the difficulties described above as limiting the extension of insurance markets. They then threaten, over the longer run, to subvert the behavior of actors in the market economy, in this way undermining its operation.

A Vicious Circle: Outlook for the 1980s?

Growth and intervention
The assignment of responsibility to government combined with the power of a conservative social welfare function threatens to subvert a variety of policies whose objective is that of assisting smooth adjustment. One recent OECD study, for example, suggests that governments have too often used adjustment assistance programs to provide complicated income support schemes. Such programs have done little to ease the underlying problems of industrial adjustment for ailing industries.[18] It is not hard to point to temporary policies which become institutionalised. Consider the 1961 Short-Term Arrangement on Cotton Textiles, which evolved into the Long-Term Arrangement Regarding International Trade in Cotton Textiles. In 1973 it simply became the Arrangement Regarding International Trade in Cotton Textiles. Twenty years after 1961 the Multifibers Arrangement was still alive – and in some ways more restrictive than its predecessors.

Sequential short-term pressures by groups adversely affected by economic circumstances may therefore cumulate to undermine the market economy, replacing it with layer over layer of frequently contradictory administrative controls. One consequence of such policies, substantially designed to maintain 'acceptable' levels of wages and benefits, increase individual job security, protect vulnerable industries and firms, supplement the incomes of those without employment and achieve a measure of regional and ethnic equality, has undoubtedly been to place a brake on the speed with which the market economy is able to operate. In particular, it may now be far harder in a number of countries for economic forces to shift labor and capital from activities where demand is declining to activities where demand is increasing. This tendency for market forces to be inhibited through the political process is quite widely seen as fundamental to the argument that economic growth will remain substantially slower over the 1980s than previously.

It is probably not feasible to attain again the pace of productivity growth achieved over the 1955–70 period . . . not so much in any physical limits to growth, but rather in the social limits to growth that we have built into our laws and institutions. In a sense the OECD societies have chosen to slow the pace of economic progress traditionally defined and measured, and tried to redirect the pattern of economic progress to one that better respects a variety of nonmarket values. At the same time they have attempted to better shield individuals and families from the vicissitudes of economic change . . . It well may be that the OECD societies in their moves to protect other values have hindered the ability of their economies to achieve more conventional kinds of productivity growth to a greater extent than they bargained.[19]

For some decades now, programs and agencies to aid industry in different ways have proliferated in industrial countries, *pari passu* with the liberalization of international trade. This is a source of concern to those who see in such practices the demise of the mixed economy, a new and covert protectionism, a source of international conflict, and an issue on which negotiated agreement may be difficult to come by.

Concern has focused on the extent to which increased state involvement in the private sector and the concomitant multiplication of direct and indirect forms of subsidization have contributed to the erosion of the validity and viability of the liberal economic concepts and assumptions upon which much of contemporary commercial diplomacy, such as takes place in the General Agreement on Tariffs and Trade, has been based. The changed relationship between governments and their private sectors has affected both the operation of firms and markets. The minimization of risk through subsidies has influenced the conditions under which international competition takes place. And active government industrial policies have challenged traditional notions of comparative advantage, thereby affecting the processes and rates at which the global distribution of industry advances.[20]

Social restraint may not be the sole source of productivity deceleration. In the US at least, the decline in production of the mining sector (rent exhaustion) and the 'baby boom' generation interacting with low rates of capital formation have been suggested as major causes. Bruno (1981) has recently provided an alternative account in terms of the increased prices of imported intermediates (notably petroleum). In addition, still unproven Schumpeterian explanations centering on a slowdown of innovation could be hypothesised. But to the extent that social restraint is a significant factor, the outlook for the Western economies is harder to reverse. Over the longer run, low rates of productivity-increase result in slower growth in total output. Structural adjustment is easier in a growing economy, not least because the assurance of alternative employment and higher living standards reduces the incentive to obstruct labor-displacing shifts in product, region or technique. Less dynamic industrial economies therefore see less room for maneuver. Given present institutional arrangements, flexibility to adjust to technical change and shifting patterns of comparative advantage is reduced. Economic stagnation is therefore itself likely to provoke increased demands for protection from foreign competition, and other forms of assistance. Countries are locked-in even more tightly to existing sectors and modes of production by the cumulative interaction between slow growth, political pressure and further legislation.

Some alternative proposals
The conclusion that existing forms of industrial policy retard rather than promote productivity increase, and weaken rather than strengthen the competitive position of assisted firms, does more than suggest the existence of a long-run vicious circle. It also argues that measures addressed to the problem of 'deindustrialisation' – the decline of the entire manufacturing base of certain countries and regions – will *need* to be unorthodox when judged by past standards. Present patterns of intervention appear unable to preserve failing enterprises indefinitely unless subsidies are extended forever. Neither is it easy to pick out, far in advance, sectors of natural advantage and concentrate resources on these, although such a policy has its adherents.

Some proposals advanced to reverse deindustrialisation are indeed unorthodox. Besides extensive nationalisation, suggestions include limiting the investment abroad of international corporations and (in the US) that workers assert their rights, possibly through trade unions, to control the investment of their pension funds.[21] Through such methods investment might indeed be temporarily retained in firms and regions less attractive to private capital, and the rate of job loss slowed in hard-hit traditional industrial areas. Yet they, too, fail to address the basic problem. In the longer run, unless wages are forced down relative to those elsewhere, reduced profitability in the 'protected' areas will lead to a fall in the surplus available for reinvestment, hence to a slowdown in capital formation. Declining areas are, in general, less able to attract capital, innovation and new industry. Reduced profitability also raises a serious potential conflict between older, less mobile workers concerned to preserve their jobs rather than to ensure the long-run solvency of their pension systems, and younger workers with the opposite priorities. It is, in addition, not clear that the overall impact on net domestic job creation of multinationals is strongly adverse: most closedowns in the US industrial 'graybelt', for example, have been observed to involve national rather than multinational American corporations.[22]

Industrial Collapse

Closure, profitability and internal organisation
Neither in the US nor in Britain can industrial collapse, and the redundancy associated with it, be considered an unusual phenomenon. Some 24,000 American firms petitioned for bankruptcy each year on average between 1970 and 1977, and in the market economy the process of firm birth, evolution, relocation and death is aptly described as one of continual flux.[23] Failure rates are higher for smaller firms than for large ones. Some 50 percent of small businesses in the US go under

within the first two years of startup and 80 percent close within five, but those surviving past this period have a sharply lowered probability of deceasing in any given period.[24] Most closures result from factors specific to the affected enterprises rather than global economic parameters, but profound shifts in economic climate affect the frequency of more significant shutdowns and condition the economic and political consequences of important closures. In a generally less buoyant sector of industry, collapses correlate across similar firms to include enterprises formerly considered as industrial leaders. Spatial shifts in the productive center, as in the draining of manufacturing from the northeastern US and the northern UK, are reflected in regional imbalances in the number of large or medium-sized closedowns and startups. Such sectoral or spatial correlation increases the difficulty of redeploying redundant workforces, a task harder still in a generally stagnant economic environment. In these circumstances the representative-democratic mode of political organisation tends to generate strong political pressure for industrial support. Depending on the balance of political forces, some concession to these pressures is at times inevitable.[25]

Are collapsed enterprises really unprofitable? This is not an easy question to answer, not least because all measures of profitability are relative. In an uncertain world, some decisions to close firms will also inevitably prove to be wrong, as will decisions to keep certain firms going. Past performance provides an imperfect guide to expected profitability as seen by the owners or managers of a closing firm, as do success records of firms restarted after closure. A careful distinction must also be drawn between a firm prior to collapse and the *potential* firm following reorganisation. The proposition that the traumatic experience of closure might actually be necessary to facilitate reorganisation is further addressed below. Considering the firm prior to collapse, shifts in relative prices, product demands, or the development of new industries able to exploit cheaper labor and raw materials, improved technology or financial incentives may be responsible for plant and equipment being written down to below its scrap or alternative use value. Such forces making for closure may be considered as exogenous to firm organisation. Slack management, an unreceptive industrial environment within the firm or within the local ambience, may also result in the firm, prior to collapse, being a chronic loser rather than a profit-making enterprise.

Not all closedowns are chronic losers however. US experience suggests that a proportion may be traced to market failures, in either capital or managerial markets, and to tax-writeoff laws. Many closures of medium-sized firms in remote industrial areas appear to have involved moderately profitable subsidiaries of large corporations unable to meet target corporate returns to equity.[26] 'Overambitious' return requirements have been singled out as a significant factor in the decapitalisation of much American industry, and a consequent contributer to 'deindustrialisation' of the US economy.[27] High yield targets are not necessarily (privately) excessive; if scarce equity can indeed return a high yield when invested in other product lines, a new Sun Belt plant or abroad, there is clearly little point in holding low-yielding plants in the Northeast Corridor. The possibility of offsetting losses against capital gains for tax purposes, or the prospect of competition from a sold-off subsidiary, may then render a total closedown more attractive to the corporate owner than sale as a going concern. The result has been closure of somewhat, although not spectacularly, profitable enterprises, often preceded by a period of running down the plant.

Contributing to such closures seems to have been the frenetic period of US corporate mergers which began in the mid-1960s. Takeovers, acquisitions and mergers resulted in patternless conglomerates, with ownership tentacles winding in seemingly random fashion across numerous unrelated industrial branches and yielding little synergic gain.[28] Some corporate owners developed sophisticated information-reporting and control systems, designed to allow scope for independent decision making at plant level while providing centralised expertise and consultant services from head offices. Others intervened directly in the management of their newly-acquired subsidiaries, influencing product, production and marketing decisions. In some cases, remote control by a management not well acquainted with local conditions or the specific requirements of the industry affected profitability adversely. Relative unprofitability or a product line not in keeping with the general 'image' of the controlling conglomerate sometimes resulted in sale as a going concern. Sometimes it led to closure.

A further factor apparently important in influencing the decision of US corporations to relocate has been a desire to escape unionisation.[29] Perceived differences in the 'labor climate' have apparently affected location decisions directly, in addition to any indirect effect in reducing current profitability. This has contributed to the steady draining of industrial employment out of the traditional graybelt over the 1960s and 1970s. Similarly, but on a nationwide scale, perceptions regarding the future course of labor relations have probably adversely influenced the decision to invest in certain other industrial economies, notably the UK.

Even chronic lossmaking is not irrevocable if due to organisational factors internal to the firm. Enough examples may be found of enterprises and industries apparently bent on commercial suicide to suggest that, in many cases, internal reorganisation, the moderating or restructuring of wage claims, labor–management consensus on the adoption of new technology or a reduction in the frequency of industrial disruption, could permit smooth adjustment to a more difficult market environment.[30] In such cases, some or all of the parties involved in the firm stand to lose significantly as a result of closure. It then represents a resolution of industrial conflict apparently inferior for all concerned parties. Why do such situations arise, and what role does the closure itself play in facilitating reorganisation? To venture briefly into this topic is necessary since the potential of interventions along the lines of cooperation is especially great when collapse is due to a failure of industrial relations.

A fourfold classification of the main elements of organisational failure may be proposed:

(a) *Dynamic conservatism*   Fostered by the existing system of industrial relations, both for workers and managers, dynamic conservatism hinders adjustment to the problems of the present through sustaining attitudes generated by, and appropriate to, past experience.[31] When combined with *informational asymmetry* (described below), dynamic conservatism acts powerfully to impede smooth adaptation of firms to reorganisation and new techniques.

(b) *Goal displacement*[32]   The observation that organisations tend to acquire lives and objectives of their own is hardly new. Important labor institutions within one particular firm may perceive its survival as a secondary goal relative to their own priorities which cut across many firms. National union objectives on pay scales and working conditions may leave little room for flexibility in negotiating firm-specific agreements. In a number of interesting cases, worker representatives have shown themselves less ready to compromise with management than have subsequent general assemblies and ballots of the workforces themselves. The split loyalty of trade union representatives – towards employees of their particular firm and to national objectives – may therefore be a significant factor inhibiting smooth adjustment. Management, too, may perceive divided loyalties and not be immune to the charge of goal displacement.

(c) *Announcement effects*   To give notice of an impending period of difficulty may be judged – correctly – as not being in the best interest of the firm. Trade credit will become more difficult to obtain as the credit rating of the enterprise falls. Loans to finance what might, after all, prove merely to be a tight but transient period would dry up, so provoking the very crisis the announcement attempted to avoid. The effects on labor morale and on employee turnover may also be unfavorable. Employees with the most saleable skills (hence the most difficult to replace) are likely to seek secure jobs elsewhere. Mobile managerial staff, rewarded mainly on the basis of current performance rather than for perspicacity in bringing notice of future difficulties to share-holders might also feel it not to be in their interests to sound alarm bells at a sufficiently early stage. In both the UK and the US short managerial planning horizons have been seen as important elements in industrial decline.[33]

(d) *Informational asymmetry and low-trust relationships* The effect of these first three factors is frequently to create a 'crisis'. Adjustment periods are telescoped into short intervals, and negotiations conducted in an environment of extreme stress. Whether a crisis is real or fictional may not, however, be equally apparent to all parties. Indeed if one party to internal negotiations – the workers – feels that the other – management – has access to superior information on the current situation and future prospects for the firm, a distinctive asymmetrical game-theoretic situation is likely to evolve. In sequential plays of the game, workers *never* find it in their interests to accept the need for concessions – until the reality of crisis is evidenced by closure, which then plays a vital role in reorganisation. The only alternative to such a strategy is perceived by the workforce to be continual exploitation. For such an outcome to result, management and labor should see themselves in generally adversarial roles – 'low-trust' relationships should dominate hierarchical interactions within the firm. Case studies described in subsequent chapters do indeed suggest that perceived informational asymmetry may be an important factor in perpetuating 'noncooperative' behavior by sections of a workforce. They also indicate that this problem is likely to be more serious the larger and more complex is the industrial unit or conglomerate to which the firm belongs.[34]

Towards regulating closures

Legislation may compress or extend the period over which adjustment takes place. On the one hand, while political considerations suppport the extension of aid to ailing enterprises, the incentive to adjust to underlying market conditions is surely blunted. Abrupt shifts in the political climate may then leave little time to revise attitudes and institutional arrangements developed over a number of years. On the other hand, legislation may prolong the crisis by limiting the prerogative traditionally held by capital to cease business. Safeguards and consultative periods may be specified to be necessary prior to closure, as in much current European legislation; the US, as noted earlier has, to date, relatively little legislation dealing with plant shutdowns. In a large number of American cases, formal notification of closure has not therefore been given, and employees have had to rely on voluntary notification and informal signals such as failure to renew plant and equipment to predict closure. Such information – rather like predictions that San Francisco will suffer a major earthquake – is of limited value, as it provides little guide to the probable time of closure.

Although most redundant workers do not suffer permanent job loss, the group is nevertheless important because many such workers are known to remain unemployed longer than average. They suffer emotional and family pressures, and are frequently in a position to voice strong opposition to their changed circumstances. The private financial losses suffered, especially by older employees with skills specific to a given industry or firm, as a result of closure, may be considerable. Estimates of such losses, computed from the discounted present value of expected earnings' streams with and without plant closure, range up to $20,000 for individuals in the US, although the expected loss will differ depending on the circumstances specific to an employee – age, degree of mobility and type of training. For young workers, job loss may actually impact *positively* on expected earning streams if plant closure impels a transfer to a more dynamic, high-paying sector.[35] Losses tend to be most serious for workers receiving a large element of firm-specific quasi-rent in their incomes, and in the 45–55 age bracket over which mobility declines substantially. The financial impact of job loss also depends on the extent to which transfer payments replace foregone earnings. US unemployment insurance typically covers 30–50 percent of pre-layoff take-home pay, but severance pay, supplemental unemployment assistance and trade adjustment assistance programs may result in a fortunate few doing better after shutdowns than before.

Some additional welfare benefit from unemployment leisure may also be gained. But evidence for the US suggests that this is unlikely to be substantial if unemployment arises from redundancy. The psychological and emotional consequences of involuntary unemployment have been investigated by a number of studies. Research into the relationship between unemployment and social–psychological stress concludes that the impact of decreased socioeconomic status due to unemployment can be considerable. Unemployment relates significantly to various stress indices: rates of mortality, homicide, admission to mental hospitals, and imprisonment. Brenner (1976) set out to make:

. . . a statistical examination of the relationships between three economic indicators (per-capita income, the rate of unemployment, and the rate of inflation) and various pathological conditions . . . economic indices were chosen for their critical influence on the level of social stability (or distress) while the pathological indices are used to gauge changes in mental health, and criminal aggression. The latter represent three outstanding and obvious areas of social cost that scientific investigators have associated with patterns of national economic changes.[36]

Brenner's results show a significant relationship between all measures of social pathology and increases in unemployment, and suggest that its longer-run social impact is considerable. His results are supported by those of other researchers. Wilcock and Franke (1963) similarly observe:

The unemployed man or woman who is responsible for his own livelihood and that of others can come to feel that there is no place for him. He can lose confidence in himself. In his search for a scapegoat he may take his frustrations out on his family.[37]

A number of other studies attest to the effect of unemployment on alcoholism, crime and intrafamily stress caused not only by pecuniary factors but by the loss of self-esteem by the displaced wage earner. And besides impacting in an individualistic manner, social distress may also acquire a communal dimension through the decline of industries central to the income-generation process in small manufacturing communities.[38] Similar research does not appear to have been done for the UK, but British surveys of the unemployed leave little doubt that, despite unemployment insurance, supplementary insurance and redundancy pay, job loss is generally seen as a highly undesirable event attended by at least a fair degree of financial hardship.[39]

These studies do not provide a basis for evaluating in monetary terms the welfare losses due to industrial closures. They do, however, lend credence to the view that whatever the objective experience might have been of individuals made redundant in specific instances, reducing the overall anticipated cost of closure as perceived by employees will not be easy. Improved programmatic cushioning and adjustment assistance can have an effect in reducing real economic hardship. They may be less successful in weakening the political drive towards limiting the prerogative of capital to close plants and, more generally, reversing the conservative social welfare function.

3 An Alternative Strategy: Cooperation

Public Intervention and the Reorganisation of Firms

Private versus public reorganisation

While public funds have in fact been used in a number of countries to assist declining firms to convert to some form of employee ownership and control, such a policy has not been part of the accepted sets of normal measures. Public funding has actually been reluctantly conceded in the face of strong spontaneous pressure for employee takeovers, an impulse which has arisen in parallel fashion across a variety of circumstances and countries. This chapter analyzes the buildup of such pressures, emphasising the 'pragmatic' response to industrial closure as opposed to ideological reaction, and outlines its importance for a pattern of job-saving public intervention which emphasises some form of employee ownership and control.

To transform the performance of a firm experiencing difficulties usually requires substantial organisational inputs, in addition to financial resources. Rescue may require the recruitment of a new management team, some new plant, a search for alternative marketing outlets and so forth. While taking over an existing firm offers potential advantages – plant perhaps available at near-breakup cost, a trained workforce with a reservoir of experience – it also poses complications. Relative to starting anew, a legacy of poor past industrial practices may prove difficult to overcome. Indeed, rescue is not always easy to distinguish from a fresh beginning, particularly when – as in several cases discussed in Chapters 4, 7, 8 – lengthy periods of closure intervene between collapse and rebirth.

The option facing government of whether to invest in subsidising the reorganisation of a firm or industry is often debated as if the choice were deterministic. However, as for any other investment, to attempt reorganisation involves a substantial element of risk. The viability of a renewed enterprise depends, as did its past bankruptcy, not only on factors internal to the firm, but on external developments none of which can be predicted with certainty. A proportion of rescue attempts, once initiated, is therefore virtually bound to fail, as would a high proportion of startups if, instead, new firms were to reemploy redundant labor.

Why, in cases where the chance of success is reasonable, do not private capital and management step in to effect the necessary re-organisation? In many cases they of course do, and the immediate problem of closure is solved or at least recedes. A number of examples may, of course, be cited to disprove any assertion that private capital always makes the right decision.[1] One interpretation of such an observation involves hypothesised imperfections in the markets for financial capital and entrepreneurial skills. An interventionist government may then be cast in the potential role of improving their functioning. Yet, this is not a very helpful approach. How could such markets genuinely be improved? Anyway, relative to what hypothetical degree of perfection are they being assessed? Under conditions of uncertainty errors are to be expected even in 'good' markets. A more reasonable and operational focus appears to be that, given the past history of 'failure' dogging any enterprise about to shut its doors, and the small likelihood that a resuscitated firm will prove to be spectacularly profitable, the expected payoff to investing funds and managerial effort in a rescue attempt may not be high enough to justify private takeover as a going concern. Any such private computation must take into account a relatively high perceived probability of failure and consequent loss of equity and managerial inputs. Even given a moderately favorable external environment and good possibilities for internal reorganisation, the expected return as judged by the criterion of private profitability may just be too low.

In contrast to the position of a potential private rescuer, society at large does incur transient, or sometimes less fleeting, losses on close-downs. These often represent the delayed realisation of cumulated erosion of competitiveness and reduced efficiency over a number of years: a portion of the overall loss has probably been suffered, almost unconsciously, long before closure. Losses to society may be categorised into four general types:

(a) Output losses reflect any fall in the value-added produced by the economy following closedown, taking into account the possibility of releasing factors of production to other uses. In the short run these losses are probably positive: as time elapses they tend to decrease and may turn negative, that is, into output gains, if reallocation prospects are reasonably good.

(b) Public budgetary costs comprise the increased volume of transfers to redundant employees and reduced taxes collected on output and incomes. They are likely to follow a profile similar to that of output losses, initially being substantial, then probably decreasing.

(c) The psychological and communal costs associated with redundancy as described in Chapter 2 also cannot be ignored.

(d) Over and above the sum of 'social' losses may be political costs, narrowly defined, as perceived by government. These depend on the size of the firm, strategic (in a political sense) characteristics of its location and workforce and the political environment and balance of forces prevailing at the time of the impending closedown.

The introduction of political costs as a separate category implies that the government of the day may be taken to possess an objective function somewhat different to the 'social' welfare function, as is further discussed in Chapters 5 and 6. In some cases of imminent closure, a combination of narrowly political factors, as well as social costs reflected through the political process, are likely to raise the costs of nonintervention, as perceived by government, considerably above those to a potential private investor. While it is difficult to compare public and private benefits and costs for the two other possible eventualities – successful and failed intervention – the probable net effect of greater public nonintervention costs is for the government's propensity to intervene to exceed that of a private investor.

This in turn implies that the 'threshold' probability of success necessary to induce government to assist an ailing firm would tend to be lower than that for a private investor. Reorganisations with public assistance should therefore fail more frequently than those able to be effected by private capital alone. Where political considerations or genuine social needs are paramount, government support may be forthcoming even when success is quite unlikely. The present objective is neither to justify nor to condemn this state of affairs; nothing guarantees that choices arrived at under representative democracy – or any other system – are 'optimal'. The degree to which government feels obliged to offer assistance to an enterprise in difficulties will depend as much on its own vulnerability to pressure from certain groups as on 'objective' economic and social criteria involving the enterprise itself. These are taken as data: the issue is then how to accommodate political pressure at minimal long-run economic and social cost.

Decentralised intervention

Whether government-assisted intervention succeeds or fails to produce a viable enterprise, in the longer run the outcome will be more favorable if the assisted firm can improve its efficiency. Not only would greater productivity increase the likelihood that intervention eventually results in an independent self-sustaining firm (as opposed to a perpetual ward of the state), but it reduces the budgetary subsidy necessary to sustain the operation of the firm for a given period. The time over which a specified total subsidy suffices to maintain the firm is inversely related to the difference between its cost levels and those of its viable competitors. Even quite small improvements in profitability or reductions in loss rates may therefore extend the benefit of public support considerably.[2]

The shortcomings of much current policy discussed in Chapter 2 suggest strongly that greater, rather than reduced, efficiency is only likely to be associated with intervention if this involves a shift in responsibility away from central government and towards those (a) most directly affected by collapse, and (b) in a position to influence the performance of a renewed enterprise. In some, although perhaps not entirely traditional, sense these, rather than central government, must hold 'equity' in the new enterprise. Local groups and affected individuals must feel responsible for the project, benefit from its success or be accountable for its failure. This follows from the difficulty of monitoring firm behavior in complex modern industry and the consequent problem of moral hazard.

The precise form of equity may be less important than the general principle. The optimal portfolio of equity will reflect, on the one hand, the risk aversion of the employees relative to two varieties of risk – profit risk and bankruptcy risk. Bankruptcy risk alone can make wages and profits close substitutes whereas profit risk makes profits less desirable to risk-averse employees. On the other hand, it reflects the need to tie incentives to economic performance because of the inability of the state to monitor and the need to avoid moral hazard. From this perspective, the assumption of a degree of profit risk by the workforce may be socially optimal even if workers are risk averse and the government is not.

A further argument for shifting responsibility away from government involves political constraints on the degree to which it can reverse its once-assumed obligations, as perceived by segments of the electorate. If collapse is due to a subsidy cut, government, as the immediate 'cause' of closure is likely to come under greater pressure to extend the subsidy than if the government role is more remote.

Decentralisation places definite constraints on the form which public intervention is required to follow. Direct intervention must be minimal regarding the policies and plans of assisted enterprises. Because government lacks the information to make correct commercial decisions and cannot easily enforce its objectives on the firm, its main role in the rescue attempt is necessarily that of creditor, bankrolling the rescue through providing loans or loan guarantees. There is a strong argument for securing these by liens on the fixed assets of the new firm. When rescue aims to prevent collapse rather than resuscitate the firm after bankruptcy, this may require the agreement of existing creditors to the assumption by the state of a prior lien.

A second role for government agencies involves the provision of technical assistance to improve the flow of information to the redundant, or about to be redundant, workforce, to potential rescuers and other individuals and organisations affected by closure. Public agencies might assess and aid plans for reorganisation, commission feasibility studies and fund the activities of management consultants. In this respect their role would fit that conventionally played by such institutions as the Economic Development Administration in the US and the Industrial Development Unit in the UK.

Spontaneous Movements to Cooperation
Decentralisation defines the responsibility assumed by lobbying groups at the receiving end of public support: management, employees, possibly suppliers, dealers and the representatives of the local community. Such groups are aptly described in the Chrysler Corporation Loan Guarantee Act (1979) as 'persons with an existing stake in the economic health of the corporation'. 'Responsibility' usually goes hand in hand with some ownership of equity and a degree of control over an enterprise. How equity is distributed over the new plant's management and workforce, the extent of holdings by 'outsiders' and the precise relationship between ownership and control will naturally differ between cases.

Reluctance on the part of 'persons with a stake' to assume such responsibility could stop decentralised intervention in its tracks before such a policy could be effected. Case studies suggest, however, considerable spontaneous pressure towards accepting responsibility in circumstances of industrial failure. Frequently this extends to demands for a degree of employee equity ownership. The managerial potential of these pressures is then available to facilitate decentralised intervention by government. Why do they arise?

In the market economy different forms of economic organisation evolve through the efforts of individuals to satisfy better their economic objectives.[3] The fact that cooperative-type firms have not come to occupy a significant place in major industrial market economies suggests that, in general, their Darwinian superiority over conventional firms is not proved over the longer term. A fair volume of evidence, surveyed briefly in Chapter 6, suggests that although extending ownership more widely within the firm opens the door to potential efficiency gains, longer run instability of the cooperative form might offset this advantage. Nevertheless, in the rather specific circumstances associated with the collapse of an enterprise, some variant of cooperation – perhaps very partial and possibly temporary – is likely to evolve because of its ability to satisfy pecuniary objectives better than other, more conventional, industrial organisational forms.

Consider firstly the case in which there is no significant productivity difference between a potential 'cooperative' and conventionally-owned firm. Rule out, too, any differences in the intrinsic agreeability of working on a cooperative, as perceived by a potential workforce, relative to that of working in the potential firm.[4] The most significant difference between the two industrial units is then the identity (perhaps partial) of cooperateurs with the owners of its equity: capitalists and workers in a conventional firm are stereotypically distinct groups. By investing in a cooperative-type enterprise, each employee contributes to the preservation of his *own* job. Pure capitalists, on the other hand, conventionally fund the means of production on which *others* work. Financial and labor markets are interlinked for the redundant workforce.

Other 'persons with a stake' similarly experience interlinking. In the US, every 100 manufacturing jobs is estimated to create about 66 additional jobs in local service and goods-supplying industries. Particularly in small communities, collapse of a sizeable firm may have repercussions far beyond its immediate effects. The Chrysler Corporation Loan Guarantee Act (1979) points to another set of linkages: creditors may be willing to make concessions (explicitly or implicitly investing in the new company) in order to increase the chances of preserving their existing stakes. Such concession could, for example, involve recognising government as a prior creditor.

For employees, the distinction between cooperative and firm may not be of great importance in a competitive labor market with 'full' or at least high levels of employment, and if social and financial barriers to geographic mobility are small. Employees will then be able to obtain jobs at the 'going wage'. Since efficiency differences between cooperatives and firms have been ruled out, the total income accruing to workers in an employee-owned enterprise cannot exceed the free-market wage plus a competitive rate of return on any capital stake in the enterprise. Asset diversification to reduce risk then argues for a diversified portfolio spread over a number of assets, rather than a portfolio concentrated in any particular firm. The risk of undiversified asset holding is especially large when the particular firm is also the source of employment. But when labor markets are not freely competitive in the sense that redundant workers cannot slightly undercut the wage of the employed, or when historical patterns of employment and location 'lock individuals in' to a limited range of options, the internalising of the capitalist's decision to invest with the worker's need of a job becomes a significant linkage. It could be noted that workers would be indifferent to redundancy in perfect labor markets. Resistance to plant closure may therefore be taken as evidence of substantial market imperfections as perceived by the workforce and of the significance of interlinking, a phenomenon most extensively analysed in the quite different context of rural markets in certain developing countries.[5]

In his capitalist role, a potentially redundant worker can invest with the object of securing desirable employment for himself, rather than merely seeking out the investment with the highest financial return. By investing outside the cooperative, one worker may help to keep another worker in a job – but this is likely to be of little consolation. Total expected returns of the joint transaction linking job and capital markets may be higher than the sum of any distinct investment and job-search activities, as the internalising of the investment–employment externality allows workers to relax constraints on the selling of their labor through a transaction in the market for capital. Similar remarks apply to other groups with a potential stake in the success of a revived enterprise.

In what circumstances and for which employees will this relaxation be significant? If a worker is confident of his ability to obtain suitable employment in a capitalist firm, there will be little point in sinking savings into a possibly risky enterprise or contributing to equity accumulation by accepting lower take-home pay. Also, there will be little incentive to buy himself a job if the welfare level obtainable from the market (or cooperative) wage is not significantly above that obtainable from the alternative combination of unemployment pay and unemployment leisure. The employee-ownership strategy is therefore most appropriate to workers who: (a) perceive a constraint on the selling of their labor at the going wage, and (b) would in principle be prepared to take suitable work for somewhat less than the going wage rather than remain unemployed. 'Suitable', in this context, relates to such attributes of the job as location as well as to type of employment.

These workers might then face a regulated labor market in which wages are held by legislation, unions, employee agreements or tacit understanding above the levels which would result from free competition in the labor market. Free competition at a given wage may also be inhibited by market segmentation due to firm-specific learning effects so that jobs offering an element of rent to firm-specific experience are rationed.[6] Alternatively, obstacles to mobility may inhibit competition for jobs. To a homeowning worker of middle age or above situated in a community remote from other centers, possible employment outside the town or its immediate vicinity may appear even less preferable than an extended spell of unemployment.

Two other points should be addressed to clarify further the potential superiority of a cooperative over other forms of reorganisation following closure. Firstly, instead of recourse to employee ownership, why is the value of the capital stock of a closing enterprise not written down until it *does* pay some capitalist to take over the plant and rehire the workers? There are two answers to this question. (a) The market for highly specific plant and equipment is often 'thin' and may take a long time to clear; factories and plant frequently remain idle for appreciable periods, particularly in depressed areas. (b) A 'new capitalist' will plausibly be subject to similar constraints on wage levels and the allocation of factors within the firm as exist generally in the industry. These constraints, together with the need to earn a return on his investment competitive with that generally available in the market, set an upper limit to the value which he will be willing to pay for the plant. This is *necessarily less* than that which would be offered by a potential cooperative of 'job constrained' workers who would be breaking a labor market constraint, and hence be willing to accept a lower expected return to their investments. The owners of the closing firm might therefore expect their best offer to come from a group of redundant employees in appropriate circumstances. But because such an offer is prompted by duress on the labor market, it would not be expected to be forthcoming prior to exhaustive attempts supported by worker representatives to find a *conventional* buyer for the closing plant. In almost all known cases of worker purchase, extensive searches for buyers were indeed made prior to the workers resigning themselves to an employee-ownership strategy.

The second arena of possible superiority of cooperative-type enterprises is their potential for overcoming constraints to the allocation of productive factors. The cases described in Chapters 4, 7 and 8 suggest that this may be considerable. In some cases pay levels fell and manning and demarcation limits went by the board, contributing to substantial cuts in operating costs. Workers cooperatives arising out of bankrupt firms have sometimes been able to reach consensus on a wider set of labor arrangements than conventional firms. In fact, the ability of so-called 'cooperatives' to overcome constraints to the setting of internal wage levels (for example, by volunteering a portion of the wage as an equity contribution) provides one explanation for their evolution out of bankruptcy in a labor constrained situation even when workers actually hold little or no equity and exert even less control.

It may well be asked in what sense such a firm is genuinely a cooperative or even employee-owned. Certainly, structures of ownership and control arising out of firm closures usually bear little resemblance to 'true' cooperatives, as defined for example by Vanek (1975). Nevertheless, if the assumption of the surface trappings of cooperation and its rhetoric permits workers to sell their labor more cheaply than they otherwise would be constrained to do, a 'pseudo-cooperative' may also appear to be superior to a conventional capitalist firm.

These factors will supplement the impact on profitability of any real efficiency gain arising out of employee ownership. But in the circumstances of industrial closure, neither they nor efficiency gains may be necessary to establish the superiority of a cooperative form from the perspective of an individual worker or affected member of the local community.

The interlinked markets explanation suggests that not all employees will press equally strongly for the conversion of their closing firm to worker-ownership. A formal model of worker self-selection for cooperative experiments and the probable attitudes of such workers to the viability of their enterprise is presented in the Annex. Here its structure and conclusions are described and related to the mode of industrial intervention.

The model focuses on individual decisionmaking units, in a framework of expected utility maximisation. Differences between individuals span a vast range of dimensions, but for analytic simplicity most interpersonal variation is suppressed. Specifically, the model abstracts from differential attitudes to risk, and supposes that most redundant workers are able to contribute a reasonable downpayment to the cooperative from savings, borrowing or redundancy pay. Funding may also be available from external (government) sources. The greater is the funding available to the potential cooperative from external sources, the smaller is the necessary contribution from its employees either in cash or in the form of foregone payments. An individual worker will only opt for a cooperative-type solution if his expected benefit from doing so exceeds that available from alternative job-search activities; the latter depends on the expected duration of unemployment and on the nature of the anticipated job.

If limited geographic mobility is not the sole constraint perceived by the redundant workforce, the attraction of being thrown onto the job market is determined by such characteristics as age, seniority within the enterprise and general demand for any marketable skills. The strong association between age and duration of unemployment spells, itself a manifestation of the general association between youth and flexibility, suggests that the attraction of 'employee ownership' relative to the alternative will be far higher for older, more established employees with stable employment histories. Unless fired by enthusiasm by the prospect of working on a novel type of enterprise or by radical leanings, younger employees are more likely to choose the alternative of seeking new avenues. Blue-collar occupations might find a cooperative option attractive relative to more occupationally mobile white-collar staff. (An empirically important exception here is that certain employees of managerial level are likely to see potential advantages in converting to a worker cooperative, and may be attracted by the prospect of large financial gains.)

Geographic ties may modify the determinants of those facing the cooperative option. Homeownership, in particular, is likely to prove an important constraint to seeking another job, as are family ties which limit the mobility of individual members. In general, however, the set of individuals favoring a cooperative solution is likely to shrink as the generosity of public assistance to the enterprise is reduced. Eventually it would be reduced to a 'hard core' composed either of workers committed to a cooperative ideal or of truly desperate individuals not seeing any prospect of alternative employment. In this way, the appropriate pitch of public assistance initiates a 'self-screening' process which tends to exclude from the group of beneficiaries individuals not really in such dire need of assistance. This screening process may also be interpreted as acting on *cases* or communities. The details of such a process are further spelled out in Chapter 6.

In another important respect the differential characteristics of individuals (and cases or communities) will cause them to be screened in the process of negotiation to establish an employee or community-owned enterprise. In a given situation, individuals will differ in their assessment of what is achievable. Some adopt a predominantly fatalistic attitude, maintaining that they exert little influence on the course of events. Others, termed 'voluntaristic' in the formal model, tend to feel that external influences are not overwhelming and that their own efforts can indeed contribute to the establishment of a viable firm. Individuals of the second type, it may reasonably be assumed, are more prepared to seek innovative solutions and, because they value their own efforts and contributions, to work harder towards their goal. 'Work effort' in this context encompasses a broad range of behavior – initiative, adaptability and commitment – in addition to more quantifiable variables such as reduced absenteeism and longer hours, which in practice may be less important in raising productivity.

Individuals in the second group are also more likely to volunteer and press for cooperative solutions, not because they necessarily have a more rosy view of the world in general, but because they see positive opportunities from the new organisation, and hence take a more favorable view of its prospects. For similar reasons, they are more willing to make economic sacrifices to help 'their' enterprise get off the ground. It is indeed noticeable that, coexisting with desperation, a fiercely independent ethic is liable to develop within workforces and communities adversely affected by industrial closure: to openly admit that continuing and open-ended subsidisation is needed is not only impolitic but a severe blow to self-esteem. The cooperation strategy exploits this ethic, rather than undermining it through wresting responsibility away from affected groups in return for aid.

This model framework suggests that managerial advantages to government of offering conversion to some form of employee ownership as a standard option for industrial assistance could be quite substantial in some circumstances. Relative to conventional policy, leakage of benefits to individuals and communities less in need will be reduced by pitching the level and terms of assistance appropriately. Strong pressures are created for operating efficiently. And because assistance is given on a 'once and for all' basis, with the government funding feasibility studies and playing the role of bank against the assurances of 'persons with a stake', collapse of the firm, should it occur a second time, is more clearly the responsibility of the workforce and local community than in the case of conventional policy.

4 Patterns of Transition to Employee Ownership

Public Involvement in the Transition

Pressure for public assistance

This chapter outlines and contrasts a number of conversions to employee ownership, with special emphasis on cases which have taken place with public assistance. This synthesis helps to assess the extent to which the cases conform to a pattern, central to the argument for public intervention along these lines. It also illustrates the considerable degree of divergence across cases, and some important differences in the characteristics of transition across countries.

Not all purchases of struggling firms by their employees involve the use of government funds. In the US for example, public assistance has actually been forthcoming in only a minority of cases. A number of factors do, however, increase the likelihood that government will be involved in the transition. These may be considered in two categories: those external to the firm and those specific to the transition itself.

Factors external to the transition include low regional or national investment, slow growth of aggregate output in the face of rapid structural change and pronounced regional shifts in industrial location. A particular case of the last effect is the swift development of competitive manufacturing capacity abroad. On the political side, circumstances which render the government of the day particularly vulnerable to organised groups exert a strong pressure, which appears to be heightened in times of acute electoral competition.

Factors more specific to a particular case either increase adjustment costs or raise the possibility of bringing these to public attention: in response to escalated tension in the adjustment process, government is likely to be drawn in. A list would include:

(a) *less favorable prospects* which reduce the probability of a purely private takeover, for example, through a managerial buyout of shareholders;

(b) *strong ties between a firm and local community*. This provides members of the ailing enterprise with ready channels of political organisation through which to solicit aid. The objective is to avoid or shift onto government the costs potentially imposed by closure. Such ties are strengthened by:

(c) *status as a major local employer.* By rendering the community dependent this evokes additional support;

(d) *a substantial proportion of older employees.* For these, costs of adjustment are high, especially in relation to the income benefits available from changing occupations over the remainder of working life;

(e) *skills not readily transferable to other enterprises.* While the less skilled face a more constrained range of reemployment opportunities, the potential income loss to the more skilled and those with considerable seniority is greater. Reemployment will often necessitate occupational downgrading and lead to lower expected income levels;

(f) *generally depressed demand for marketable skills of the workforce,* possibly associated with high local unemployment;

(g) *size.* Not only is the collapse of a single large employer more noticeable than the unsynchronised closures of many small firms but, to the extent that redundancy is not phased, it also increases the difficulty of re-employment (especially locally) because of the clogging of the job market. The greater political weight of organised employees in large-scale industry also increases their chances of receiving state assistance. This, in turn, provides an additional incentive to lobby harder. With the notable exception of Chrysler Corporation, the US cases considered here are small relative to the size of the overall economy, as are all the British cases. But the size dimension may, in the case of small economies, extend beyond the above factors to encompass a degree of dependence of the entire economy on the fortunes of one or two large enterprises.

The difficulties facing the tiny Maltese economy following the run-down of the British defense establishment led Maltese premier Dom Mintoff to initiate imaginative examples of the employee takeover strategy in the British Naval Dockyards (a vital employer and key source of foreign exchange) and in a number of other enterprises in the early 1970s. The Maltese example is, in many ways, similar to those of other transitions to employee ownership which have occurred in larger economies. However, the size factor and consequent involvement of government are particular structural characteristics which render it an unusual case. It is therefore outlined separately, at the end of this chapter.

Cross-Country Patterns of Employee Takeovers

Case studies

Case studies of employee buyouts are most freely available for the US. Prominent American examples include Vermont Asbestos Group, which was acquired by its workforce in 1974 following a spell of low asbestos prices and the need to introduce improved safety equipment, Saratoga Knitting Mill (February 1975), and South Bend Lathe, an Indiana enterprise bought by its workforce in the early 1970s. These and a number of other cases are described in Stern and Hammer (1978), Zwerdling (1978, 1980), Frieden (1979), Gurdon (1979), Ross (1980), the Senate Report for the Select Committee on Small Business (1979), and Rothschild-Whitt (1981). They have been important in influencing the trends in US legislation described in Chapter 5. Stern *et al* (1979) also describe in detail the experience of the library furniture factory at Herkimer, New York. A recent conversion to employee ownership – that of Rath Pork Packing Co., of Waterloo, Iowa – is also included.[1] Canadian examples include the Edmonton-based company of Byers Transport[1], and Pioneer Chain Saw Manufacturers[2]. A controversial case was that of the Tembec pulp mills at Temiscaming, Quebec.[2] British transitions to (rather nominally) worker-owned enterprises include Upper Clyde Shipbuilders (1972)[3] and the three 'Benn' co-operatives established in 1974: Meriden motorcycles, Kirkby Manufacturing and the Glasgow-based Scottish Daily News.[4]

In a large, but uncertain, number of cases transitions to employee ownership have been mooted but did not actually occur. Youngstown Iron and Steel and the Ford plant in Sheffield Alabama are two prominent US examples, with Triang and Imperial Typewriters in the UK.[5]

France, with its well-established cooperative tradition, and an associated infrastructure to assist conversions, has seen a considerable number of employee takeovers. Notable cases include the large watch manufacturers of Lip,[6] and the Manuest furniture factory.[7] Lip stands out as a particularly controversial takeover, an illegal occupation by the workers having eventually to be terminated by the riot police. Employee takeovers are also fairly prevalent in Italy and Spain: Oakeshott (1978) cites a number of other European cases, such as that of Valencia Omnibus.

Factors impeding adjustment
Data coverage differs greatly between cases and it is not easy to judge, other than subjectively, the extent to which characteristics (b) to (g) listed earlier as likely to impede adjustment were important in any one instance. Nevertheless, an attempt is made to indicate their relative strengths for a number of cases in Table 4.1, which in some instances draws on only incomplete information. Strong relationships are indicated by two stars, weaker, but discernible interactions by one star. In each instance a number of case-specific criteria are clearly satisfied.

Grouping cases by country, a definite pattern emerges regarding the nature of the main barriers seen as inhibiting smooth adjustment and accommodation to closure by the redundant workforces. Distinguishing the selected North American examples is a particularly strong link with their local communities. This was related to their status as major local employers. As explained in Chapter 5, the firm-community linkage plays an especially large role in the US because of the decentralised American political system. It thus provides a natural focus for attempts to obtain assistance. The two French cases listed also had strong links with their local communities, Manuest because of its isolation, and Lip because of its size relative to the local economy. The watchmaking industry employed some 12,000 persons in a fairly remote area of the Ardennes. Only Upper Clyde Shipbuilders among the British cases can be considered as a significant local employer. UCS employed 13,000 workers and although situated in a generally industrialised part of Scotland, the decline, over a number of years, of industry in general, and of shipbuilding in particular, had left the area dependent on a limited number of still-surviving large plants.

The firms preceeding Meriden, Kirkby Manufacturing, and the Scottish Daily News had employed only 1,750, 1,200 and 1,942 before their respective closures, and none of the three can be considered as having been located in a remote or isolated environment. Kirkby and the Scottish Daily News were, however, situated in exceptionally depressed localities. In the mid-1970s Glaswegian unemployment stood at almost twice the national average for the UK, and redundant newspaper employees could anticipate little opportunity in a declining and overmanned industry. After surveying the desolate appearance of the Kirkby industrial estate on the outskirts of Liverpool, no-one would find it hard to understand an attachment to the ungainly plant producing radiators and soft drinks as 'employer of the last resort'.

Age and a history of generally stable local employment are known to have played a role in limiting mobility in several cases. Workers over 50 years of age represented 47 percent of the workforce of the Scottish Daily News, those below 30, only some 6 percent. The average Tembec worker was aged 49 and had spent twenty-four years working at the Temiscaming mill. Library Bureau workers, too, averaged 49, and had worked for the company on average for seventeen years. One year previously, 650 workers in a similar craft had lost their jobs owing to the closure of the Standard Desk company in Herkimer. Many workers at the Saratoga Mill had over thirty years service, although the low wages of the textile industry led, too, to a transient proportion among the labor force. Manuest, in contrast, contained a high proportion of young workers, many of whom had immigrated to the region between six and fourteen years previously. An unusual factor limiting mobility was, however, a substantial proportion of two-earner families with husband and wife working in the same plant.

Table 4.1 Characteristics of some transitions

Case	Before collapse				Collapse	Employee-owned enterprise							
	Strong community linkage	Vital local employer	Craft skill	Skill in depressed demand		Factory occupation	Attempt to find buyer	Strong union initiative	Worker/community equity	Reduced pay	Large manning cuts	Diminished union role	Productivity increase
US													
Vermont Asbestos Group	**	**	No	**		No	**	*	**	No	No	No	No
Saratoga Knitting Mills	**	*	No	**		No	**	No	**	No	No	No	*
South Bend Lathe	**	**	**	**		No	**	*	**	No³	No	No	**
Library Bureau	**	**	**	**		No	**	*	**	No	No	U	No
Rath Pork Pkg. Co.	*	*	No	*		No	***5	**	**	**	No	No	*

Canada															
Tembec Mills	**	**	**	**	**	**[2]	**	**	**	**	**	*	**	**	**
Pioneer Chain Saw	**	*	**	**	**	**	**	**	**	**	**	**	U	U	**
UK															
UCS	**	*	*	**	No	**	No	No[1]	**	**	No	**	**	U	
Meriden Motorcycles	*	No	**	**	**	**	No[1]	**	**	**	No	**	**	U	
Kirkby Manufacturing	*	No	*	**	No[1]	**	**	*	*	*	**	*			
Scottish Daily News	*	No	**	**	**	**	**	**	**	**	**	**			
France															
Lip	**	**	**	**	*	U	U	U	No	U					
Manuest	**	**	**	**	*	No[4]	**	**	No	*					

U = Unknown; [1] Token participation; [2] Similar protests: see Chapter 7; [3] Pension rights were given up for ESOP, to detriment of some older workers; [4] A number of nominally re-employed workers were supported by unemployment pay while working; [5] Employees' offer accepted over that of potential buyers.

The protest phase

Demonstrations, factory occupations and other similar forms of protest at the loss of jobs were far more characteristic of employee takeovers outside North America. Of known US examples, only the abortive attempt to establish an employee-owned steel plant at Youngstown was marked by violent demonstration. Of the cases listed in Table 4.1, only Tembec relied heavily on such tactics and on their attendant publicity designed to embarrass the Liberal Quebec government into extending support. Tembec workers aided by the local community blockaded the Ottawa River and occupied a vital bridge between Quebec and Ontario. One factor important in sparing the US this kind of experience appears to have been quite general acceptance on the part of American unions of the prerogative of plant owners to close their doors; in line with an absence of radical criticism the rights of capital are less contested in the US than in Europe.[8] The American reaction to impending closure was therefore directed far more towards seeking constructive solutions to the problem than protesting against it.

This marks a clear distinction from patterns of protest observed elsewhere. All of the British examples experienced significant 'political' activity during transitions to worker ownership. But only UCS based its petition for support on a prominent local and national campaign. Twice, thousands of workers and community leaders took to the Glasgow streets in demonstrations.[9] The other three British co-operatives did not need to rely on such tactics (although they too were preceded by sit-ins and demonstrations) because of the timely appointment of a staunch cooperative patron, Tony Benn, as Secretary of State for Industry in the February 1974 Labour government.

Despite the illegality of factory occupations at Lip and Manuest, these were staunchly supported by their local communities. School halls and church premises were opened to the redundant workforces providing fora for meetings. Watches produced by Lip workers in occupation were distributed through a clandestine local underground network of sympathisers. Support for Manuest was forthcoming from the mayor, council and local deputé of the Assemblée Générale. As in isolated American communities, the quest to save jobs proceeded with the support of a wide range of local private and public organisations.

Outside the US in particular, and North America in general, such forms of protest were invariably spearheaded by trade unions. Union leaders such as Allister Mackie of the Scottish Daily New, Jack Spriggs of Kirkby, and Pierre Montesinos at Manuest came to personify the spirit of resistance and determination to save jobs. The impulses towards employee ownership, however, came more from local than from national union levels. Not all US plants taken over by workers were unionised. The purchase of Saratoga Mill, a non-union plant, was instrumented primarily by Donald Cox, general manager of the mill and vice president of the van Raalte division of the controlling conglomerate Cluett Peabody. Cox's philosophical stance has been identified as consonant with the anti-socialist, anti-big business strand in American political ideology, important in promoting the legislative drive towards employee purchases as described in Chapter 5.[10] At the local level, American unions frequently played an important supporting role, although they did not generally lead the drive to purchase closing firms. The two locals of the International Union of Electrical, Radio and Machine Workers (IUE) were central in the drive to raise the downpayment for the Herkimer plant, for example, although the purchase was led by a group of local investors. At the national level, American unions approached employee purchases cautiously, adopted a 'wait and see' attitude towards the change of ownership and generally were unwilling to extend themselves to help, without being openly hostile.

The search for a buyer and the alternatives
The initial response on learning of the decision to close the firm invariably involved a search for capitalist buyers. An exception here seems to have been Upper Clyde Shipbuilders, where such a search might have seemed futile. The American cases tended to be in far better shape financially, but with few exceptions these searches proved to be unsuccessful; outside buyers were not forthcoming to puchase and run the firm along traditional capitalist lines. In the case of Byers Transport Company of Edmonton, Alberta, six offers were indeed made for the company. These were low, partly because of its poor financial record and difficult labor-management relationship, characterised by insensitive management and militant trade unionism. Several bidders had poor reputations in making takeovers, often having been known to release over half of an acquired firm's employees. On learning that the employees had also made a bid for the company, four of the offers were withdrawn, and, in accord with the predictions of the model in Chapter 3, the employees' bid was the highest of the remaining offers.[11]

In the process of searching for alternatives, feasibility studies were carried out for a large proportion of cases. Although generally emphasising commercial viability rather than social concerns, these did more than assess the profitability of a resuscitated plant. They provided a forum for debate and discussion of alternative strategies for preserving jobs. By reducing at least the perception of asymmetric information, they encouraged the emergence of a consensus over the appropriate action to be taken by the redundant workforce and community. Where social concerns explicitly entered the cost-benefit calculus (as in the case of the assessment of the Youngstown steel workers),[12] studies included the impact of closure versus employee ownership on the local community and the direct fiscal consequences. Effects of an economy-wide nature and possible gains from resource allocation in the long run were seldom emphasised. Consensus on the need for a new enterprise to be profitable and, to a degree, on the requirements for this, appears to have smoothed the process of fundamental reorganisation considerably where this was needed to set the new firm on a better footing.

Despite intense effort, the intervals between closure and restart were sometimes lengthy. The Scottish Daily News, Meriden, and Kirkby operated at best, intermittently during reorganisation phases lasting for eighteen, fourteen and twelve months, respectively. Manuest ceased production for six months. Over a year elapsed between the closure of the Kipwa mill by Canadian International Paper and the opening of Tembec, its replacement. Smooth transitions were more characteristic of cases occurring in the US. South Bend Lathe and the library furniture factory at Herkimer, for example, maintained flows of orders and production. A clear pattern emerges in this comparison: takeovers of less commercially viable firms and those more dependent on government assistance have tended to be less smooth than employee purchases of firms close to commercial viability even when these have needed public assistance.

During the phase of transition, negotiations and appeals for funds usually involved virtually every conceivable party: the departing employers and employees, their friends, neighbors and relatives, trade unions and related organisations, local, state and sometimes national governments, and possible sources of private capital. In all known cases the overwhelming initial objective appears to have been jobs. In the British, Canadian and French cases, ideology, whether that viewing cooperatives as a third option to capitalism and socialism, or orthodox left wing, tended to be attracted by the controversy surrounding attempts to save jobs rather than to be generated *within* the collapsing enterprise. Radical criticism of the capitalist system, when it arose, reflected the channels through which financial support was elicited. Consequently, it was most evident in the rhetoric of outsiders and in media reports, some of which were deeply resented by employees intent only on saving their jobs.[13] Radical ideology was similarly muted in the US. American examples do, however, suggest a strong populist ideological critique of 'big' business. The origins of this sentiment and its impact on legislation are discussed in Chapter 5. The more complex issue, of whether the action of implementing some form of worker ownership leads to substantial radical criticism of capitalism (including traditional control structures in the new firm), is taken up later.

An emphasis on viability

In all the cases investigated, both in the US and outside it, it is interesting to note the strong emphasis on the need to develop a commercially viable enterprise. This apparently was accepted by all parties in negotiations, including employees. The need to be viable was general and central, not only in cases where the outlook for the new firm was relatively favorable. Even in the shakiest venture, strong commitment was generated in the course of the struggle to save jobs. 'You will have to work like you never worked before,' exhorted Jack Spriggs, the worker chairman of Kirkby Manufacturing.[14] Otherwise unsympathetic commentaries on the British Benn cooperatives noting 'a clear and strong desire to succeed',[15] are echoed in accounts of other experiments. Opinions from outside the workforce that restarted firms would not prove to be viable were met with alternative feasibility studies, more optimistic projections and a reiterated position, common to all workforces, that they *could* indeed succeed.[16]

The significance of this widespread feature extends beyond the obvious point that to admit in public to a high probability of failure would be impolitic while lobbying for private or government funds. The process of self-conviction played a vital role in the need to maintain self respect, so basic a factor in the drive for jobs. Despite the poor labor relations record of a number of the failed or closing units and restrictive union agreements on labor allocation which raised costs and inhibited the introduction of new technology (which undoubtedly had been factors in the decline of certain enterprises, especially the British cases), workers were inclined to attribute the major cause of closure to poor management, or to consider closure as not justified.[17] If ownership were to change and workers given some say in the firm's operation viability would surely follow. Determined optimism on the part of the workforce and their attribution of responsibility for failure are consistent.

Cutting costs

To reduce operating costs was less immediately important in those American cases which involved corporate divestitures of moderately profitable firms. There was also less need to resort to drastic manning cuts when inappropriate management by previous corporate owners had been largely responsible for the financial straits of the company about to be taken over.[18] Many American conversions therefore involved relatively little structural change. But for weaker enterprises this was vital to present even a modest case for viability. Substantial savings were indeed effected in many cases, particularly where agreements with unions had inhibited adjustment to new technology and resulted in chronic overmanning. This was especially marked in

Britain: the Scottish Daily News saw its workforce cut from 1,942 to 500. Meriden and Kirkby after the transition employed, respectively, only 36 percent and 65 percent of their previous workforces. According to Eccles (1981), Kirkby manning could have been further reduced, but the cut was nevertheless considerable. Manuest and Tembec also cut their workforces substantially, but rebuilt them as business picked up after the restart. Laurent, the managing director of Manuest, was constrained by the workers' insistence that all 250 employees participating in the factory occupation be reemployed, but this still represented only 40 percent of the previous workforce, and many nominally reemployed workers were actually supported by unemployment pay while contributing to the output of the firm.

Pioneer provides a particularly interesting example of a workforce responding to a new responsibility. Before closure it employed 450. When asked by Joseph Mason, its future managing director and major stockholder, to estimate the minimal number of employees needed to run the business the workers debated for three weeks. 'That question blew their minds out,' recalled Mason. 'No one had ever asked them that before, and they couldn't cope with it.' The workers' estimate, at 130–135, proved to be too low. Pioneer was able to reemploy 150.[19]

Over quite a wide range of cases, only about half of the original workforces were therefore able to preserve their jobs. Evidence is scarce on the characteristics of the selected, or self-selecting 'cooperative' workers. Nevertheless, the age profile of Scottish Daily News workers and accounts of other conversions suggest that these tended to be rather less occupationally or geographically mobile than other ex-employees, some of whom had already migrated in search of alternative opportunities.

Outside the US, lowered hourly labor costs frequently contributed to cut operating expenses. The three 'Benn' cooperatives saw unit labor costs fall by about 20–30 percent, relative to levels prevailing on similar conventional firms. At Meriden, for example, all differentials were eliminated, the workforce accepting a relatively low, uniform weekly wage in an attempt to convince Harold Wilson's 1974 Labour government of their desire to be viable. At Tembec, too, pay concessions were seen to be vital in negotiation for assistance with Federal and Provincial governments. Relative to pay levels projected under the ownership of Canadian International Paper, basic hourly wage rates were to be trimmed by some 18 percent.[20] Elimination of shift premia and cuts in a range of fringe benefits were estimated to lower total hourly wage costs, relative to those otherwise projected, by 26 percent, a saving over three years of almost Can $3 million. The Pioneer workforce, too, accepted a $2 cut in basic hourly wages and gave up a number of fringe benefits including overtime and certain paid holidays. Paid overtime similarly disappeared in two of the three 'Benn' cooperatives although hours worked undoubtedly rose. The US cases listed in the table did not experience similar pressure to cut hourly rates, although South Bend Lathe workers gave up their pensions in return for participation in the new firm's Employee Stock Ownership Plan. Nevertheless, Rath Packing workers of Waterloo, Iowa conceded approximately $2,000 each in fringe benefits, including half their vacation and holiday pay, to enable them to buy stocks and improve the cash flow of the new company.[21] The Chrysler rescue, too, involved concessions on pay compensated by ownership of Chrysler stock.

Towards greater productivity

Did employees actually work harder after conversion, and was any such effect attributable to the form of employee ownership assumed by the company? Systematic studies of changes in work intensity are rare, so this question cannot be answered generally. A survey of the Scottish Daily News (see Chapter 8), suggests that over 60 percent of the workforce considered that they worked more intensively on the co-operative than they had under Beaverbrook, the owner of the previous Scottish Daily Express. Many claimed to have worked over ten hours extra weekly. Accounts of Meriden and Tembec also suggest a shift towards more intensive work associated with a reduction in demarcation rules. In the British examples, this particularly reflected massive manning cuts. Increased work intensity does not appear to have been a prominent feature in North American cases. Rather than attributing greater work intensity *directly* to some form of employee ownership, it therefore appears that a link may arise through the extent of reorganisation and streamlining effected in the transition.

The initial impact, at least, of worker takeover can be to raise productivity measured in output/man.[22] This does not automatically occur, however, and cannot easily be directly attributed to any specific form of ownership and control. A number of effects can contribute to raise productivity, including improvements in management of a conventional nature, greater worker motivation and collaboration with supervisors. The alignment of employee goals with that of the firm has many dimensions. These range from active intervention to improve the production process to passive acceptance of new working arrangements and technology, or from mutual support and peer group reinforcement among employees to reduced absenteeism and shorter breaks volunteered on an individual basis. An undetermined combination of such effects appears to have assisted labor productivity increases estimated at 30–40 percent at Tembec, Meriden, and Pioneer. Kirkby, despite the cut in manning, actually increased output from 7,000 to 13,000 radiators per week, considerably increasing its share of the UK market.

The cut in manning levels of the Scottish Daily News speaks for itself and would have been the envy of conventional British newspaper management.

Productivity (and profitability) increases have been documented in a number of American firms converting to employee ownership. There was no evidence of productivity improvement at Vermont Asbestos Group and the Library Bureau. At South Bend Lathe, however, waste due to rejected material fell by 70 percent within one month of employee purchase, and productivity was estimated to have increased by 25 percent after a year.[23] Sales rose by 53 percent over its first few years and after-tax profits more than quintupled to over $1 million – a figure which understates its new-found profitability by excluding a further $1 million contributed in 1979 to the Employee Stock Ownership Trust. Wages could thus be increased 35 percent over the first three years. The attribution of this turnaround between better labor relations, new equipment and fortuitous orders is, however, not clear. As noted later, labor relations appeared to have deteriorated at South Bend Lathe after the first few years of employee ownership. At Saratoga Mill, pilferage was eliminated and scrap material began to be salvaged soon after employee purchase. Within two years the value of common stock had appreciated by over 200 percent. The transition at Byers Transport, too, appears to have resulted in greater employee care in using company equipment and in their work generally. The figure for claims against the company for lost or damaged freight was estimated to have fallen from 5.1 percent of freight volume to 2.1 percent while pounds loaded per manhour rose slightly, by some five percent. Byers workers, it appears, did not necessarily work harder or longer hours; their attitude had, however, improved and this resulted in more efficient operation and lower employee turnover. The potential of worker ownership for raising productivity and profitability is also demonstrated by the Australian experience of Hart of the West, which acquired the Perth firm of S.W. Hart & Co. from its parent company.[24] This followed uncertainty and loss of morale among employees owing to a history of three takeovers within two years. About sixty percent of the 350 employees were shareholders in the company: after the first year of trading earnings per share almost quintupled and product quality is currently reputed to be well above average for the industry.

To raise productivity, and especially to operate plants with greatly reduced manning, sometimes required quite substantial relaxation of outdated conventions on job demarcation and changes in management style. Workers at Kirkby Manufacturing accepted that, when skilled tradesmen's work was not available, skilled personnel could be switched to unskilled tasks. Workers also 'dropped the traditional opposition to working on a flexible basis, which means that machines do not have to be stopped during breaks. This, it was suggested, increased radiator output by approximately 1,000 per week.'[25] Meriden's submission for public assistance stressed that craftsmen would handle several trades and production workers would 'fetch their own materials and sweep up after themselves . . . on the shop floor there would be . . . no foremen, no union rule book, job delineation no longer applies, and men move flexibly from one job to another'.[26] Pioneer Chain Saw was able to reduce quality control personnel from 57 to 10 without increasing defective product rates. At Tembec, lead operators replaced foremen, and job demarcation was similarly relaxed to give workers greater flexibility in repairing their equipment and carrying out preventative maintenance. Despite the advanced age of much of its machinery, Tembec had the least down-time over 1976–7 of all Canadian pulp mills. Reductions in the Scottish Daily News workforce especially emphasised cuts in the number of production workers and supervisory staff – without any apparent adverse consequences.

There is some evidence to suggest that mutual reinforcement between employees promoted the 'work ethic', following a number of transitions. 'We used to have one foreman, now we have fifty,' commented one Byers transport employee.[27] Surveys indicated that Tembec and Scottish Daily News workers, too, were clearly far less tolerant of fellow workers who refused to pull their weight.[28] Even the Sixth Report of the Committee on Public Accounts, otherwise scathing on the decision to fund Meriden, Kirkby, and the Scottish Daily News, noted the commitment with which workers in general went about their jobs.

Improved performance did not require solely passive accommodation. Worker initiatives proved able, in a number of cases, to contribute towards improved profitability. An outstanding example here is perhaps that of press conversion from broadsheet to tabloid on the *Scottish Daily News*. Outside engineers had previously indicated that this would not only be costly but require at least a month's closedown. The workers converted the presses in three weeks while maintaining full production. The initiative of Tembec workers was similarly significant in speeding the reopening of the plant and keeping old machinery running. Meriden Triumph workers contributed to product design by producing an improved motorcycle gearchange. Active worker support for, and greater identification with, their new enterprises are also indicated by reductions in absenteeism, shorter breaks, fewer grievances, and a low incidence of industrial disruption following transitions.

Inequality of ownership and possible reversion
Such improvements in the climate of labor relations may be temporary,

in Table 4.1 came from public sources. But there were private investors from whom limited funds could also be obtained. These may be grouped into three categories:

(a)   *Sympathy capital* could sometimes be raised from individuals concerned at the loss of jobs among friends, neighbors and relatives. This capital source was sometimes important in the US too, as in the case of the Library Bureau. Library Bureau workers were encouraged to locate six investors each, and it is significant that of the 3,396 equity subscribers, 2,265 invested only $100 each.[31] The Scottish Daily News relied considerably upon sympathy capital, generally contributed in small sums. Survey evidence described in Chapter 8 shows that the small outside SDN investors were well aware of the risk involved and that their contributions included a sizeable charitable element, in the sense that their expected return on the risky investment was not anticipated to exceed that on such regular, secure investments as post office deposits.

(b)   *Linked capital* – that provided by persons and organisations with an existing stake in the survival of the enterprise – is sometimes hard to distinguish from sympathy capital. The locals of Temiscaming, Quebec and local firms contributed Can $200,000 to the Tembec pulp mill for an initial stake of 8 percent of the equity. The clearest case of linked capital is perhaps that of the Chrysler rescue, where suppliers, dealers and existing creditors of the company were required to make financial concessions totalling at least $280 million under the terms of the Chrysler Corporation Loan Guarantee Act (1979). Concessions and capital from local authorities, concerned at the evaporation of their tax bases, are also appropriately seen as linked capital.

(c)   *Capital plus management*   In three cases, those of Tembec, Pioneer Chain Saw and the Scottish Daily News, a highly personalised package of entrepreneurial capital was attracted in the form of individuals who recognised the potential of the transition for trimming operating costs and raising efficiency. These were able to place themselves in strong positions of control by providing desperately needed skills and cash. For a collective contribution of only Can $100,000 the Tembec 'founders', George Petty, Jim Chantler, Frank Dottori and Jack Stevens were able to secure 39 percent of the equity and effective control of a plant whose net worth by 1978 had risen to Can $18.7 million. The British entrepreneur, Robert Maxwell, secured a strong foothold in the Scottish Daily News for an investment of £100,000. Shortly thereafter he seized the opportunity afforded by its desperate circumstances to gain effective control. Had it survived, Maxwell would have secured a national newspaper for very little. Joseph Mason contributed Can $250,000 to Pioneer, securing 51 percent of control of

Granton Corporation, which itself controlled 51 percent of the shares of Pioneer, a company with assets estimated to be in the region of Can $10 million.

Conversion and trade unionism

A number of examples outside the US suggest a tendency for individual trade unions to lose a degree of bargaining power after conversion. Ninety-five percent of the Manuest workforce was unionised prior to employee takeover; the unionised proportion subsequently fell to only forty percent. Surveys for Manuest and the Scottish Daily News confirm this tendency to a reduced union role, as do accounts of Meriden and the national union reaction to the experience of Tembec. This is not, however, to suggest that the establishment of some form of employee ownership spells the end of trade unionism. Stern (1978) and Long (1979) cite evidence to the effect that American transitions have not led to a reduced perception of the need for unions in US plants. In Long's (1979) longitudinal study the perceived necessity for a union actually increased after the initial period of transition, and, in the only known case of union decertification – that at Jeanrette Glass – a plant-based union was formed to replace the decertified national union.

These observations are not necessarily inconsistent. They point to the change in the union role necessary for unions to flourish under worker ownership (a theme developed also by Long, 1979), and also relate to the unequal distribution of power in most existing firms, even those substantially owned by their employees. While a union role is especially necessary in firms characterised by unequal equity holdings and nondemocratic structures of control, transitions to employee ownership appear to be able to potentially weaken the nationwide, traditional role of trade unionism as representative of the working class through the mechanism of collective bargaining. Worker buyouts of collapsing firms present national trade unions with a microcosmic version of the general problem faced by unions in their attempts to raise living standards of their members – how to take into account the prospect that greater demands may lead to members being made redundant through competition in labor or product markets. The role of trade unions in worker-run enterprises may be no less problematic than the union role among the unemployed.

Successes and failures

The survival record of the cases listed in Table 4.1 is mixed. Considering those outside the US, Kirkby Manufacturing, Lip and the Scottish Daily News failed. The last-mentioned case survived for only six months because of a market worse than had been anticipated by even official feasibility studies, and unexpectedly low advertising revenues.

After a long and uncertain struggle, by 1981 Meriden had improved its profitability; UCS reverted to more traditional forms of state support. Tembec, Pioneer Chain Saw and Manuest survive, all in more or less their original form.

The survival record of American transition has been remarkable. Of the 50 to 60 buyouts of conventional closing firms in the 1970s, none was known to have failed by the end of the decade.[32] In most cases, as noted above, conversion was possible without state support, which suggests that many resembled conventional 'managerial buyouts' of potentially quite competitive firms, but a number (including the cases in Table 4.1) would not have been possible without public backing.

In assessing this mixed record it must be recalled that the British cases, especially, started under severe handicaps. Markets and distributorships had to be revived following substantial periods of shutdown. Uncertainty over their prospects hampered their ability to raise normal working capital and trade credit: they were thus constrained more than would have been anticipated on the basis of normal trading relationships. Their origin in political compromise (see Chapter 5) implied that little attention was given in rescue plans to upgrading and renewing capital equipment.

On the other hand, at least a part of the success of a number of examples may be attributed to unanticipated and favorable market developments. Pulp prices, Can $165/ton at the time of the closure of the Kipwa mill, soared to $500 in the beginning of 1974, providing a welcome cash infusion into Tembec. Pioneer benefited from the boom in the chain saw market resulting from an increased demand for wood-burning fires in North America following the oil crisis. South Bend Lathe was perhaps fortunate to land the largest order in its history shortly after purchase by its employees. And the worker-shareholders of Vermont Asbestos Group surely owed a great deal to extraordinarily favorable developments in the asbestos market, which, soon after purchase, boosted the value of a $250 shareholding to $10,000.

These divergent experiences highlight the element of risk in the decision to restart a closing firm. As discussed in Chapter 3, a high proportion of failures in government-assisted takeovers does not necessarily indicate misguided industrial policy. What does seem to indicate sound policy, however, is an intervention strategy capable of encouraging the streamlining of assisted firms and generating a high degree of consensus on the need to be viable – necessary, but of course not sufficient, preconditions for success. On this score, the evidence appears to be favorable to employee takeovers – even for the failures. If these appear overemphasised in this chapter and in the weighting of case study material in Chapters 7 and 8, it is in an attempt to provide a more rigorous basis for assessing the suggested pattern of intervention.

The Maltese Experience

The Maltese drydocks

Malta was presented to the Knights of St John by Philip of Spain as an island with a strategic position but limited natural resources. Following World War II, the mainstay of the Maltese economy until the mid-1960s was the British defense establishment, which employed 24 percent of the workforce in 1958. This shrank to 6 percent by 1970, during which period an intensive industrialisation program raised the proportion of workers in nondefense industry from 10 to 23 percent. Labor unrest mounted in the late 1960s following Maltese independence in 1964 – the number of days lost by strikes rose from 4,000 in 1965 to 148,000 by 1970. Ominously, the number of days was tending to increase more rapidly than the number of workers involved.[33]

In 1971 the Malta Labour party under Dom Mintoff won the General Election in coalition with the General Workers Union (GWU), the largest workers' union. By 1970 the GWU comprised 69 percent of the total unionised workforce which itself amounted to 45 percent of all workers. However, the trade unions operated in a decentralised manner, with strong organisation at plant levels which possessed a high degree of autonomy. Collective bargaining emphasised wages and working conditions with unemployment a constant threat. Over the 1970s, as worker militancy increased, perception of the need for widespread participation in industry appears to have become fairly general, although the definition and scope of worker participation naturally differed between the Nationalist and Labour parties, and the unions and employers association. Mintoff and the Labour party were said to have been against the ideological imposition of participation and convinced that 'it had to grow from the shop floor'. Participation was emphasised especially in the public enterprise sector, and was initiated by the government or GWU. Independently, however, participatory movements evolved in certain private enterprises.[34]

Kester (1980) cites five instances of worker participation initiated after the coming to power of the Labour government. Of these, by far the most significant concerned the parastatal drydocks which had been a major political issue since it had been taken over by Baileys Shipyards in 1959, following the rundown of the British defense establishment. The GWU had pressured Baileys into accepting a workforce of 6,000 from the Admiralty's roll of 12,000, but even this was excessive in relation to the work available. The period 1965–7 was relatively quiet, but following the breakdown of negotiation in 1968 the dockyards were nationalised in April with the assurance of the Nationalist government that all jobs would be preserved. Wage leapfrogging between industrial and nonindustrial workers led to claims for wage increases of up to 63 percent. Negotiations broke down, and a work to rule was followed by a strike of some fifty employees in key trades. The resulting industrial standstill continued for seven months and was by far the most serious in Malta's history. Over the four year period since nationalisation, losses had totalled £M9 million. About a quarter of total outstanding public debt was accounted for by advances to the dockyard.

The dockyard thus was a significant issue in the 1971 election. Labour proceeded to put its plans into practice, appointing three Trade Union and three government representatives to the Board of Directors, with a neutral chairman. Although worker participation had been introduced, the Prime Minister argued that workers could not share in profits before the debts of the drydock were paid. Under the drydocks legislation, Mintoff still retained great power to direct the Board after consultation.

Misapprehension between union leaders and drydock workers over the new participation situation increased, however, and union representatives accustomed to playing an adversarial role found themselves in a delicate situation with their members who had difficulty in adjusting to the new situation. Towards the end of 1972 it was becoming clear that losses of the drydocks would amount to far more than the anticipated £M1.5 million. The government decided to take drastic action. The Prime Minister Dom Mintoff, put forward the alternatives to the senior and executive staff of the drydocks. These were, either to accept bankruptcy, to close it down for a period or to cut the salaries and number of management personnel and accept other measures. Management accepted the last option. The measures proposed proved unacceptable, however, to the union delegation – these included abolition of the shift system, acceptance of absolute occupational flexibility, unpaid overtime and a levy on pay.

Mintoff then appealed directly to the drydock workers at a mass meeting. He outlined the causes of its financial difficulties, including the lack of flexibility in working arrangements, and the consequences for the Maltese economy:

I am not referring to the time when Bailey was owner. At that time you did well to take all you could. Now you are not taking anything from anyone else but your own brothers, your children and your neighbors . . . You industrial workers maintain that you have made sacrifices . . . it is not true . . . it is also not true that you work hard . . .[35]

Mintoff then appealed directly to the drydock workers, placing on their shoulders the burden of decision: 'You have three choices to consider: whether you want me to continue to be your leader, whether you want the drydocks to be closed down or whether . . . everyone accepts to carry his share of the burden.'[36] Despite an initial fierce reaction to the terms outlined, Mintoff's position was supported by the vote of a massed assembly. In return for wide-ranging concessions, he guaranteed that future profits should be saved on behalf of the workforce. This provided the catalyst for a process of negotiation between government and the GWU, which eventually conceded that the agreement reached was the best in the situation and that in its opinion government had introduced a sincere method to put the yard on a sound economic footing for the eventual benefit of the workers themselves.

At the end of a half-year austerity period it appeared that the economic effect of the agreement had been fully achieved. The losses of the drydocks had been completely eliminated. This provided the basis for a new agreement between the drydocks management, the Government and the GWU. The major achievement in this new agreement was the adoption of the proposed wage restructuring which had been for so long a major issue.

The Maltese experience is of interest in assessing the managerial potential of interventions involving changes in the structure of asset ownership and the introduction of participatory decisionmaking. It illustrates – rather like Chrysler in the US and British Leyland in the UK – how the size of an enterprise facing difficulty may compel government to intervene: the drydocks alone employed five percent of the Maltese labor force. Mintoff's use of the participatory approach may also be seen as an example of the shifting of responsibility away from government and towards the mass of workers involved in the drydock, which included strategically placed groups probably more vulnerable to peer pressure than to government directives. While workers were not asked to come up with their own solutions, the strategy resembles, in many respects, interventions analyzed earlier in this chapter.

5   The United States and Britain Compared

Pragmatic and Ideological Perspectives

Controversy and reaction
In any capitalist economy, the spectacle of workers buying their own jobs is unusual. Even smooth transitions to employee ownership attract some publicity – and, when tension escalates to the point of sit-ins, demonstrations and protest marches, worker takeovers are indeed newsworthy events at local and even national level. But, despite strong underlying similarities between individual instances, the slant of media treatment and general view of the events differ considerably across countries.

In the US, attempts by workers to buy their closing firms have received sympathetic (if often skeptical) support from a range of political persuasions, from Eastern Democrats to Southern Republicans. Legislation to assist such buyouts has advanced. In Britain, on the other hand, worker takeovers have encountered hostility, not only Conservative, but also from much of the Labour Party and the extreme left wing.

This difference is important in that the American reaction is more conducive to experiments with worker ownership as a constructive response to some cases of plant closure. However, because the US has seen less pressure for intervention along European lines, worker takeovers have not been advocated from the standpoint of improving national industrial policy relative to conventional methods.

Only to a minor extent do varying perspectives appear to reflect different objectives and ideological stances adopted by redundant workforces. Far more important are cross-country differences in the balance and nature of conservative and radical ideologies. These differences are reflected in the institutions through which workers have funded or otherwise assisted their takeovers. In comparing the American and British responses to attempts by employees to purchase their firms the experience of each country may be broken down under two headings: firstly, the development of ideology insofar as it bears on cooperation; secondly, the implications of this development for practical policy. The American reaction cannot be addressed without reference to the origins and nature of 'American Exceptionalism' – the failure of class-based political movements to assume a dominant place in the US despite its status as a preeminent capitalist power. Exceptionalism reflects clearly in recent legislative trends towards instituting worker takeovers as acceptable candidates for public assistance, and an almost unconscious acceptance of the implications for the structure of asset ownership of the Chrysler Corporation Loan Guarantee Act (1979).

As described in Chapter 4, many US transitions have stemmed from corporate divestitures and closures of somewhat isolated enterprises. The right of capital to close plants has not been ideologically disputed and, in line with the pluralistic, almost populist ethos further described below, any ideological reaction has been directed against 'big business' rather than the capitalist system itself. The pluralistic, localised strand of American political thought and structure is an important feature in the origins of support for worker takeovers. It facilitates the coming together of normally disparate interests temporarily united by threatened firm closure. Paradoxically, cooperation has been shielded from a radical complexion through its association with the individualistic, frontier ethic which is thought still to exert a powerful influence on American political ideology.

Opposition to a potential role for government in assisting employee takeovers has stemmed from three sources. Conservative reservations tend to be dominated by aversion to the use of public funds to intervene into industry. That the new enterprises take a 'cooperative' form seems less of an issue, partly, no doubt, because of the legitimation of the cooperative response as 'small business', partly perhaps because of the faith in marketplace incentives, so pervasive in conservative American ideology. It is hard to disagree with the *principle* of employee ownership on conservative grounds. Not unnaturally, the prospect of control leaving orthodox capitalist hands prompts disagreement from traditional sources of capital, which have in some cases insisted upon conventional patterns of control as a precondition for their participation. Ideological objections aside, this may also be viewed as a consequence of skepticism over the commercial viability of the cooperative form which is only partly tempered by faith in incentives.[1] A second source of opposition stemmed from a trade union movement uncertain of its role under employee ownership, and not favorable to alternative modes of employee representation.[2] Thirdly, belief that public funds could better be employed in alternative uses (such as retraining) has prompted opposition to policies supporting existing industries and firms.

Britain, in contrast to the US, has been splintered over the desirability of takeovers. This reflects a greater degree of ideological polarisation.

Neither Conservative, Labour, nor mainstream left wing has emphasised employee ownership, and even the Institute for Workers' Control portrays it in conflictual as opposed to puralistic terms. Unlike the US, Britain cannot point to clear legislative trends involving the worker takeover strategy. Despite considerable current interest in the potential of such a policy – or indeed, of *any* policy! – in combatting unemployment, the recent political perspective on the strategy was most prominently reflected in a period of ideological controversy accompanying the establishment, in 1974, of three worker cooperatives by the Labour government. This controversy, provoked primarily by the political route through which state support was elicited, has detracted from merits of the procedures through which the cooperatives were financed, and obscured the potential of similar procedures for industrial support and possible regeneration.

As in the US, Britain had no centralised institution to assist conversions until recently. Negotiations with central government for funding were far more crucial in obtaining backing than support from local communities. Central government assistance was indeed forthcoming in three cases, but was granted primarily on ideological grounds rather than as a pragmatic response to save jobs. This route to funding the cooperatives initiated a wave of conservative hostility despite the fact that the impulses towards cooperativism were not, in the first instance, primarily radical. Cooperatives in the US unified disparate interest groups; in the UK they generated ideological polarisation between a faction of the Labour party and virtually the rest of the country.

Without suitable institutions to assist transitions to employee ownership, the impact of legislation may be small. In contrast to America and Britain, France has a well-developed agency for facilitating conversions of bankrupt firms to worker ownership.[3] However, in the wake of a wave of US transitions in the 1970s, institutions to assist are being established and parallel the main directions of legislative evolution. These and recent British initiatives are briefly and selectively reviewed in this chapter.

American Pragmatism and Attitudes to Employee Takeovers[4]

American exceptionalism
The pragmatic reaction to cooperatives in the US has its roots in certain aspects of American industrial history. At the turn of the century American industrialisation appeared to develop along similar lines to that of Europe with regard to class consciousness and conflict. From the 1930s onwards, however, US responses to economic crises prompted a different path of development. The US developed a

pluralist society, with a variety of competing groups united by a common rejection of socialism. No significant group maintained a socialist perspective. This, it was thought, would perpetuate capitalism through the cyclical upsets within the economy. Optimism in this prescription is still sustained today although considerably modified in form.

Explanations for the divergent path of ideological development include the absence of feudalism in North America, which therefore lacked the seeds of a class-based society; the overlapping of immigrant and status boundaries within the working class; job, as opposed to class, consciousness; political agnosticism of the AFL under Samuel Gompers; the ethics of 'rugged individualism' and the frontier thesis; the continuing vigor of US capitalist growth, a relatively high wage economy, and the socially mobile nature of American society. According to Hartz (1955):

One of the central characteristics of a nonfeudal society is that it lacks a genuine revolutionary tradition for a society which begins with Locke, and then transforms him, stays with Locke . . . and becomes indifferent to the challenge of socialism in the late era as it was unfamiliar with the heritage of feudalism in the earlier one.[5]

Conformism and consensus underlie American ideology since the point of entry to the American 'experience' is common to most waves of immigrants. Consensus is therefore so deeply rooted that it is 'unknown'. Rather than a superstructural variable in the Marxist sense, ideology appears as an infrastructural determinant. Industrialism may be a factor common to all advanced societies, but a nearly neutral model of production leaves society to be interpreted through ideology. The American 'end of ideology' thesis saw 'industrialisation' as a global model of production with certain implications for the division of labor rather than viewing capitalism as a distinct socioeconomic form with particular contradictions.[6]

Relative to the UK, American trade unions, as typified by the AFL, have a reputation for economism and lack of interest in issues of industrial control. Grob (1961), not unlike the UK 'Oxford School',[7] views US unions as working to establish stable collective bargaining relationships:

The trade unions . . . accepted their environment, and sought to take advantage of the relative scarcity of labor . . . Hence they emphasised the collective bargaining functions of labor organisations, tacitly accepting the workers wage status.[8]

The high-wage economy was thus sufficient to 'buy off' workers' demands for control.

Personal philosophies of the AFL leaders were important in influencing trade union policy at crucial stages, noticeably when they engineered the rejection of socialist principles.[9] Although Clegg (1976) suggests that 'the old AFL had a high regard for political action but though the best results would be achieved by avoiding party ties',[10] Gompers, in his efforts to secure stable union organisation, became suspicious of any political programming. He held that the effect of the socialist party was to divert the attention of the American working people from the immediate need and struggle to something remote.[11] Hoxie (1966) also draws attention to the opportunistic, short-run nature of union objectives.

In the *History of Labor in the United States*, Commons (1921) provides a broader analysis of the development of American labor which emphasises pragmatism. Commons not only pointed to the 'voluntarist' nature of American unionism, but also charted the demise of syndicalism.[12] Commons, like Gompers, concluded that because economic and political methods diverged, each type of unionism would sap the other's strength. Moreover, he drew attention to the fact that the AFL was an extremely limited organisation, remaining 'mainly the organisation of the upper and median strata among the native and Americanised wage earners'.[13]

Perlman (1928) paid attention to the importance of 'intellectuals' and how labor movements were the poorer for their absence, suggesting that the 'perpetual struggle to keep the organisation from going to pieces for want of inner cohesiveness' was based upon the identification of American labor:

. . . in outlook, interest and action with the great lower middle class, the farmers, the small manufacturers and businessmen – in a word the 'producing' classes and their periodic 'anti-monopoly' campaigns.[14]

The weakness of labor was based on having to contend with a wide distribution of private property:

. . . in the American community, labor is a minority, and is facing a nation of property holders, actual or potential.[15]

This also explains the disinclination of labor movements to form a permanent political alliance. In explaining the absence of class consciousness, Perlman cited several factors among which was immigration:

To workers employed in a given industry, a new wave of immigrants, generally of a new nationality, meant a competitive menace to be fought off and to be kept out of industry . . .[16]

Bell (1962) uses Perlman's analysis in his explanation of the failure of socialism and supplements this with the observation that immigration heightened needs for conformism. 'Americanism' then offered a substitute for 'socialism', appearing to transcend class conflict and demanding normative obedience. This relates closely to Hartz's explanation in terms of a lack of a feudal stage of development.

The rugged frontier spirit, too, was transmitted into anti-collectivist sentiments within the 'collective' environment of the twentieth century:

The normative aspirations of the majority have served to buttress the position of employers in their opposition to trade unions; the folklore of 'rugged individualism' and the ideology of the 'open shop' are inextricably connected.[17]

Individualism was supported by the AFL and 'business unions' in order to oppose monopoly power. Roosevelt and Wilson similarly opposed monopoly.

The great monopoly of this country is the money monopoly . . . all of our activities are in the hands of a few men . . . who necessarily, by very reason of their own limitations, chill and check and destroy genuine economic freedom.[18]

The genesis of American exceptionalism goes a long way towards explaining the different local union roles in North American and European transitions described in Chapter 4. In both environments, the possibility of workers purchasing their firm does, however, raise a degree of tension between local and national-level unionism for similar reasons. Outside the US, more 'political' union movements are conscious of the threat to their objective of representing labor through party political channels, in addition to the concern, common also in the US, at the erosion of nation-wide or industry-wide collective bargaining. Their more pragmatic orientation has, however, made employee ownership more palatable to American unions and there are signs that opposition is being replaced by cautious acceptance.

To sum up, characterisation of the US as an ideological vacuum relative to other mature industrial economies is for present purposes neither necessary nor sufficient. What appears significant is its distinctive balance in the pattern of alliances and alignments – less class-based, more local, strongly individualistic and with a significant anti-monopoly, rather than anti-capitalist undertone. 'American exceptionalism' manifests itself, in the present context, in a generally pragmatic approach towards employee stock ownership and worker control, and in the linking of legislative movements in these directions with the interests of small business against monopoly capital and conglomeration.[19]

Employee-Ownership in Recent US Legislation

Two legislative strands
The spread of employee ownership and formation of worker co-

operatives *per se* has thus not been a focus of significant ideological controversy in the US. Debate intensifies, however, at the point where government becomes involved in their funding. A large state role in transitions to employee ownership conflicts somewhat with the individualistic, populist appeal of the cooperative firm. Nevertheless, because of the relatively pragmatic, economistic attitude to worker ownership in the US, legislation to further this form of organisation is far more developed than in the UK.

It is possible to distinguish, in the US legislative drive, two quite distinct strands linked by political expediency as well as objectives. The first relates to the Employee Stock Ownership Plan (ESOP): a specific mechanism for promoting employee ownership which may be introduced in a wide variety of circumstances. Support for the ESOP draws on the strong populist tradition of the US, is closely aligned to the powerful small business lobby and has been spearheaded by Senator Russell Long, chairman of the Senate Finance Committee. The second, more recent, legislative strand is that involving support for declining industries and motivated by concern at the drain of manufacturing jobs from the 'gray belt' – the industrialised Northeast Corridor. The legislator perhaps most closely associated with this drive for 'community stabilisation' has been Congressman Peter Kostmayer, of Pennsylvania.

To distinguish these strands, it could be noted that ESOP legislation primarily seeks tax concessions to incentivate a shift in the patterns of equity ownership, while 'community stabilisation' legislation emphasised the disbursement of public funds through such existing channels as the Economic Development Administration to assist worker buyouts, specifically of firms about to close their doors. 'Community Stabilisation' legislation has so far advanced haltingly. In contrast, since 1973, Congress has passed, and three separate administrators have signed into law, fourteen Bills promoting the use of ESOPs.

Employee ownerships and ESOPs

The tendency for capitalism to concentrate economic power in relatively few hands, and the implication of this for social and political influence, has been of concern in the US from Jefferson to Reagan.[20] There has thus been a long and generalised desire to expand the social basis of asset ownership, but in ways compatible with the capitalist system. The signing in the nineteenth century of the Homestead Act by Abraham Lincoln, a series of loan programs included in the Farmers Home Administration and the Small Business Administration, as well as other measures, are directed towards this end.

Support for ESOPs falls very much within this tradition.

. . . for the majority of American families their most important asset is their right some day to draw a social security payment from the Federal Government . . . That is a poor showing for a nation who prides itself on a strong private property approach to economic matters . . .[21]

In terms of stock ownership, about one percent of our people own about 50 percent of it. About six percent own 80 percent, but the shocking part is that about 80 percent of our people don't own any investment at all in productive wealth. That is something that concerns those of us who believe in a strong capitalist system.[22]

ESOPs therefore are seen by their proponents as a mechanism for redistributing income at source, through the redistribution of asset ownership, rather than through increased transfer payments financed out of an evermore concentrated distribution of income. The intention, however, is less to redistribute existing wealth than to give incentives for newly-created capital to be more broadly owned and to provide an expanded source of equity financing for corporations.

ESOPs are largely the effort of Louis Kelso, a San Francisco attorney. Under such a plan, a company establishes an Employee Stock Ownership Trust (ESOT) which then arranges a loan from a bank or other source to fund the capital needs of the company. The Trust is fully guaranteed by the company, and uses its funds to purchase company stock. This then is owned by the Trust; the company pledges to pay to the Trust sufficient to repay principal and interest on the loan. Whereas conventionally only interest payments are tax-deductible, both interest and principal payments to the ESOT are deductible up to certain limits. Thus, a company in a 46 percent tax bracket will in effect pay only 54 percent of the entire program. Stock is vested with the employees as the loan is repaid, generally beginning after a few years. Employees receive their stock when they retire, die or leave the company. Unless a contribution plan is arranged, they may pay nothing for their stock during employment.

In many cases, however, ESOPs have come to replace, rather than supplement, other forms of employee benefits linked to retirement. For this reason, the operation of specific ESOPs has attracted criticism as possibly not being in the best interests of their supposed beneficiaries, the workforces, as is further described in Chapter 6. ESOPs are nevertheless undoubtedly the widest formal vehicle through which worker shareholdings have been effected in the US. One recent estimate put the number of firms with ESOPs at around four thousand.

Surveys of firms owned through ESOPs (rather than directly) reveal significant differences in the dimensions of ownership. Hourly-paid employees in firms directly owned by their workers are far more likely to own a majority of shares than are similar workers in ESOP firms, which are forced, for reasons of tax advantage, to distribute stock in proportion to salary. The motivations for adopting ESOPs – tax advantage and employee incentive – also differ from the most usual factor impelling direct ownership – a desire to keep the firm alive.

Industrial closure and employee ownership

Legislative impulses in this direction date from early 1977. On 1 March 1978 Congressman Kostmayer, from Pennsylvania, together with Congressmen Stanley Lundine and Matthew McHugh of New York, introduced the *Voluntary Job Preservation and Community Stabilisation Act* HR12094 which 'provides loans to employee and employee-community groups to purchase firms due to shut down.'[23] The bill was authorised:

in response to the problems of plant shutdowns which in the past decade have hurt increasing numbers of Americans and threatened the economic stability of their communities. When a firm closes employees often lose more than their jobs. The economic hardship and uncertainty can wreck families, affect mental health, and cause extended personal suffering. Idleness may last for months and many workers require substantial retraining before they are again employable. The costs to society are staggering.[24]

Limitations of conventional federal and state government intervention are suggested.

The government can spend money on unemployment compensation, welfare or expensive job training programs, but these . . . do not combat the basic problem – preserving jobs . . . We believe one alternative to plant closings is ownership by employees or the residents of the affected community. Where plants would otherwise be abandoned, our bill would help interested groups of employees and community residents purchase the firms and try to run them profitably . . . The bill has four purposes: First, to preserve jobs . . .[25]

The Bill introducing the Act provided for technical assistance to help the startup of the new company and for evaluation of the feasibility of the prospective enterprise. It would have created a $100 million loan fund in the Economic Development Administration (EDA) to make loans to employees and employee organisations to purchase industrial plants which otherwise would close or relocate.[26] The bill subsequently became part of Title II of the National Public Works and Economic Development Act (1979), HR-2063. This bill passed the House by a substantial majority on 14 November and the Senate by a lesser margin on 1 August 1980. Disagreement arose over aspects of the bill unrelated to worker ownership in the House-Senate conference committee; it thus failed to become law.

In a simultaneous initiative, Kostmayer and associates had aligned themselves with Long and the small business lobby, introducing the Small Business Ownership Act (1980), which provided for loans of up to $500,000 administered through the Small Business Administration. These loans were to finance employee buyouts of closing firms and employee ownership of new firms. As Title V of the Small Business Development Act (1980), the bill passed the Senate unanimously on 1 May 1979. The new bill (S-2698), signed into law by President Carter on 2 July 1980, authorised the SBA to make and guarantee loans for worker-owned firms as part of all its existing programs. The criteria for worker ownership are laid down in guidelines adopted by the Joint House-Senate conference report.[27] The strength of bipartisan support for small business and associated worker ownership schemes has implied continuing support for the program despite the change of US administration.

Another important piece of legislation is the Chrysler Corporation Loan Guarantee Act of 1979. In a number of respects the Chrysler rescue attempt resembles the pattern of industrial intervention described in Chapters 3 and 4. In particular, it was not dissimilar to the pattern adopted in the case of the Scottish Daily News as described in Chapter 8. Federal loan guarantees not exceeding $1.5 billion were conditional upon matching contributions totaling $2 billion from a broad class of individuals and institutions characterised as 'persons with an existing economic stake in the health of the Corporation'. Unionised employees were to contribute $460 million, nonunionised workers $125 million in the form of concessions on pay increases, and creditors $500 million. In return, employees would acquire equity in Chrysler, through the inclusion into legislation of an employee stock ownership plan. Federal funding was in principle 'once and for all', but to be subject to continuous review by a committee established to monitor Chrysler's performance. To secure its investments the federal government also assumed liens on Chrysler's assets prior to those of many existing creditors.[28]

It is interesting to observe that opposition to the Chrysler bill emphasised (a) conservative opposition to any form of state intervention into the ailing auto industry, and (b) failure to adopt a more forward-looking industrial policy emphasising the development of new industries. One of the most articulate oppositions to the Chrysler Act along the latter lines came from Senator Adlai Stevenson. The rescue was seen as:

a waste of federal resources and the misallocation of private credit to the politically powerful instead of the economically viable . . .[29]

At stake here is whether we will go the British route and mortgage prosperity to the expediences of the present . . . The British have made support for geriatric industrial sectors a national labor and, led by the labor unions, have dragged their economy into a spiral of decline.[30]

It is possible to sympathise with Stevenson's opposition while at the same time supporting the general method through which the Chrysler bailout was effected, as an appropriate means of implementing a second-best policy. The first-best policy – closure of Chrysler and a shift in resources to more buoyant sectors – was clearly not politically feasible in the circumstances then prevailing. But even Stevenson's opposition did not focus on the issue of worker shareholding – in the UK, intervention itself would possibly have been less controversial than the implications of the package for changes in ownership structure and perhaps ultimately worker control.

Worker Ownership as a Radical Response: A British View?

Pragmatic acceptance versus radicalisation

Britain is commonly seen as a society more polarised than the US and more divided along class lines. Over the 1950s and 1960s, British political sociology was dominated by debate over the effect of increasing prosperity on working class attitudes. This period saw the development of the 'pragmatic acceptance hypothesis' and the reappraisal by Marxists of the utility of the Marxist-Leninist notions of true and false consciousness. The thesis of pragmatic acceptance was that working class 'conservatives' could not be considered as cultural dupes. They were 'pragmatists': individuals who supported the status quo because they believed it was in their material interest to do so. Pragmatic acceptance concluded that there was no potential for radical change in Britain among the working class.

A particularly significant work arguing along these lines was *The Affluent Worker Study* due to Goldthorpe *et al* (1968–69) which focused on workers in the automobile industry. Variants of the hypothesis stress the accommodative nature of pragmatic acceptance to existing social and economic arrangements.[31] Increasingly, the British working class is 'privatised', individuals focusing on their immediate personal circumstances rather than adopting a class position. Whatever class consciousness exists, it is argued, is limited to class identity, and even this is undercut by economism. Formulated within a common ideology dedicated to preserving the capitalist system, government policy correspondingly views conflict between groups as normal. Indeed, conflict can sometimes be useful, manifesting itself in support of a strand of managerialism which emphasises the necessary role of economic growth in improving social conditions. This phase of development in British social thought has a clear, though not perfect, parallel in the pragmatic, accommodative stance of American labor towards the capitalist system, described previously.

Meanwhile Marxism was in retreat and took the form of defensive theories centered on the so-called 'cash nexus hypothesis' argued by, among others, Westergaard (1970). Westergaard argues that there exists a fair amount of evidence in studies such as McKensie and Silver (1968) and Goldthorpe *et al* (1968-9) to demonstrate that 'social criticism coexists with "social apathy" in contemporary British working class consciousness',[32] and attacks the Affluent Worker Study's validation of pragmatic acceptance. While he supports the thesis of the study that workers are tied to jobs primarily by monetary considerations and that, for most workers, work itself holds no intrinsic interests, he argues that the one-dimensional link between pecuniary and social stability must be seen as the reason for potential radicalism rather than a sign of acceptance. Thus:

should the amount and dependability of the money be threatened, his [the worker's] resigned toleration of the lack of discretion, control and 'meaning' attached to the job could no longer be guaranteed. The cash nexus may snap just because it is only a cash nexus, because it is single stranded, and, if it does snap there is nothing else to bind the worker to acceptance of the situation.[33]

Ideological radicalism will thus follow the snapping of the cash nexus and lead to radical action. Westergaard, therefore, implies that spontaneous actions of workers engaged in their immediate struggles will lead to the transcendence of capitalism.

The cash nexus hypothesis is difficult to apply as an analytical tool because of its historicist origins which throw no light on the mechanism of its operation. There remains the critical and still unresolved question of whether ideological radicalism precedes or is induced by radical action which is not understood at the time: the latter course of events is suggested by, among others, Moorhouse (1976) and Lane and Roberts (1971). Also absent from discussion of the cash nexus hypothesis is any specification of the magnitude and nature of the nexus break necessary to generate radicalism. Marxists, furthermore, appear not to allow for the possibility of 'pragmatic rejection' of the unknown. Following the postulates of pragmatic acceptance, workers might plausibly accommodate to even an unpleasant reality because of a rational appreciation of their position. Failure, in some senses, of capitalism therefore need not imply an ideological shift to radical alternatives. In addressing this issue, it is essential to consider individual circumstances and options, rather than merely a class position, since the constraints to class action may actually be those perceived by the specific groups within the class affected by the snapping of the nexus.

It would therefore be appropriate to assess evidence drawn from periods of economic decline to see the extent to which the theory is valid for Britain. The early 1970s would be one period in which we might expect the defensive Marxist formulations of the 1960s to manifest themselves. In the early 1970s, inflation rose to 30 percent per annum, unemployment rose, and there were, increasingly, significant closures.[34]

For three reasons, redundancy through closures, rather than simply layoffs, is especially significant in relation to the cash nexus hypothesis. Firstly, it represents a very definite snapping of the cash nexus, removing the possibility that labor can be reemployed by the firm. Secondly, large numbers of workers are thrown into the job market in specific geographical areas. This heightens the difficulty of finding new jobs and increases the probability that occupational downgrading will have to be accepted. Thirdly, it decreases trade union power. Without the continued presence of the employer, the scope for union action on behalf of the redundant workers is limited. At a critical time, the worker is let down by the major worker organisations of the pluralist system. The concentration of redundancy facilitates communication among the redundant and the growth of alternative organisations. As the managerial promises of the 1960s, so vital to pluralist ideology, became less easy to sustain, many British workers therefore took their own defensive action and occupied factories threatened by closure. Gretton (1972) cites thirty cases of worker occupations in South Lancashire alone in spring 1972, involving, in total, between 25,000 and 30,000 workers.

Ideology and worker control
Both in North America and Europe the emergence of 'employee-owned' enterprises can therefore possibly be seen as manifestation of radical reaction – of a challenge to the existing order – following industrial decline. It may also be explained as an accommodative response to threatened redundancy, initiated as the best pragmatic attempt to restore the 'cash nexus', as analyzed in Chapter 3. In the US the latter view was overwhelming. Most observers considered the spectacle of workers buying their jobs sympathetically, albeit sometimes skeptically, as an appropriate response to closure. In Britain on the other hand, experiments at cooperation were attacked as 'wasteful projects' which would only encourage 'creeping militancy'. 'A diet of sub-Trotskyism' commented the *Daily Telegraph*,[35] enraged by the establishment of the Scottish Daily News. Michael Heseltine, then Conservative Spokesman for Industry, strongly attacked Labour's support for the cooperatives, suggesting that they encouraged

others to follow these illegal precedents, commit national resources to wasteful projects, and create a growing sense of injustice among the overwhelming majority of hard working, law-abiding citizens who totally fail to understand why creeping militancy should attract government support at their expense.[36]

There was criticism too from less obviously politically partisan sources. The *Sixth Report of the Committee on Public Accounts*,[37] for example, criticised the Department of Industry for backing the three 1974 cooperatives, concluding that they were not viable and thus a waste of public money.

Not only the conservative view, but that of the majority of the Labour party was hostile. The evolution of official Labour policy on worker participation explains the lack of mainstream Labour support for cooperative forms in general. Policy statements have emphasised the need for reliance on traditional trade-union institutions to further the power of workers, and even expressed a degree of antagonism towards alternative methods of achieving similar objectives. These, it has been held, will weaken the trade-union channel of representation[38] and lead, ultimately, to a reduction in the cohesion and strength of the working class.

Official Labour policy in fact dismissed both company works councils and worker shareholders as viable alternatives to union-led collective bargaining. The latter was ruled out on the grounds that workers would be insufficiently diversified against risk. Although the problem of risk diversification is indeed a serious one for cooperateurs, a further, very probable, reason for downplaying their potential role would seem to be the difficulties posed by such a prospect for trade-union representation and, indeed, for the trade-union movement as a whole.[39]

The attitude of a significant portion of the left was also skeptical. Marxists argued that worker control was illusory and insignificant and suggested that workers '. . . cannot implement decisions taken (at factory level) against the operation of market laws'.[40] It was further declared to be 'impossible to build islands of socialism in a sea of capitalism'.[41] Ironically, mainstream leftists accurately perceived the nature of the forces making for the transition as those of pragmatic accommodation to (in their view) an undesirable socioeconomic order, and recognised the managerial potential of the strategy more clearly than did conservative opinion.

Insofar as there exists a British 'orthodoxy' of radical workers' control, it is represented by the Institute for Workers Control (IWC), which was formed in 1969 as a 'research and educational body' covering all matters related to the democratisation of British industry. The IWC holds that 'aggressive encroachments' on managerial prerogatives will progressively lead to a transformation of the current political and social order and to workers' self-management. Worker control arises from a tug-of-war between workers and management which takes place 'factory by factory and industry by industry'.[42] According to Coates (1971): 'the main battleground of the real status war is . . . the factory, the office and the enterprise'.[43] Social training must take place at the level of the factory in order that individuals form the necessary attitudes and psychological qualities of democracy. Worker control, in the view of this fragment of the left, has thus an educative and sensitising function in support of an ultimate, radical, objective.

The Cooperative Experiments of 1974

An origin in compromise
The British cooperative experiments actually involved workers overwhelmingly motivated by pragmatic, as opposed to radical, objectives. All documentary studies of the 1974 attempts to establish worker-controlled firms emphasise a perceived need for employment as the central motivating force,[44] as do our own surveys reported in Chapter 8. Alister Mackie, militant trade unionist and initiator of the Scottish Daily News worker committee, himself observed regretfully that: 'The bulk of our workforce was more concerned about a weekly wage than they were about cooperative.'[45] The moving figure behind their funding, Tony Benn, then Secretary of State for Industry, recognised the employment drive behind the cooperatives. Benn also argued, however, that the demands of the workers at Meriden, Kirkby and the Scottish Daily News went 'beyond protest about job loss and have begun to think out how they could actually organise and run their own enterprise'.[46] As further described below, Benn was ideologically committed to workers control and substantially adopted the Institute for Workers' Control view of transitions to cooperatives as useful opportunities for social education.

That the British cooperatives, like their American counterparts, had rather conservative origins does not detract from the fact that they were popularly perceived as radical because of their 'appropriation' by certain leftist elements of the Labour Party. The British cooperatives were more idiosyncratic than the American, and less in line with trends in national policy. Consequent political struggle at a national level contributed to their ultimate demise and has also inhibited consideration of cooperation as a potential policy tool in circumstances of plant closedowns.

Surprisingly, the process of political compromise underlying the funding decision shaped a pattern of intervention rather appropriate to such problems from present perspectives. The pattern also resembled that of certain American interventions – without any of the parties involved in the struggle advocating or even outlining such a pattern on pragmatic, managerial grounds. Compromise appears to have involved three distinct political interests: the mainstream Labour Party leadership, Tony Benn, then Secretary of State for Industry, and the professional Civil Service and Treasury. Their respective positions must be analyzed with an appreciation of the political and economic position of Labour between the two 1974 general elections, in addition to the broader ideological questions raised by workers' control. To piece together the determinants of support has not been straightforward, owing to the restrictions placed on information relating to Cabinet decisions.[47]

Government, trade unions and industrial democracy
The majority Labour view of worker control through non-union channels has been discussed above. In the context of the 1974 co-operatives, this translated into a lack of approval and perhaps crystallised into more active opposition because of the fear of being seen to favor leftist policies shortly before the October 1974 election. Nevertheless, Labour leadership supported Benn's initiatives largely for reasons of temporary political expediency, as further described below.

Benn's ideology and workers' action
The British cooperatives all resulted from militant grassroot reaction to mass redundancy arising from plant closures. While, in such circumstances, the mediating role of trade unions and their traditional weapon of the strike are of little use, sit-ins immobilise assets, so preventing resource transfers between economic enterprises. Moreover, the predicament of workers about to be abandoned by their employers can be raised to the level of a public issue.[48] However, Meriden, Kirkby and the Scottish Daily News were vulnerable because they did not rely on substantial local or national campaigns. Rank and file labour action converged with Benn's ideological leanings, and culminated in his enthusiastic support. Benn's willingness to fund 'workers instead of firms' provided a short cut to financial assistance, but caused the cooperatives to be associated with a relatively radical ideology which did not command majority support even within the Labour Cabinet.

At the time of the Labour government's funding of the three co-operatives, Benn was the undisputed leader and ideologue of Labour's left wing, with a substantial rank and file trade union power base and sincerely committed to worker control on radical ideological grounds. Perhaps more than any other Labour minister, Benn could be identified with the position of the Institute for Workers' Control, seeing in the process of rank and file mobilisation a counterweight to conservative policies. These he viewed as a danger organised and engineered at the top whether by Labour or Conservative leadership.

against this is posed the concept of workers' control and industrial democracy – which is what the Labour movement in a less-often quoted phase talks about as the best obtainable means of popular administration[49]

In his capacity as Secretary of State for Industry, Benn gave the 1974 cooperative experiments every encouragement. Firstly, he was ideologically committed to worker control. According to a ministerial colleague:

If Benn controlled appointments . . . I think we would see these kinds of policies on a much bigger scale . . . In his mind this was an experiment for something which could be much bigger.[50]

Secondly, cooperative structure was not without financial appeal to Benn, who anticipated increased efficiency as one of the payoffs to industrial democracy: 'If productivity can be increased through industrial democracy and supply more goods at a lower unit cost it would help reduce inflation.'[51] Thirdly, given increasing rank-and-file labor pressure against both the Conservatives and the Labour establishment, it might be argued that support for the cooperatives was necessary for Benn to preserve credibility with his own power base.

The Treasury and the civil service

Formally apolitical, but, in practice, staunch bastions of British conservatism, the Treasury and higher civil service are known to have bitterly opposed the fundings. Their open opposition was expressed on economic grounds in terms similar to those of the Sixth Report of the Committee on Public Accounts: that nonviable cooperatives were a waste of taxpayers' money. Neither the Treasury nor Benn's economic advisers can, however, be seen as politically neutral and their opposition is believed to have been fundamentally ideological.[52] This interpretation is especially plausible given Benn's emphasis on the importance of such ventures in radically transforming society. The stringency of the conditions set on cooperative funding are thus best understood as an attempt to prevent the success of the experiments, a strategy which must, in retrospect, itself be seen as quite successful. Participants, when interviewed, all made reference to their impact in limiting the availability of normal trade credit.

Those people in Whitehall who wanted to kill these projects were well aware . . . Keep them (the cooperatives) on a short string and the normal private, commercial market doesn't operate because they regard it as short term and too risky. It's a way of surreptitiously defeating the projects without overtly blocking them.[53]

This is not to say that greater access to credit would have assured the success of any of the 1974 cooperatives. But whatever their longer-term viability might have been, the combination of low initial working capital and difficult access to credit markets would have inhibited investment and rendered survival over an initial loss-making period extremely difficult.

Between elections: Labour's politico-economic conjuncture

The political and economic circumstances of mid-1974 Britain provided the cooperatives' advocates with unusual, but temporary influence over their less radical Labour Cabinet colleagues. They thus set
a critical stage for the interaction of the three principal interests.

The February Labour government assumed office at the difficult
time of a looming world economic recession. Two days before the
February election it had been learned that the January trade deficit had
reached £382 million. February and March deficits were even higher.
Harold Wilson, then Prime Minister, faced an annual deficit of around
£4,000 million after the February election. Crucial passages in
Labour's February 1974 manifesto referred to these difficulties, in
particular to mounting inflation and to rising unemployment. The
Treasury estimated that Britain urgently needed £10,000 million in
international loans.[54] Here it is important to bear in mind that the
Labour government was doubly disadvantaged: while in opposition it
had aggravated sources of international capital and appeared to have
placed itself in a bad position to borrow from abroad. There was,
nevertheless, little doubt that Wilson would secure necessary financing
from the International Monetary Fund. The government was commonly seen to be bound by external commitments to prevent any
significant wage increases and to impose a fierce brake on public
spending.[55]

At the same time, however, the Labour Party faced an unpreced-
ented growth in grassroots worker militancy and showed signs of
serious domestic splits and internal difficulties. Militancy can partly be
ascribed to the serious and growing problem of unemployment. But an
important contributory factor had been the polarising effect of the prior
February election, called by Edward Heath, then leader of the Conservative government, following the coalminers' strike. The Conservatives had argued that the major choice for the British people was
between moderation and extremism alleging that: 'The moderates
within Labour's ranks have lost control and the real power in the
Labour Party has been taken over, for the first time ever, by the
extreme left wing.'[56] Labour nevertheless won the election, and the
minority government settled the miners' dispute, ending the 'three-day
week' by agreeing to their demands.[57]

The net result of the failure of the Conservatives 'Suez of the
Seventies' policy of confrontation was a mood of optimism among trade
unionists and a distinct strengthening of Labour's left wing, which was
seen to have secured a more powerful mandate at the polls. Some form
of concession was necessary both to secure Labour's unity until the
October election and because of the importance placed on the so-called
'social contract' emphasising voluntary wage restraint as the major

element in Labour's prescription for Britain's economic ailments.[58]

The short to medium-term impact of wage and price controls will almost inevitably be felt largely in real wage reductions. These were seen as necessary to reduce domestic absorption of goods and services and to improve Britain's 1974 trade balance. Compensation for lowered living standards cannot, of course, be provided in a material form: to ensure Labour's acquiescence to the voluntary controls of the social contract, political concessions were therefore necessary. Indeed, at least one prominent economist has pronounced the major danger arising out of such wage controls to be the extent to which political concessions are likely to be needed to maintain them.[59] Benn's appointment as Secretary of State for Industry may be seen as part of this process of political concession to grassroots labor, a process not without risk to the Labour party. Fears that the Labour government would be defeated in October as a result of openly adopting socialist policies were, however, outweighed by the immediate difficulties which would arise through the dropping of Benn and the open rejection of his views. Such an event, allegedly planned in advance by Wilson, would have split the Cabinet and greatly diminished the possibility of reaching agreement on the 'social contract'. This, too, would have jeopardised Labour's chances of victory in the October election. Benn was therefore in a strong position, even if only temporarily.

There were also, apparently, certain specific influences which were important in securing the Cabinet's approval of the support operations. While in opposition Wilson had personally been involved with the fate of the Kirkby cooperative, which was situated in the constituency next to his own, and had been instrumental in obtaining financial support for the enterprise. Wilson was not, in principle, in favor of the cooperatives. Nevertheless, he could not risk such a U-turn immediately on assuming office. Meriden too had powerful friends, notably Jack Jones, General Secretary of the Transport and General Workers Union, and Geoffrey Robinson, former Managing Director of Jaguar and the cooperative's financial adviser. As one of the principal architects of the 'social contract', Jones was in an influential position. Robinson's success at Jaguar, and his argument that Meriden was indeed commercially feasible, appears to have gained the support of at least one Cabinet minister. Harold Lever, then Wilson's economic adviser, was reputedly convinced by Jones and Robinson. While the Scottish Daily News did not appear to have powerful backing other than that of Benn, Labour was disturbed at the increasing support for the Scottish Nationalist Party.[60] In requesting government assistance, Allister Mackie had indicated that the editorial policy of the paper was to be 'left of center' and a vehicle for fighting both the Conservatives and the 'new enemy', the Scottish Nationalist Party. Scottish Nationalsm does not appear to have been the major influence in persuading the Cabinet to support the newspaper, but it undoubtedly did play a role.

As described in more detail in Chapter 8, the overriding character-istics of the government loan to the Scottish Daily News were (1) the stringency of its conditions, which hampered the raising of other funds and (2) the very explicit limitation on state support. Condition (1), by forcing the commercially inexperienced workers into collaboration with a financier, jeopardised the ideological significance of workers' control from the outset. The limitation of support derived from the fact that the government and Treasury viewed their obligation as temporary - a consequence of the temporarily strong position of Benn, itself caused by the need for the Labour party to strike a political balance between its own supporters before the October election. In line with the trade union movement, most of the Labour Cabinet was markedly unenthusiastic about this particular form of worker control: the lack of support for the newspaper by trade unions in general and the (conservative) print unions in particular is evident in their meager contributions to the enterprise, while the trade union movement was relatively hostile to Kirkby. The role of the Treasury in seeking to limit the existence of the cooperatives, which it opposed, appears to have been supported by Wilson, who, reputedly, had long planned Benn's exit from the Department of Industry. And no cooperative impulses came from Eric Varley, Benn's replacement.

All parties gained something from the compromise. The Treasury, although not successful in preventing the cooperatives' establishment, achieved a brake on continuing support and forced them to operate under tight financial constraints. Labour won the October election, preserving its united facade, and, perhaps, a greater measure of worker support for its industrial prescriptions than it might otherwise have done without making any long-term economic or political concessions to its left wing. Benn, from a fundamentally weak position, managed to set up three cooperatives in a brief period, although he himself admitted that the 'conditions were so tough that it would have been almost impossible . . . to succeed'.[61]

Why, finally, did Benn agree to such restrictive conditions? He might have done so because he hoped to continue at the Department of Industry after the October 1974 election, and to be able to influence the situation once the cooperatives had been initiated. This view gains credibility from the account of one of Benn's ministerial colleagues, who argued that the 'once and for all' conditions were not necessarily what they might have appeared because:

one learns in Whitehall that such things are political hopes. The Treasury would always like it to be like that. Governments are subject to pressures and in face of pressures there is no doubt that statements like 'once and for all' do get changed. This happens repeatedly.[62]

Organisations to Facilitate Employee Ownership

It is important to emphasise that, in the US and Britain, attempts to convert failing firms into cooperatives have been made on an *ad hoc* basis, generally with little communication or collaboration between them. The potential for an organisation to arrange worker puchases is shown in France which has had, for a substantial period, such an advanced and centralised organisation, the Confédération Générale des Sociétés Ouvrières de Production (SCOP). The genesis of this movement was the intellectual idealist tradition of Fourier and Buchez in the early nineteenth century and Napoleon's ambition to beautify Paris. The landmarks of French cooperative history are associated with state initiatives. As early as 1867 a legal form for cooperatives was established in France. Interestingly, Napoleon conceded to cooperative demands to win working class support through the introduction of social measures, believing that he could appease potential worker militancy by encouraging cooperative societies. Thus, worker cooperatives were established in the building industry under Napoleon's public works projects. These also facilitated his ambitions to rebuild and beautify Paris, and decrease unemployment.[63]

This paved the way for cooperatives to receive state contracts and the establishment in 1884 of a central organisation which later became the Confédération Générale des Sociétiés Ouvrières de Production (SCOP).[64] Currently, the number of cooperatives related to SCOP exceeds 500. These employ over 30,000 workers and, although their composition still reflects its origins in the construction sector, SCOP cooperatives span a diverse set of industrial activities. SCOP's role in the transition to employee ownership is, firstly, to locate funds to assist worker purchase and, secondly, to provide management skills through the phase of transition. To illustrate the latter role, the case of Manuest is surveyed in Chapter 7.

In the US, conversions to employee ownership have been hampered by the absence of organisations specifically charged with the function of facilitating them. While government loans for worker purchases have been made – through 1979 the Small Business Administration had made three, the Economic Development Administration, nine, and the Farmers Home Administration, one – loans have been made reluctantly. The SBA emphasises small business rather than employee takeovers, while the EDA had to give priority to companies suffering from the effects of disasters, defense realignments and government regulation. Only companies in towns of less than 25,000 inhabitants were eligible for FmHA loans.

However, organisations to encourage worker buyouts have emerged following the wave of cooperatives in the 1970s. While they share a broad common mandate, they differ in their emphasis on forms of worker control and routes to employee ownership. The Industrial Cooperative Association (ICA) in Massachusetts, for example, now boasts a full-time staff of eleven, and provides legal and financial assistance to troubled companies in the New England area who might contemplate worker ownership as a means of survival. It emphasises the creation of Mondragon-style[65] cooperatives controlled on the basis of one worker, one vote. Regional associations to promote local labor-management on a broad basis include (among others) the Jamestown Area Labor Management Committee.[66] This was founded in February 1972 in response to a steady decline in the number of local manu-facturing jobs over the previous two decades accelerated by a record of poor labor relations. The committee brought together government advisers, management and labor representatives, and was instrumental in the reorganisation of several declining firms. It also succeeded in attracting the first new company to join the Jamestown manufacturing base for over fifty years – a division of the Cummins Engine Company, with job potential of between 1,500 and 2,000 – and in reversing the twenty-year slide in the number of jobs in Jamestown.

At a national level, and concerned with more wide-ranging issues is the National Center for Employee Ownership, a tax-exempt, nonprofit organisation designed to promote a better understanding of employee ownership. The center, closely identified with the position of the Small Business Lobby, acts as a clearing house for individuals concerned with the subject, researches, advises employers and employees and dissem-inates literature.

Two institutions have recently become prominent in Britain. Job Ownership Limited (JOL) is privately funded whereas the Cooperative Development Agency (CDA) is a public body. Both primarily provide consulting services, and JOL in particular takes Mondragon as its model and works towards legislative change. It was formed in 1978 with a grant from the Rowntree Social Service Trust.

The CDA, rather like the funding of the Benn cooperatives, appears as somewhat of an anachronism. It originated in left-wing elements of the Labour Party in the late 1960s, proposals being included in Labour's Economic Strategy for 1969, and in its 1973 and 1974 election manifestoes. By 1977, James Callaghan, then Prime Minister and facing the difficult task of holding disparate factions of the Party together, promised to legislate for the Agency. As in the case of the Benn cooperatives, appeasement was possible at little cost: the CDA was established in March 1978 with total funding of only £900,000, which was expected to sustain its operation over three years. In view of this limitation, the Conservative Government of Margaret Thatcher had little need to revoke its mandate on coming to power two years later.[67]

6 Worker Ownership as Industrial Policy

A Social Compromise

Four dimensions of case studies
Preceding chapters and the case studies of Chapters 7 and 8 indicate considerable commonality across conversions of declining firms to employee ownership. Such an option has been assessed from viewpoints of the local community and employees of the firm,[1] typically in contrast to the alternative of doing nothing. This option, in practice, may be politically unfeasible. Chapter 5 has, in addition, addressed the cross-country relationship between perceptions of worker ownership as industrial policy and the predominant ideologies. The present chapter aims to evaluate the strategy broadly from the viewpoint of various social groups and the government, as a possible complement to conventional policies directed towards supporting affected industries.

Case studies, firstly, suggest that the impulses towards employee takeovers are primarily accommodative, and may be assessed from within the framework of the existing socioeconomic system, rather than being a radical challenge. Such is the present focus of assessment. This is not to say that in the long run declining capitalism would be stable. Mounting unemployment and failure to raise living standards in line with expectations might well provoke labor unrest, repressive reaction and a truly radical counter-response, especially if a broad and organisationally cohesive section of the working population were affected. But, in most instances of employee takeover, the immediate circumstances and isolation of those individuals for whom the 'cash nexus' has snapped makes it unlikely that closures will lead *directly* to ideological reaction. Advanced age, stable employment history and geographic dispersion are hardly fertile seedbeds for radical ideology.

Case studies also indicate four dimensions of firms undergoing transition. Firstly, they range from those close to commercial viability to virtually hopeless cases. The position on this spectrum of commercial viability relates to that in the second dimension – the degree of political protest, controversy and perhaps even violence. The nearer is the closing company to full commercial viability, the less controversial, and the smoother, is likely to be an employee takeover. Also, the less pressure there is likely to be for government to become involved. Restricting employee takeovers to such cases will, however, result in this form of industrial policy assuming only a peripheral role, confined to correcting minor aberrations in capital and managerial markets. Meanwhile, less viable firms and industries will be buttressed, possibly at large budgetary and economic cost, by conventional forms of subsidy, and thus *de facto* become ever more dependent on the state.

A third dimension is the capital intensity of an affected firm. The greater average job cost/man, the more costly is the prevention of a given number of redundancies likely to prove. From this perspective, steel plants (such as the Youngstown case) are not prime candidates for rescue. More suitable might be relatively labor-intensive activities such as textiles or craft-based industries.

The fourth dimension is the extent to which closure is politically unacceptable for genuine social reasons, as opposed to immediate political pressures which cause government to adopt a 'survival' welfare function. Canadian, British and French examples suggest the latter situation is likely to arise at times of particularly delicate political balance. The resulting stresses then cause the priorities of the 'government of the day' to deviate from their regular pattern. The objective of support differs somewhat, depending on the balance between social and political factors. If the former are dominant, the task of intervention is to support economic and social welfare at least cost. This may, or may not, require the preservation of an existing firm or community. If permanent subsidisation is not acceptable, intervention must be primarily directed towards improving the local environment from the viewpoint of investment, a function poorly performed by conventional policies and controls. When the imperative to intervene is primarily a result of political stress, emphasis shifts to the problem of accommodating short-term political pressures at minimal longer-run economic cost. This is not, however, a clear-cut argument for public handouts, temporary protection or open-ended subsidisation as it is difficult for government to withdraw from responsibilities which it had been widely seen as willing to accept. To minimise budgetary costs and prevent an undue deterioration in economy-wide use of productive resources, the method of intervention still needs to avoid inducing X-inefficiency through moral hazard effects.

Survival: a common denominator
An announcement of the intention to close an industrial plant is likely to have a catalytic effect, bringing together a number of normally disparate groups. Workers and employees with managerial responsibilities are similarly faced with job loss. Trade union representatives, without a viable enterprise in which to organise, decrease in effectiveness. If closure results from bankruptcy rather than relocation, local banks and other financial institutions may face losses; in any event they

are likely to lose future business. Substantial chunks of the local tax base threaten to evaporate. A succession of closures stamps the region as 'declining', and increases the skepticism of potential investors invited to initiate new enterprises in the future. In many cases, the announcement of closure therefore triggers a broad spectrum of local opposition to complement the natural reaction of employees, who unify in the face of adversity.

While alternative sources of income and employment may be sought by individuals and canvassed by local leaders, the principal objective of protest is to maintain the ailing plant. This is not only because adjustment incurs private and social costs but because pressure groups are most powerful when provided with readily available channels of organisation and protest. These reflect the existing nature and structure of production, employment and community. This lends a strong 'conservative' bias to local demands. Especially when an employer's 'right' to close is not unquestioned in the eyes of labor representatives, factory occupations are likely. This form of protest is preferred by labor because it hinders the sale of a doomed plant, at the same time buying time for the workers and other adversely affected groups to organise against the closure. Marches and rallies also may have value, depending on political circumstances, in embarrassing governments into a sympathetic response and bringing the plight of the workers and community to public notice. The first attempt to avoid closure is invariably to attract conventional capitalist buyers to take over the plant as a going concern. Generally this is not successful. When it is, the reputations of prospective buyers may not be acceptable to the workforce and management who then might initiate a dialogue with government agencies seeking public support.

The way in which this dialogue proceeds is crucial for successful intervention. 'Successful' in this context refers to improved performance of an assisted enterprise whether or not the resulting plant eventually proves to be commercially viable. The response of government to such initiatives appears, in the successful cases studied, to have a distinctive characteristic, which may be termed 'reactive'. Responsibility for preserving jobs was established with individuals and communities most seriously affected by impending closure, rather than assumed by government. This assignment did not always need to proceed directly. In certain cases, entrepreneurs aware of the potential afforded by a combination of (a) an established plant about to be sold at scrap value, (b) a desperate workforce and (c) pressure on government, assumed a major share of formal managerial responsibility. They then were able to transmit this sense to their new workforces because the latter, rather than government or owners, had initiated attempts to save the plant. For government to pursue a 'reactive' role appears not to have been too difficult because groups affected by closure accepted and stressed the need for a viable source of employment: in no case was the demand one for charitable handouts. This assignment of responsibility contrasts strongly with that obtained under traditional measures (such as protection from foreign competition) where the responsibility to support industry is that of the state through regulation, and individual firms incur no obligation whatsoever.

The managerial advantages to intervention through employee take-overs therefore arise through a marriage of local initiative and responsibility and government bankrolling. In this sense it represents a social compromise between society as a whole (as represented by government) and certain of its members, who themselves are forced to compromise *vis à vis* the claims of each other to secure state support. Government agencies may play an additional valuable role in improving the flow of information to groups affected by closure, by financing feasibility studies and helping to bring the investment opportunity to the attention of potential sources of private capital and management. But, at an early stage, initiatives stemming from the redundant work-force or local community are likely to be referred back by the government on the grounds that the proposed enterprise is not sufficiently likely to prove viable to warrant support.

In the subsequent iterative dialogue between government and local interest groups, suggestions will come from a wide variety of sources. Those stemming from employees – particularly those below managerial levels – are likely to differ from those of traditional management. They may be limited in scope – production workers, for example, cannot be expected to bring to the debate an informed perspective on marketing possibilities. Examples of employee takeover suggest that workforce initiatives are likely to be valuable in broaching suggestions for re-organisation and cutting production costs which management cannot or will not insist on, partly for fear of alienating a potential workforce and partly because they lack necessary information. The substantial element of labor–capital distrust prevalent in many industrial units combined with labor perception of informational asymmetry will result in such suggestions being strongly resisted if they originate from initiatives not fully supported by the workforce. To abolish unnecessary job demarcation, for example, it is probably more effective to rely on peer pressure to resolve competing claims than to attack the problem, and the trade union concerned, head on.

That production level labor can indeed make a contribution to more efficient industrial organisation is demonstrated by the upsurge, both in North America and Europe, of worker groups set up to propose improvements in the quality of working life. Quality circles are one example of the way in which employee knowledge is harnessed to increase efficiency and reduce production costs, somewhat along the lines of the Japanese model.[2]

Negotiation between workers and the government may result in a cost level, and an associated probability of survival, which is acceptable to government. Closure would result in government incurring the burden of unemployment and possibly suffering political embarrassment. The expected return from investment in the firm will, however, possibly be inadequate to attract private capital. By securing any contribution by a prior lien on the fixed assets the government can, of course, raise its expected return considerably. The divergence of the return acceptable to government from that required by private investors provides a rough guide to the sum of political imperative and social costs as reflected through the political process.

As only part of the total cost of restart is covered by government loans or loan guarantees, the burden of equity mobilisation is thrown back onto employees, local community and, indeed, all those with a stake in the enterprise. This tends to *force* the new venture towards some form of employee ownership, possibly even towards a true cooperative. Especially in more capital-intensive industrial activities, worker savings may nevertheless only finance a small part of the necessary equity. As described in Chapter 3, worker contributions will be forthcoming because financial transactions linking capital and labor markets require a lower return than that needed to attract conventional investors. A part of the employee contribution may be forthcoming in cash and concessions on accrued benefits, a part in the form of deductions from future wages. The indirect inducement of employee ownership by the government's action in pitching and structuring its own capital commitment appropriately accords well with the need to decentralise responsibility, and with the necessary assignment of incentives to efficient operation.

The first consequence of such an iterative process is to screen out from the new enterprise those individuals finding the terms established for government support unacceptable. As the attractiveness of the prospective firm is judged relative to that of the alternative of seeking other unemployment, individuals accepting the offer of limited loan assistance effectively conditional on an equity contribution are likely to see fewer employment opportunities and to be less mobile. Their opportunity costs in the form of resources drawn away from other branches of the economy will therefore probably be lower; their redundancy will involve a correspondingly larger social cost. A similar screening can be considered to apply at firm and community levels, the community contribution to the enterprise being indicative of its revealed preference for survival.

At first sight, individuals screened out by the selection process might also include the most risk-averse, because of the need to contribute some form of capital to the enterprise. In many cases this may be so, but not necessarily since the alternative of seeking employment in an uncertain labor market involves an element of risk too, especially in circumstances of high unemployment. Clearly, asset holdings concentrated in a single firm imply a more risky portfolio than one diversified over many, but, at the same time, worker ownership may imply a degree of job security not felt in traditional firms. In imperfect labor markets, the combination of capital and labor-income risk on a worker-run enterprise could well be less than that envisaged from a diversified portfolio and conventional employment.

A second effect of interventions along the general lines described in this book has been to generate substantial pressure *internal* to the firm, towards efficiency. This appears to have arisen as a consequence of employee involvement, although the latter must be interpreted in a broad sense. The return on worker shares, narrowly defined, is unlikely to have been sufficient to motivate nonmanagerial employees in the majority of cases. The most spectacular benefits to employee shareholders, those at Vermont Asbestos Group, arose out of fortunate developments in the product market, which similarly favored a number of other cases such as Tembec. However, in some cases, increased identification of workforces with their reconstituted enterprises, and consciousness of the dependence of their jobs and communities on their endeavors, appear to have contributed significantly to improved performance. The example of the Scottish Daily News (see Chapter 8) suggests a link between the worker screening and the increase in productivity. Screening selects 'voluntarist' workers (and communities?): those characterised by a belief in their ability to turn their enterprises from potential failure to success. This belief appears to have been important in translating a strong desire for employment into action.

A period of actual closure between collapse and resuscitation therefore has advantages and disadvantages. On the positive side, it reinforces the screening effect and increases commitment for fundamental change. But on the other, closure renders it necessary to recapture markets, greatly increasing the difficulties facing the new enterprise. The importance of this will vary depending on the characteristics of the industry, especially the marketing of its product. Tembec, arguably, was not greatly hindered by its year of closure, where Chrysler Corporation, should it once have shut down, would probably have ceased trading forever.[3]

Formal government control is relinquished at the inception of the new firm. This is because state assistance is extended conditional upon the explicit acknowledgement by the recipients that it is provided 'once and for all'. This feature is important for two reasons. Firstly, withdrawal of support, should the new enterprise fail, is automatic. Government is seen to have acted on the face value of the assurances from its workforce and local community that it will indeed be viable. A second collapse, should it occur, is therefore not the responsibility of the government. No amount of assurances can provide a cast-iron guarantee that further pressure for support will not be forthcoming, but enhancement of the ability to withdraw support is a distinctive feature of the proposed support strategy.[4] Public assistance is also more clearly separated from the *ex post* observed profitability of the new enterprise. This further avoids weakening the incentives towards its efficiency.

Assessing the Social Compromise

Capitalist and capital

The real interests of individual capitalists and 'institutional' capital as a whole are not easy to distinguish. A Marxist view would see both as similarly determined by the objective relationship to the means of production. Milliband's (1969) Weberian analysis, with an emphasis on subjective, as opposed to objective, determinants, would point to a similar conclusion. The perspective of individual capitalists generally accords with that of the capitalist state, although in exceptional circumstances deviant behavior is possible. Socialisation of individual capitalists into the capitalist ethic may not, however, be so extensive as to totally circumscribe the quest for immediate profit, even when the profitable activity is likely to prove deleterious to capitalism in some longer-run sense. This explains actions of individual capitalists which are not condoned by the capitalist establishment. Individual capitalists, for example, lobby extensively for preferential treatment and state support in forms which, if widely conceded, would spell the end of the capitalist state as currently established.

To an individual capitalist faced with an increasingly less profitable enterprise, subsidisation or other conventional forms of support are possibly more attractive financially than conversion to employee ownership and formation of a new, possibly competing, firm. Conversion might also be less attractive than outright nationalisation, although this would depend on official compensation policy. Excepting possible state compensation, the highest offer for plant and equipment is, however, likely to come from a group of 'job-constrained' workers in exactly the circumstances generating pressure for employee ownership. This may therefore prove to be more attractive than the alternative of no intervention at all for owners of the closing industrial plant. Beaverbrook's attitude to the sale of the Scottish Daily News to the Albion Street workers provides some support for this position.[5] Against it, may, however, be cited the reluctance of some owners of closing firms in the US to accept worker offers of takeover for a variety of reasons, not all of which are clear. The first relates to tax advantages from sale after closure. Potential competition from a new enterprise has also been a factor in some cases. Not all reservations may be strictly financial.[6]

The Canadian experience in particular demonstrates that transitions to employee ownership may open up enormous opportunities to a limited set of astute entrepreneurs able to offer technical and managerial expertise together with investable funds. Such a role may not appeal to 'establishment' capitalists. The Tembec founder-millionaires are more appropriately seen as upwardly mobile high-level managerial employees while Robert Maxwell of the Scottish Daily News had long been considered a 'maverick' by the British capitalist establishment. At a time when many capitalists had serious reservations about investing in British industry, Joseph Mason roamed Britain in search of collapsed enterprises where Pioneer-type revivals could be initiated.

Workers, the community and labor
From the perspective of the majority of the employees of a closing firm and the dependent community, conversion to worker ownership may appear to be less attractive than straight nationalisation or continued assistance on generous terms. This judgement depends on whether employee or employee-community ownership leads to a welfare gain independently of material rewards. In this connection it could be noted that employee ownership is a popular concept, at least in the United States, with considerable broad ideological appeal.[7] From an individual (as distinct from a community) perspective, the extent to which the strategy is preferable to that of no intervention at all depends also on how unemployment leisure is valued. If highly, then the attraction of working for potentially lower payments is correspondingly reduced. Case study evidence argues strongly against the view that unemployment leisure caused by involuntary redundancy is highly, indeed positively, valued. In any event, since participation in an employee-owned enterprise is voluntary, individuals valuing leisure highly are simply less likely to volunteer if its terms are significantly less favorable than those previously obtained. It is difficult to view the extension of the range of choice offered by the option to convert to employee ownership as *reducing* welfare to below its level in the absence of intervention. The true potential financial loss of workers and, perhaps, of their communities (rather like that of an individual capitalist) results from the ability of the state to deflect political pressure without resorting to possibly more generous policies.

A criticism might be that to facilitate employee takeovers of firms in difficulty is morally indefensible since failures and financial losses are inevitable. Individuals might indeed be better off with some more generous compensation, but the critique fails to identify the ranges of choice open to government and individuals. It is not possible to insulate all adversely affected by all closures. The strategy at least increases the range of choice by offering an alternative to redundancy.

From the perspective of trade unions, the consequences of a movement towards employee ownership are uncertain. As described in Chapter 4, transitions to employee ownership in the US, at least, have not spelled the end to plant-level unionism, and the perceived need for a union does not appear to diminish subsequent to the transition. This may be partly due to the fact that most employee takeovers have not, in fact, involved a significant move to worker control and that shareholding has typically been highly unequal. Traditional patterns of adversarial industrial relations have therefore tended to reappear between six and twelve months after employee takeover.

For its survival under more democratic worker ownership, plant-level unionism does, however, appear to require a shift in role, away from adversary and towards critical but essentially loyal opposition. In its new role, the union may contribute substantially towards maintaining the *de facto* balance of power and ensuring that work and pay norms are not unreasonable.[8] Such a role may be permanently necessary, given an inherently unequal distribution over the population of managerial talent, which implies a tendency for permanent managerial strata to emerge.[9]

At national level, agreements on collective bargaining and restrictive labor agreements have been seen as necessary to protect the bulk of union membership. In an adversarial system of labor relations, labor must continually seek to limit the prerogatives of capital which otherwise can undermine collective agreements in a variety of ways. Worker buyouts therefore cause stress between local and national trade unionism. In the UK, for example, the leading role of local union leaders and support of the Scottish Trades Union Congress stands in marked contrast to the position of the national Trades Union Congress. The US position is not dissimilar, except that the more pragmatic, less ideologically adversarial American national unions have recently begun to show signs of accommodating worker buyouts, and of relaxing restrictions on plant-level negotiations in the face of difficult economic circumstances.[10]

Towards a cooperative economy?

In assessing the longer-run implications of worker buyouts, one important issue is whether any efficiency improvements realised in the transition to employee ownership are likely to persist. Important, too, is the probability that such takeovers could pave the way to a co-operative economy, or introduce a substantial worker-managed sector into the existing economic system.

Most case study research into the commercial viability of employee-owned firms in a mature capitalist economy has been carried out for the US, although other experiences, notably that of the Mondragon group in Spain have also been analyzed in some detail. The American examples can be roughly divided into three broad groups. Only a limited number of worker cooperatives of significant size have lengthy histories, the most notable being the Plywood cooperatives of the Pacific Northwest. The earliest of these originated in the early 1920s following the arrival of Scandinavian immigrants with a cooperative tradition.[11] Roughly eighty percent of all firms substantially owned by their employees and currently in operation date, however, from the 1970s. In line with the two trends in US legislation described in Chapter 5, two categories of ownership patterns have evolved. The first operates within quite specific legal bounds through Employee Stock Ownership plans, the second involves relatively *ad hoc* worker buyouts of closing firms, which result in a variety of forms of ownership and control.

Some thirty-two plywood cooperatives are known to have been started since 1930, and by 1978 sixteen were still surviving. Overall, they seem to have been successful. Productivity levels 30 percent above average for the industry were cited as justifying payment levels some 25 percent greater than those paid by competing firms. After investigation by the Internal Revenue Service, who were concerned that tax advantages might be gained by artificially lowering reported profits, this claim was fully accepted.

In no known US case of employee takeover stemming from corporate divestiture over the 1970s have the employees lost their interests because of closure of the worker-owned enterprise,[12] although the returns to worker equity have sometimes been low. This too argues in favor of generally efficient operation of employee-owned firms. The total direct job-preserving effect of US employee takeovers has been estimated at between 50,000 and 100,000.[13] Multiplier effects could increase this figure considerably. Despite the less favorable experience of the UK, British cases suggest that in the process of transition significant cost-cutting may indeed be effected, and that part of this is associated with improvement in productive efficiency. This may not, however, be sufficient to save firms starting from extremely weak competitive positions.

In their investigation of US employee-owned firms, Conte and Tannenbaum (1978) analyzed a panel of 98 firms with substantial employee ownership, 68 'beneficially owned' through ESOPs and 30 through direct employee holding of equity. In three quarters of the

ESOP-owned firms, employees actually owned half or more of the total equity, yet only in 38 percent of these firms did workers sit on boards. At 77 percent, the proportion of companies with workers on boards was far higher for directly-owned firms. In such firms it also was more common for employees to vote their stock. Despite these limitations on their power, in 77 percent of directly employee-owned firms, and half of ESOP owned firms, employees were felt to influence 'important' decisions.

Employee ownership also appeared to be profitable. Conte and Tannenbaum compared the ratio of profits/sales for the 30 firms reporting such information to average ratios for conventional firms in matching industries. In a number of cases, considerably higher pay levels on the employee-owned enterprises reduced reported profitability to below its level as most appropriately measured for comparison. To take this effect into account, adjusted profit/sales ratios were also computed. Both ratios showed considerable cross-firm variability even within the same industry, which prevented means between the conventional control group and the sample of employee-owned firms from being different at a high level of statistical significance. Unadjusted profitability for employee-owned firms averaged 1.5 times that for control firms while the ratio for adjusted profitability was 1.7. The only structural characteristic significantly associated with higher profitability *within* the employee-owned sample was the share of equity owned by employees, although correlations between a number of characteristics made a conclusive attribution difficult. In the subsample of 30 firms for which the more extensive analysis of profitability could be performed, there was, interestingly, little correlation between the share of equity owned by employees and the percentage of employees owning equity. This reflected the highly concentrated pattern of much employee shareholding. Many employees typically owned little or no equity, even in firms owned mostly by employees.

Conte and Tannenbaum also report a positive attitude to employee ownership on the part of management. Good industrial relations were generally felt to prevail on employee-owned firms. Grievances were few, and improved employee cooperation was frequently observed to have contributed to reduced levels of wastage. Management representatives were questioned about the effect of employee ownership on productivity and profit. Their replies were, on average, supportive of employee ownership, to which they were ready to attribute significantly improved attitudes of employees towards their jobs.

Conte and Tannenbaum's results must be interpreted with a degree of caution in inferring causality. Management perceptive and progressive enough to reap the benefits of some employee participation through employee stockholding might also be able to realise greater profitability for other reasons. The sentiments of their study are, however, echoed in the testimony of major corporations before the Senate Committee on Finance,[14] which credits employee ownership with potential advantages, not only from the viewpoint of the firm but from the perspectives of employee and national interest. The experience of the Mondragon cooperative group in the Basque provinces of Spain also provides evidence in favor of fully participatory worker cooperatives. The group has an impressive history of expansion and job creation, and has been judged as outperforming the surrounding capitalist environment quite significantly.[15]

American evidence, together with studies of cooperatively-run enterprises in other countries therefore, presents a very favorable view of employee-owned firms, despite the fact that part of the appeal of ESOPs in the US undoubtedly lies in their tax advantages. However, the record also suggests that employee ownership may not be a stable organisational form in the longer run. Aldrich and Stern (1978) document well over 500 cooperative or worker-owned production firms over the period 1790–1970 in the United States, yet the survival of these enterprises has been unimpressive.[16]

Paradoxically, part of the reason for failure to survive in cooperative form appears to have been economic success, which, by raising the value of employee shareholdings, placed them out of reach to new entrants to the job market aspiring to join the cooperatives. Several 'failures' of this kind have been documented for the plywood co-operatives. Employee ownership of American industry has involved individual shareholding, either directly or through a trust, rather than 'socially-owned' capital, as in the case of Yugoslavia where workers have no claim to the capital resources of their individual firms. A switch to the latter form of ownership would certainly ease the difficulties occasioned by retirement and new entry, but it also could reduce the incentivating effect of employee ownership through breaking the link between performance and effective ownership of equity.

A second source of instability of the employee-owned structure which stems from success is the natural limit on capital availability for expansion. Such was the difficulty in the firm preceding the present Amana Corporation. As Amana reached the point where it needed finance to order to expand its facilities, necessary equity was only possible through selling the company to private investors.[17] Rather like family enterprises, successful employee-owned firms may be forced by the scale requirements of production to abandon their ownership structure and 'go public'.

The above two sources of instability relate to employee-owned firms in general. A third potential factor is perhaps more specific to worker buyouts of declining enterprises: the failure of the working environment to satisfy expectations raised by the transition itself and by the new-found status of the workers as 'owners'.

Undoubtedly the transition is likely to change the view of at least some employees, who feel that their equity holdings should provide them with more of a say in the operation of the company. While participation in such a venture may not induce ideological criticism along the lines postulated by Moorhouse (1976) and Lane and Roberts (1971), some demand for a greater measure of job control and for a more responsive style of management is quite likely.[18] Failure to introduce a more democratic working environment may then cause a resurgence of traditional labor-management (although not strictly labor-capital) animosity. It may also contribute to a decision of employees to sell their stock to outside investors should the terms of their holdings permit them to do so.

The problem of introducing management practices consonant with the pattern of equity holding is likely to prove particularly problematic because of the speed with which declining firms must be restructured. Closedowns do not select the most promising candidates for experiments in democratic management. True worker involvement appears to require not merely the assumption of an organisational form, but a process of socialisation and education of workers and management into a cooperative ethic. This is borne out by the experience of the Mondragon group, which both screens prospective members according to 'social' criteria prior to entry, and operates a substantial program of education in the cooperative ideal for established members. Employee-owned firms born out of conventional closures do not have the screening possibilities open to Mondragon, neither are they generally equipped to socialise their members appropriately, a process which anyway, would take time.

That the transforming of the work environment of a plant is a lengthy and fairly costly process is demonstrated by the experience of Rath Packing Company (see Chapter 7). Rath started with certain advantages – an orderly and lengthy transition avoiding the trauma of bankruptcy, and the experience of prior conversions. Measures were adopted from the start to prevent the re-emergence of adversarial labor-management relations. Overall, the participatory innovations appear to be functioning well at Rath. But, two years after the transition, employee morale is low following declines in the market and, under economic stress, there are signs that the old antagonisms are re-emerging.

For a number of reasons, employee purchase of declining firms may therefore not lead directly to a substantially worker-owned or 'co-operative' economy, even if a high proportion of such rescue attempts proves to be successful. In many cases worker ownership may appear as a transient phase lasting several years in the overall cycle of industrial decline, renewal and renovation. Such a conclusion in no way weakens the case for state intervention through the restructuring of ownership patterns along the lines described above. A change in the pattern of ownership, even if temporary, may offer the best prospects for an interventionist strategy, should one prove necessary for social or political reasons, to effect the necessary improvement in industrial performance.

7 Some 'Successful' Transitions to Employee Ownership

Overview

Transitions to employee ownership fell into a spectrum, from outstanding commercial successes to failures. Typically, cases in the US have evolved from corporate divestitures of firms which, prior to employee ownership, had been moderately, although not spectacularly, profitable. Indeed, US legislation in support of employee purchases has been advocated only for clearly viable concerns.[1] In the UK, employee ownership has been attempted for abject failures. Canadian and French examples, though generally successful, could be considered to combine elements of American and British experience.

Case studies described in this book need not emphasise the 'successful' US transitions. Already their main characteristics have been introduced, supporting legislation reviewed, and an explanation provided for the contrasting approaches to employee ownership in the US and the UK. Furthermore, US cases have been well documented relative to cases in other countries.[2] In the light of the central theme of this book, it is also unhelpful to concentrate too intensively on the US examples. American transitions emphasise more the correcting of imperfections in managerial and capital markets while the thrust of the present argument for employee ownership concerns the restructuring of ailing industry. This chapter, therefore, will only discuss US cases briefly.

Relative to the US, the Canadian experience regarding declining industry and employee ownership is underresearched. Tembec, the Canadian example below shows certain similarities to the US cases, but differs significantly with respect to the political dimension. The chapter concludes with the furniture factory Manuest, a transition to employee ownership in the small French town of Chatenoir. While representing a strong community reaction to plant closure and being relatively successful commercially (as are its US counterparts), in its struggle to survive Manuest includes features more reminiscent of British examples.

Corporate Divestitures and Small Communities: the US Experience

At the beginning of the 1980s recent US experience promises to continue the trend towards worker purchases established in the early 1970s. Whereas early cases tended to cluster in traditionally hard-hit industries – textiles and smaller craft-based industry – the start of the 1980s has seen a slow but steady extension of worker takeovers into the ailing auto industry, formerly an industrial leader, and frequent reports of actual or attempted takeovers in the national press.

Starting from financial positions stronger than that of Chrysler (which had accepted a measure of worker ownership through the Chrysler Corporation Loan Guarantee Act (1979), both Ford and General Motors were involved in 1981 in negotiations to sell less profitable plants to their workforces. Offered a choice between accepting a 50 percent wage reduction, purchasing their plant or seeing it close, the 1,100 employees at Ford's Sheffield, Ala. aluminium casting plant opted for closure despite the local unemployment rate of 12 percent. Given industry-wide agreements entered into with the United Auto Workers Union (UAW), employee purchase was in fact the sole option to reduce pay levels sufficiently to return the plant to profitability. In an atmosphere of suspicion, union leaders required Ford to pay early retirement benefits to workers as part of any purchase arrangement. Negotiation proceeded in a low-trust environment, possibly because the initiative to sell the plant emanated from Ford management rather than the employees, whose options were constrained by tight time limits.

In contrast, 1,200 workers at the General Motors roller ball-bearing plant in Clark, N.J. contributed $100 each to fund a feasibility study of the prospects for a worker-owned plant, after GM's attempts to sell out for $100 million failed. The worker-owners' viability plan involved reducing manning to 800 and cutting salary and benefits by 25 percent, so halving total labor costs. Underlying the projected 50 percent increase in labor productivity appears to have been a significant accommodation of the Clark UAW local:

. . . the unions helped create an atmosphere where people . . . did four hours work. That's appropriate when GM is making billions in profits – but it is no longer appropriate. They will do a day's work for a day's pay.[3]

The employees negotiated the purchase of the plant at favorable terms: $30 million cash (raised by loans with GM's assistance) and $28 million in paper held by GM. Employees are to hold equal shares in the plant whose working arrangements and compensation package focus heavily on incentives.

Worker takeovers may thus permit local deviations from arrangements reached through nationwide collective bargaining which fail to accommodate to less profitable segments of the respective industries.

They therefore promise to have an impact on labor relations even in conventional firms. Without more flexible industry-wide arrangements, the trend in the 1980s promises to strengthen that of the early 1970s which saw a considerable number of actual and attempted employee purchases.

Some of those more prominent in influencing US legislation directed towards promoting ESOP purchases and slowing or reversing community decline, are now briefly reviewed. Examples include the library furniture manufacturer in Herkimer, New York, Jamestown Metal Company, A1 Tech Speciality Steel Corporation, South Bend Lathe, Vermont Asbestos Group and Saratoga Knitting Mills.

Herkimer

This case is perhaps the best documented, by Stern, *et al* (1979). In line with the focus of US research in the area, this study adopts a worker-community, rather than national or class perspective. An interesting feature of Herkimer was the widespread shareholding among small local investors, which resembles the pattern of Scottish Daily News shareholding (see Chapter 8). The Library Bureau reverted to conventional ownership in 1980, a phenomenon no doubt deplored by advocates of participatory industrial structures, but not out of line with the thesis developed here.

Jamestown Metal Products Company

This is another example cited in the Voluntary Job Preservation legislation which was purchased by its employees in 1973. Impending closure, and the absence of any conventional takeover, forced workers to mobilise resources to buy the company themselves. Within a month of the decision to close, a purchase plan was drawn up involving financially about three-quarters of the 120 workers. Initially, the new employee-owned company experienced problems associated with a steel shortage and unrealistic pricing arrangements inherited from the previous owners. However, it weathered these difficulties and gradually picked up. To date, its sales have increased some 55 percent and the book value of the company has tripled.[4]

Al Tech

Congressman Stanley Lundine of New York, one of the sponsors of 'Voluntary Job Preservation and Community Stabilisation' Bills HR12094 and HR2203, drew attention to the case of a speciality steel plant which after fifteen years of 'heavy losses' was ready to close, forcing redundancy on some 2,000 workers in Dunkirk, N.Y. With no prospective buyer the only option perceived by employees was to purchase the plant themselves. However, with the company's poor commercial history and a dearth of management expertise among the workers, 'it was absolutely impossible to obtain any long-term finance'. Eventually 35 employees were able to meet finance requirements with the help of a $10 million loan from EDA. The new company, Al Tech Speciality Steel Corporation represented more a management buyout than a broad based employee purchase. It increased in size as productivity rose by some nine percent, and despite significantly increased pressure from imports it proved to be profitable.[5]

South Bend Lathe
Nationally, one of the most well-known worker buyouts is the case of South Bend Lathe in South Bend, Indiana. Beginning as a small family business in 1906, within forty years it had developed into an important machine tool manufacturer employing some 500 workers and supplying lathes to the US Navy. In 1959 it was taken over by the Chicago-based Amsted Industries and its fortunes quickly plummeted. Many local manufacturing industries, including the famous automobile manufacturer Studebaker which employed some ten percent of the local workforce, experienced serious financial difficulties and closed. In the early 1970s, as the recession in the machine tool industry began to take effect, Amsted announced its intention to sell.

With the exception of a scrap dealer there were no prospective buyers. At this point the company president Richard Boulis, supported by unions, bankers, municipal officials and the EDA, called in Louis Kelso, a leading proponent of employee stock ownership. Together they formulated a worker ownership plan for the stricken company. EDA furnished a $5 million grant to the town of South Bend, which was immediately loaned to the workers who undertook to repay it within 25 years at 3 percent interest. The employee trust borrowed another $5 million from three different banks at commercial interest rates. With this capital the workers bought the company from Amsted, issued 10,000 shares and deposited them with the employee trust to serve as collateral for the $10 million in loans. Individual employees, therefore, did not immediately become beneficiaries of shares. Each year the company distributes a portion of the profits to the employee trust which, in turn, repays the long-term debt. As loans are repaid the company stock is released to the employees. Each employee receives a number of shares in proportion to his salary level and duration of employment.

After the transition, output/man rose significantly even on unchanged equipment. Quality of work improved as did the level of trust between management and workers despite the absence of significant changes in organisational control. According to surveys, 58 percent of the employees perceived an improvement in internal communication, while 48 percent perceived higher worker morale. In its first year of trading, the company secured the biggest order of its seventy year history: to supply 236 lathes to Tennessee schools. As a result it was able to increase average wages considerably and distribute large profits.

While South Bend Lathe provides a good example of workers who grasped an opportunity to buy themselves jobs, it also illustrates the potential for disillusion following an employee takeover.[6] Management style did not respond to the new pattern of ownership. Profitable trading coexisted with increasing industrial unrest which eventually resulted in employees striking against their own management.

Vermont Asbestos Group

The transition at Vermont Asbestos Group is another interesting example of pragmatic response to firm closure. In 1974 GAF, an asbestos mining company employing some 175 workers and situated in an isolated region in Vermont, decided to close. The decision was prompted by declining profits and the Environmental Protection Agency's (EPA) insistence that the mine should install safety equipment costing some $1 million. Prospects for the affected workers and community alike were bleak since the mine constituted the only source of industrial employment in an already depressed area.[7]

In response to the announced closure a fifteen-man worker-community committee was formed composed equally of managers, workers and community representatives. It nominated a five-man executive which was responsible for organising the opposition to the impending closure. At one meeting, attracting some 400 people including the state governor, opposition to the closure included individual testimonies submitting that asbestos fiber was not in fact hazardous to health. There was an overwhelming call for the EPA to withdraw its demands and allow the company to continue trading.

Failing to influence the EPA the committee unsuccessfully attempted to lobby the offices of the President, the State Governor and Agency for the Development of Community Affairs to exercise their influence to get the EPA's demands lifted. The Agency did, however, carry out a feasibility study which suggested that a six-year supply of asbestos remained in the mine. The committee, encouraged by this conclusion, endeavoured, unsuccessfully, to attract a capitalist to take it over.

With failure to find a conventional solution to corporate withdrawal, John Lupien, a former maintenance engineer, proposed an employee takeover and gained the overwhelming support of the workforce. Lupien had little interest in employee participation in management, and neither had the workers any desire to manage the company.[8] Despite a generous offer from the parent company to sell at a reasonable price[9] and to place orders worth some $7 million with the new company, there was institutional reluctance to invest. Traditional sources of capital had insufficient confidence in the workers' ability to manage and were reluctant to furnish loans to a group without collateral.

It was agreed to sell 51 percent of the company's stock to workers at $50 a share, constraining any one individual to a maximum of $5,000 share capital. Thus, majority control would be dispersed over the workforce. With annual earnings below $9,000 however, workers were reluctant to purchase shares. The committee therefore made them available to the local community. 'Institutionally-linked capital', largely from traders associated with the company, flowed in and the campaign spearheaded by the committee raised some $78,000.

There then followed two significant breakthroughs. The Vermont Agency for Development and Community Affairs agreed to guarantee 80 percent of any bank loan to the mine, and the Vermont Industrial Development Authority issued a 100 percent loan guarantee. Only then did a consortium of seven banks hesitantly agree to loan the workers sufficient capital to purchase the company.[10] During the first year of trading under worker ownership, the price of asbestos fortuitously soared by some 65 percent. The company declared profits of $5 million. By 1976, shares had increased in value by 7,000 percent, from $50 to $3,500, and workers had awarded themselves a 20 percent wage increase. The success of the new company was established.

At the height of its success, however, discontent over control issues surfaced among the workforce rather as they had at South Bend Lathe.[11] Vermont Asbestos has a two-tier board. One tier, originally composed of seven workers, seven managerial staff and a local political representative, but later reconstructed with only four worker representatives, is responsible for any corporate expenditure in excess of $7,000. Day-to-day control is delegated to the second tier, a five-man executive which consists essentially of the same management as ran the previous company. Zwerdling (1978) suggests that some workers, protesting their lack of control, sold their shares to a private investor, who in 1978 was voted onto the board. Vermont Asbestos thus illustrates again the possibility of an employee-owned company reverting to a conventional capitalist firm.

However, given the original pragmatic orientation of the employees from which sprang the idea of worker ownership, it is not so clear that workers sold their shares solely in protest. Workers 'by no means demanded that they take over management'. They overwhelmingly supported John Lupien who 'had no interest in encouraging worker participation'.[12] Surprised by the rapid increase in the value of their shares, many very probably, and wisely, cashed them in. An initial investment of $250 had increased in three years to more than the average annual salary of a mine worker before the closure.

Saratoga Knitting Mill

The *Saratoga Textile Company* was started in 1906 by the Clark family to produce silk gloves. After an attempt at unionisation in 1919, the plant was closed and sold to the van Raalte Company. For reasons which are not altogether clear, the plant closed again for four years in 1927,[13] when some of its machinery was sold and the remainder relocated to other plants.

When the plant reopened, in 1931, its fervently anti-union management successfully re-oriented its products towards man-made fibers. By 1960, van Raalte was one of the largest local industrial employers, with a workforce of some 700. At this stage in its development, the company expanded, establishing three sewing machine plants in Puerto Rico where labor costs were substantially below the US levels. Van Raalte also diversified and bought stock in other corporations. Shortly after, the company experienced serious financial difficulty brought about by loss of sales volume. Major shifts in women's fashions led to a depressed demand for lingerie. New management restored the company to a sound financial footing and, in 1968, when it was taken over by Cluett Peabody, its sales were in the region of $72 million and net income was $4.2 million.

The new management introduced changes in the company's marketing strategy. Old equipment was not replaced, there was little expenditure on maintenance, and production volume dropped significantly.[14] Labour distrust of management therefore grew. Van Raalte's sales plummeted to just $20 million in 1974, involving a $9 million loss for the division during the same period. In February 1975 Cluett management informed Donald Cox, vice-president of van Raalte and general manager of the Saratoga Mill, of its decision to sell and instructed him to lay off half of the 145 workers who had been required to complete outstanding orders. Cluett found it difficult to divest itself totally of the van Raalte division and attempted to sell off its sixteen mills separately. With the general decline of the textile industry, no capitalist buyers were interested in the Saratoga Knitting Mill. Thus, Cluett decided to close down the plant completely.

The decision came as a shock to the 17,000 local residents of this small town in rural upstate New York who already were concerned about the gradual decline of manufacturing industries in the area. Now, 145 workers stood to lose their jobs in a region which was seen to offer few prospects of alternative employment.[15] Community reaction to the closure was spearheaded by the incumbent general manager, Donald Cox. After being approached to help with an employee takeover, Cox

acted swiftly, enlisting the collaboration of local banks and representatives from the shop floor. Cox ideologically opposed big business,
trade unions and the government's industrial policy, and was conscious
of the distrust between workers and managers which had developed in
the mill under Cluett's management.

the relationship between the workforce and its management . . . is largely
adversary. If we continue down the road of democratic capitalism with this
adversary relationship between employees and management, we are certainly
going to end up in the same position as many of the European countries which
now have evolved to the point of democratic socialism. This is because the
employee group is always by circumstance forced to the position of having to
demand the increase in their fair share of the earnings in industry.[16]

Convinced by rank and file support Cox and his associates[17] put
together 'a viable financial package . . . which gave some encouragement to the belief that a deal just might be pulled off if a substantial sum
could be raised from employees'.[18] The bulk of the funds to purchase
the company came from the state, as shown in Table 7.1. Employee
contributions averaged about $1,000 per head.

Table 7.1   Saratoga Knitting Mill's sources of finance

		%
Adirondack Trust Co. (51.6%) and N.Y. Business Development Corp[19]	$387,500	53.0
N.Y. Business Development Corporation, Capital Corp.	$ 12,500	1.7
N.Y.B.D.C. (Mortgage)	$100,000	13.7
Job Development Authority (Second Mortgage)	$ 80,000	10.9
	$580,000	
Shareholders' Equity (1,500 shares at $100)	$150,000	20.5
TOTAL	$730,000	100

The final transfer took place on 21 June 1975. Since then Saratoga
Mill has been a significant success. Shortly after the transition, Cox
initiated an aggressive marketing campaign. New equipment was
purchased. The enterprise employs some 140 workers and, unlike its
competitors in the textile industry, the new Saratoga Knitting Mill has
not had to lay off any employees.

Saratoga Mill is a classic example of a corporate divestiture leading to
a transition to worker ownership. It also illustrates the proposition that
remote, absentee control may prove inferior to local management, a
contention important to the populist small-business lobby seeking to

reverse the trend to corporate gigantism. The structure of shareholding is, however, highly concentrated. About half of the employee-held stock is in the hands of sixteen managers while only twenty-five production workers control the other half. However, the company has launched an ESOP which allows a large number of employees to participate financially.

Rath Pork Packing Company

One of the newest experiments in employee purchase – and one of the few involving a degree of pre-planned industrial democracy – is Rath Pork Packing Company of Waterloo, Iowa.[20] Rath is significant in the American context for four reasons. Firstly, it was saved before bankruptcy. Secondly, union members rather than managerial employees initiated and led the rescue attempt, which was preferred by the workforce to sale to a conventional entrepreneur. Thirdly, workers vote their block of shares (60 percent of all stock) through representatives elected on a one-man one-vote basis. Fourthly, active measures were taken from the start to encourage and develop worker participation in decision-making. It is too early to forecast the longer-run performance of the Rath experiment but, in its thorough planning, the Rath transition represents a significant step forward from earlier, largely *ad hoc* buyouts.

Founded in 1891, Rath had become the world's largest and most modern packing-house by the 1940's, with a slaughtering capacity of 12,000 animals per day. But by the mid-1960s the picture had changed. Machinery was outdated, and competition fierce. Losses totalled $20 million by the end of the 1970s. An average employee age of 53 boosted pensions and medical payments as well as inhibiting prospective mobility of workers. Closure of Rath and redundancy of its 2,200 workers would have come as a heavy blow to Waterloo, a city of some 110,000 inhabitants.

The impulse for employee purchase came from Lyle Taylor, President, and Chuck Mueller, Chief Steward of Local 46 of United Food and Commercial Workers Union, representing 77 percent of Rath Workers. Taylor and Mueller benefited from past American experience with worker buyouts by contacting individuals and institutions which had been involved in previous conversions and legislative development.

Employees contributed wage cuts of $20/week to purchase stock, agreed to forgo wages, half of their vacation pay and three days of sick pay. The company was allowed to postpone payments into their pension fund. By June 1980, when stockholders and employees had finalised and approved a takeover plan, the fund to purchase stock stood at $8 million. This was used to secure a Housing and Urban Development Loan of $4.6 million at 3 percent interest over 10 years.

The loan was to finance a new bacon processing plant, the first modernisation in nearly twenty years.

Rath workers, as a condition of their Employee Stock Ownership Trust, were able to choose trustees to vote their stock *en bloc* according to directions. The Union was empowered to nominate a majority to the Board of Directors. Some $40,000 was allocated to develop innovative arrangements to encourage worker participation. Action Research Teams composed of between five and ten members meet regularly and are co-chaired by management and union representatives. The Teams are modelled after Japanese quality circles.

For the fiscal year ending in September 1980, Rath reported its first profit in six years, largely because of the wages and benefits forgone by its workforce. Absenteeism dropped and improvements in productivity have been reported, although it is not yet clear to what extent these reflect improved labor relations. However, ten percent of American slaughterhouses closed over 1980–81. In deteriorating market conditions Rath lost $9.6 million in the year ending October 1981, dashing hopes of a speedy turnaround in the company's prospects. While participatory systems appear to be functioning satisfactorily, failure to restore lost pay and benefits appears to be resulting in low morale in some quarters of the workforce.

Avoiding Worker Control: Tembec, a Canadian Example
Tembec Forest Products almost caricatures the difficulties sometimes accompanying industrial dislocation.[21] It indicates the potential of imaginative state-community cooperation for preserving employment without reducing incentives for industrial efficiency and committing the state to a program of indefinite support. Tembec also occupies an intermediate point in the spectrum, running from obviously profitable to clearly unviable opportunities for employee takeover. In many respects it conforms to the US pattern of small plants abandoned by conglomerates, having in particular, a strong worker-community relationship. But other facets, notably elements of political compromise underlying its establishment, may come closer to the British cooperative example described in the next chapter.

The background
Three hundred and fifty miles to the northeast of Montreal on the Ottawa river, Temiscaming, Quebec had been a company town since 1919 when the Riordan family started the Kipwa mill, one of the first sulphite pulp mills in North America. In 1921 the mill was sold to Canadian International Paper (CIP), the largest employer in the Quebec pulp and paper industry, and a subsidiary of International Paper of New York. At the beginning of the 1970s, world pulp markets

began to soften, provoking layoffs, but this in itself was not too unusual. Then came the bombshell. On 31 January 1972, CIP announced its intention to close the mill forever, in four months – the minimum advance notice of closure to which the workforce was legally entitled.

A number of factors were cited by CIP in its decision to close the Kipwa mill – excess pulp capacity, alleged low productivity and costly environmental regulation. Tariff cuts between Canada and the US had also rendered American-produced pulp more competitive locally. This increased the incentive to shift pulp production to CIP's new mill in Natchez, Mississippi. Closure of the Kipwa mill may therefore be considered as part of the general process of industrial rationalisation accompanying a reduction in barriers to international trade. Such a process is generally accepted as necessary to reap scale and specialisation advantages made possible by trade liberalisation – but sometimes, as in the case of Temiscaming, the rationalisation process involved high social costs.

Temiscaming's mill was directly responsible for 540 jobs and indirectly for several hundred more in associated lumbering operations. The prospective career and geographical mobility of its redundant workforce would have been unusually low. At the date of closure the average worker was aged forty-nine and had been continuously employed by the mill for twenty-four years. Mobility was further lowered by the action of CIP over the preceding ten years in selling off company houses to its workforce.[22] Without the mill, the houses would have been almost valueless. This would have further hindered worker mobility through raising the costs of moving, relative to staying in Temiscaming.

Five days after closure was announced, a Temiscaming citizens' committee was formed to investigate the alternatives facing the town. Leading members included Charlie Carpenter, for the past six years president of Local 233 of the Canadian Paperworkers Union, Frank Dottori, general superintendent of the mill, Bill Clarke, the town pharmacist, and Dr. Gilbert Theberge, town dentist and member of the Quebec legislative assembly. The committee rapidly concluded, after a review of the options, that there were essentially none. The sole chance of saving Temiscaming would be to re-open the mill.

It was soon discovered that CIP could not be prevailed upon to continue production even with the possibility of certain grants from the province of Quebec. Neither was government willing to become directly involved in the pulp business by taking over the mill. However, the committee did find, in Montreal, a group of entrepreneurs interested in restarting and modernising the mill and able to substitute the management and selling functions soon to be abandoned by CIP. The group was led by George Petty, formerly CIP's Vice-President of Sales, who had left the company six years earlier. Jack Stevens had been CIP's Director of Corporate Planning, while the third member, Jim Chantler had managed the Kipwa mill until the previous year when he and Stevens had left CIP because of the company's refusal to modernise the plant. Dottori was invited to join the triumvirate, to form a new management team to found a new company – Tembec – to revitalise the mill.

Negotiation

Then began a lengthy process of negotiation between the management group, Quebec and federal governments, CIP, commercial banks, the local community and the Kipwa workers represented by the Montreal office of their union. Studies financed by the Quebec government indicated that modernisation would, initially, require about $12 million in capital investment.[23] The workers, while living off their unemployment insurance, pledged their severance pay – about $2,000 per man – towards the new company. They also agreed to cuts in basic pay and fringe benefits, in return for which they would get ten percent of the profits from the new enterprise. These agreements were seen by the union and management as a major asset in negotiating for aid from the state and federal governments.

Equally large assets were the embarrassment to the Liberal government in Quebec, and to the Federal Liberal government, concerned at the rise of French separation. A general climate of unease was perceived to prevail among working class Quebecois. The workers held demonstrations in Montreal, Quebec City, Ottawa, Trois Rivières, Hawkesbury and Gatineau, the last three being sites of other CIP operations. In November 1972 a mutual agreement was signed between the embryonic Tembec and the Canadian Paperworkers Union, concerning terms and conditions of work on the new enterprise. While these were accepted with some misgivings by the Union, they served as evidence to the media, provincial and federal governments, of the serious intent and mutual goodwill of workers and management.

Potential competition from Tembec plus the embarrassment of seeing the Kipwa mill operating again – perhaps successfully – made CIP reluctant to sell it to any party intending to restart it. The sale was therefore linked by CIP to that of its surrounding forest concessions, for which a high price was demanded. Following a picket of CIP's head office in Montreal, and a threat to expropriate CIP's forest concessions by the Quebec Minister of Lands and Forest, CIP agreed to sell the mill and seventeen company houses separately, all for $2.4 million, in February 1973. Shortly thereafter, the Quebec government offered aid on condition that assistance was also provided by the federal government and that the workers and local population subscribe to capital. In April came the announcement of a grant from the Federal Department of Regional Economic Expansion (DREE).

CIP still, however, owned its forest concessions. Since the closure a year before, 60,000 cunits of wood had accumulated in the Ottawa River above Temiscaming. On St Jean-Baptiste day it decided to release the booms and float the wood to its Gatineau mill, 200 miles downstream. Without wood Tembec could not function. With a flotilla of fishing boats, Temiscaming citizens organised a five-week blockade of the Ottawa River. CIP was granted an injunction by the Quebec courts to stop the blockade – but it merely moved to the Ontario side of the river not covered by the injunction. To attract publicity the bridge between Quebec and Ontario was occupied by almost the entire town, which resisted efforts by the Quebec police to clear a passage. Further embarrassed by publicity, the Quebec government negotiated a settlement with CIP. Tembec purchased the forest concessions for $6 million.

Financial structure

On 31 July 1975, a financial package totalling $25 million was signed between Tembec, the Quebec government and REXFOR, a Federal Crown Corporation for the recovery of wood. The major financial investors in Tembec were to be the Quebec and federal governments. The former would provide $13.5 million, $10 million in loans, $1 million in grants and $2.5 million in preferred shares. The federal government would contribute $4.4 million in grants through DREE and provide $6 million in loan guarantees to private sector creditors to enable normal bank credit to be obtained.

Far smaller contributions came from the management team, workers and local population. The four managers invested $25,000 each, for a total stake of $100,000. Direct investment by workers came to $400,000, about $1,000 per man. The workforce also agreed to concessions on future pay and benefit levels. $200,000 was, finally, to be subscribed by local nonbank private investors.

Equity and control

Relative to most other branches of manufacturing, sulphite-pulp milling is a fairly capital-intensive activity with a high capital cost/job ratio of about $100,000 in 1976. Asymmetry between state and private contributions to Tembec was therefore necessary for the project to get off the ground. The structure of Tembec's ownership and control was also asymmetric – but biased in the opposite direction. Thirty-nine percent of the equity was to be held by management, who also held four seats on the board of directors. The workers, through their holding company AKTWA, held 31 percent of the equity and controlled two board seats. REXFOR held 10 percent of the equity and appointed two board representatives, while private investors – the banks and local population – were to hold 20 percent of the equity and have one representative on the board.

The asymmetry between contribution, ownership and control patterns demonstrate that government, while willing to support Tembec given a delicate political situation and the very considerable budgetary burden of supporting Temiscaming on welfare, was unwilling to become directly involved in operating or owning the plant. Neither, however, was it prepared to see in Tembec a genuinely worker-owned and controlled enterprise. During negotiations this point was clearly brought home to union representatives, and accounts for the rewarding of the management group with *equity* and *control* rather than through more orthodox, performance-related, incentives. Tembec had to be given away to someone – but not to the workers.

The equity and voting power accorded to management coincided with the provision for management rights in the 1972 union-management agreement.

The union agrees that the company must operate in the most efficient manner possible and has the exclusive power to determine how work will be organised and carried out and how operating time will be scheduled with no limitations other than ones provided by law.[24]

In subsequent agreements this statement was softened, yet the mandate of management to secure efficient operation is still prominent. Although it may represent a significant improvement, from the viewpoint of participation and worker involvement over similar conventional enterprises, Tembec is far from being a model of worker control or, indeed, co-ownership.

Labor costs and profitsharing

The agreement between Tembec management and the Paperworkers Union negotiated reductions in unit labor costs, to be effective over 1973–75. Pay levels at Tembec were not to be completely fixed, but could be revised depending on the profitability of the company, which, in turn, would mainly reflect developments in the world pulp and paper markets. Relative to pay levels expected under CIP ownership, basic hourly wages were to be trimmed by 16 percent in 1973, 18 percent in 1974, and 20 percent in 1975. Elimination of shift premia, and cuts in paid holidays, life insurance, pension, indemnity, jury duty and call-in pay as well as in other fringe benefits were estimated to reduce total unit labor costs by 24 percent in 1973, 25 percent in 1974, and 27 percent by 1975.[25] The savings expected over the three-year period would come to almost $3 million. Management pay levels, too, were set below conventional rates.

These concessions were seen as vital in negotiation with the provincial and federal governments. In return, workers were to receive 10 percent of Tembec profits for distribution while employed, independently of their role as shareholders. Was this tradeoff of present pay against future profits seen as a high-yielding investment for the average worker? As the stream of profits would cease upon retirement, both the age of a worker and the expected profit of the enterprise determined his rate of return. Computation made at the time of negotiations show an expected rate of return on forgone pay to be 7 percent for a worker with a 30-year horizon, 5.6 percent for one with a 20-year horizon, and only 0.2 percent for a worker expecting to retire in ten years.[26] Even assuming a successful company, most Tembec workers would not have been eligible to receive profits for much over fifteen years. Financial concessions by employees were not simply pay cuts because of their link with equity, but neither were they conventional investments. Rather, their role, as described in Chapter 3, was to furnish capital at low expected rates of return to the new enterprise to unlock constraints in the labor market experienced by its prospective workforce.

Representation and communication

Quite substantial moves were made at Tembec to improve labor-management communications and involve workers in the operation of the plant. Nevertheless, the 'marriage of necessity' between management and labor has not always proved to be easy to sustain. In the years following the heady period of 1974–75, Tembec appears, if anything, to have partially reverted to a more traditional management style.

The two worker representatives on the Tembec Board are the directors of AKTWA, the worker holding company. Although formally distinct, AKTWA and Local 233 of the Union are effectively identical. Following a change in Quebec law in 1975, the worker representatives have full voting board membership; before then, they were constrained to participate as observers. Worker participation in the running of Tembec is provided through their membership on eleven joint manager-worker committees, where they and management have parity. The committees cover a broad spectrum of mill operation – hiring, discipline, leave, technology change, mill costs, security and job classification.

The nature of sulphite mill technology impedes attempts at substantial job enrichment. However, Tembec's initiation was marked by organisational changes suggestive of greater job control and autonomy. Frontline supervisors were reduced by half and lead operators replaced foremen in a number of cases. Monthly meetings were held between

workers and management, and bulletins detailing production performance, listing problems and exhorting the workforce to greater efforts
were circulated to workers. Continuous negotiation replaced the past
practice of negotiations at fixed periods, apparently with considerable
success. When, for example, management and unions met in November 1975 to renegotiate wages eroded by inflation, their proposals
matched exactly. The second Tembec agreement covering pay and
working conditions over three years was signed in September 1976 after
only three and a half days of formal bargaining: the following round of
negotiation also was accomplished rapidly and effectively.

The relatively smooth bargaining process at Tembec reflects, in part,
the lesser degree of information asymmetry between management and
workers relative to CIP days. Because the Kipwa mill was only one
plant of a Canadian subsidiary of a US multinational corporation, its
profitability could not easily be gauged by the workers from consol-
idated statements. Union demands had therefore to be inflated to
permit management's attitude, and the profitability of the plant, to be
inferred through the negotiation process itself. This difficulty was less
on Tembec, as its profits and losses not only were more easily verifiable,
but were publicised by its management.

Efficiency, participation and profitability

It's a beautiful party it is true, but you know as well as I do that it won't last like
this. The interests of the management and our own interests are the two ends of
the stick.[27]

Tembec was lucky. In 1974 the depressed pulp market sprang into
life just as production was reaching capacity. Pulp, which had sold a
year earlier for $165 per ton, fetched $500, and sometimes $600
on world markets. In June Tembec held a party for customers and
suppliers from New York, to celebrate its official opening – the climax
of their struggle to keep their town alive. The party cost $200,000
which included a specially-chartered Boeing 707 to fetch and carry
important guests. Profitability soared with the rise in pulp prices. In
1974 profits for distribution among the workforce totalled $1 million,
equivalent to a distribution of $2,000 per man. Such an amount put
Tembec total pay on a level with that of other pulp workers in Quebec.

Pulp prices declined after 1974; so did profitability and distributed
profits. However, all through the ups and downs of the pulp market
operation continued at full capacity, with a high level of efficiency. It is
difficult to separate changes in Tembec efficiency levels due to plant
modernisation from those due to attitudinal changes, and still harder to
decompose the latter into those due to ownership, profitsharing or to
the heightened realisation of the dependence of jobs – and the town

itself – on profitable operation of the mill. Productivity is generally agreed to be high at Tembec, and to have increased by over twenty percent from levels reached under CIP. Several factors argue that at least a part of this is due to attitudinal change on the part of the workforce.

Even before the installation of new machinery, determination to restart the plant led to its re-opening well ahead of schedule. Despite the advanced age of much of its machinery, Tembec mill had the least downtime over 1976–77 of all Canadian pulp mills. This appears to have been due to an increased sense of cooperation and teamwork and better reporting of malfunctioning equipment. Improvement took place despite a reduction in supervisory staff, and along with a relaxation of job demarcation. The latter gave workers greater flexibility to repair their machines and to exercise preventive maintenance. Relative to other Quebec pulp mills, where a strong divide prevails between workers and management, Tembec workers worked more willingly, and are believed to have exercised far more initiative.

Over 1975–77 absenteeism declined to less than half the six percent averaged by the Canadian pulp and paper industry. Observers of Tembec noted the shortness of lunch breaks and the extremely low level of labor turnover, although the last feature owes partly to the lack of alternative employment responsible for Tembec's very existence. A degree of peer pressure to work well, unusual in pulp mills, agrees with the results of all attitude surveys conducted at Tembec, in which some sixty percent of respondents claimed to feel responsible, to a large or substantial degree, for the success of the plant. None claimed not to feel responsible. Grievances reported within the plant also declined very substantially. Whereas previously eight or ten per day was not an uncommon figure, this fell to around four per month with the new company.

Does Tembec point the way towards worker-managed enterprises? The evidence argues strongly against this view. Management style at Tembec is to accord workers a substantial measure of job control relative to similar conventional enterprise, and a degree of say in the choosing of their immediate supervisors. Commented one critical observer: 'Workers are no longer left to the discretion of the "small bosses" sold to the bosses.' However, worker shareholding and board representation are insufficient to give them control over the key decisions affecting the plant. Unlike the case of genuine worker co-operatives, such as those in Mondragon, Spain, Tembec management is not the 'delegated authority of the workers' to any but a small degree.

Recognition of this fact, and of their more ambiguous role within the enterprise has indeed caused a degree of disillusion in union ranks, and led to skepticism regarding the long-run prospects for worker-management cooperation in the plant. Worker involvement has not been the first step to true co-ownership or control as had originally been hoped by some union officials. Management commitment to worker involvement is functional rather than ideological, the objective being to raise productivity. On the other hand, it still seems, some years after its establishment, that the proportion of Tembec workers seriously concerned at their lack of control is small. It may possibly be little higher than on any conventional enterprise.

Manuest: A French Comparator[28]

The background

In 1974 Société Breuil Girandel et Cie: Manuest, a manufacturer of kitchen equipment situated in the Neuchateau area of the Vosges in northeastern France announced that, because of financial and liquidity problems, it would have to close. In this isolated, little-industrialised area there were two main enterprises, both of which had recently been forced to lay off workers – the larger, 'Eaux de Vittel', producing mineral water, had reduced its workforce of 2,000 by twenty percent. Before liquidation on 30 October 1974, Manuest had employed 600 workers and was the major source of employment for the town of Chatenois (population 2,000) which derived half of its rates from the fifteen-year-old firm.

In the French market for kitchen and bathroom white wood furniture the largest forty enterprises accounted for some eighty percent of sales. Manuest itself had satisfied five percent of the market. At its peak in 1969 it had employed 790 workers, having expanded during a period of favorable market conditions. Profits were distributed rather than re-invested in the company, and as a result it failed to diversify. By the early 1970s management's response to steadily deteriorating performance was increasingly to employ immigrant labor from Turkey, Spain, Italy and North Africa, which was housed in appalling conditions. Reform could be postponed but not for long. In response to a poor working environment the power of the Confédération Française Démocratique du Travail (CFDT) – the union representing the workers – strengthened. Union density rose to ninety-one percent and strikes and disruption emerged. In 1971 the Breuil management was ousted by Robert Vey and Christian Mercier, who tried, unsuccessfully, to revive the company.

In April 1973, in response to the desperate situation, the Société de Développement Regional injected approximately $250,000 and ordered the company to be audited. Audits revealed a catastrophic financial position and, in addition, fraudulent balance sheets. Attempts to reorganise under new management failed – in June 1974 creditors began legal proceedings against Manuest, whose liabilities were to exceed assets by some $4 million in October 1974.

Occupation

On 30 October 1974 about 250 of the 600 redundant employees occupied the factory, led by Pierre Montesinos, a militant shop steward. The workers formed an action committee and explored avenues to remain trading. They also produced a 'livre blanc', a chronicle of mismanagement. Apparently a number of irregularities had occurred, among them payments to 'female employees' who had never set foot in the plant and deliveries of furniture which had never been invoiced.[29]

The government's desire to prevent Manuest from degenerating into a Lip-type situation, where riot police were needed to evict occupying workers, prompted an industrial solution. The Secretary of State for the Treasury and Deputé of the Assemblée Nationale approached the Confédération Générale des Sociétés Ouvrières de Production (SCOP) requesting the organisation to carry out a feasibility study, which was completed in February 1975. The study, conducted by two SCOP officials, Georges Laurent and Patrick Lasry, concluded that a co-operative-type solution was possible with significant reductions in manning levels and reorientation of the company's marketing policy. That the new company registered as a cooperative did not endear it to the local municipality since under French law cooperatives are exempt from rates. Thus, an uneasy alliance developed between the new enterprise and local officials. Manuest was needed to stabilise the community, but the latter did not benefit as much as it would have done had Manuest registered as a conventional firm.

Efforts were made to raise needed capital, estimated at FF 13 million. Manuest was in an unusual situation. The plant was mortgaged to creditors, hence could not be used as security. Workers agreed to contribute FF 500,000 redundancy pay, plus five percent of their wages: this was matched by contributions of the Cooperative Movement. A development grant of FF 1.5 million was procured from the Social and Economic Development Fund which was supplemented by a FF 1.6 million regional development bonus and an employment subsidy of FF 2.5 million. The remainder of needed capital was granted by the local municipal council and obtained from banks, despite political opposition. The Cooperative Movement also supported Manuest with orders amounting to FF 6 million in 1975 – small in relation to the 1974 turnover of FF 42 million, but important to the new firm.

Although the workforce, in transition to a cooperative, had been reduced by sixty percent, this was not still to the satisfaction of

Laurent, who had assumed the position of managing director of the new company, although he knew little about the industry. Laurent and Lasry were later to resign from SCOP in order to devote their entire time to Manuest. Laurent was forced by the local branch of the CFDT under Montesinos' leadership to reemploy all 250 of the occupying workforce within the first year of operation. In the event, a compromise was reached whereby a proportion of employees worked in the enterprise whilst benefiting from unemployment and welfare payments in lieu of wages.

The case of Manuest therefore displays characteristics similar to both typical US and British examples. Rather as in the American cases, a major barrier inhibiting adjustment to closure was the isolated and declining environment and the status of Manuest as the major local employer. On the other hand, as in the British cases, Manuest involved political activity, factory occupation (illegal in France), substantial manning cuts, some reduction in wages and a very small worker equity contribution.

The survey

Information on Manuest was assisted by an attitudinal survey of its workforce conducted in early 1979; in-depth interviewing of management and union personnel complemented the survey. One hundred and thirty responses to the questionnaire were obtained – a response rate of 52 percent – which provide a useful perspective on the takeover. Perhaps surprisingly, many respondents were fairly young. Nevertheless they had, on average, lived in the area for fifteen years. A proportion of more recent workers consisted of immigrants some of whom had difficulty expressing themselves in French. Some 30 percent were females – relative immobility of the Manuest workforce appears to have been increased by a high proportion (65 percent) of two-earner families.

Manuest workers were clearly motivated by pragmatic considerations rather than radical ideology. Ninety-two percent joined the cooperative for employment, and 62 percent would readily have taken another local job instead had it been available: 57 percent saw the cooperative as their only employment opportunity. Those few individuals who declared themselves to be motivated by the fact that Manuest was a cooperative rather than a conventional firm would not have accepted similar work elsewhere, had it been available. Despite this orientation, the cooperative was popularly viewed as: 'radical with a distinctive left-wing bias', and was the subject of:

many newspaper articles which . . . suggested that Manuest had incompetent management, paid low wages to its workers, and was a place of anarchy.[30]

Although Manuest workers did not appear to be particularly enthusiastic about their enterprise (which was viewed by many respondents as far from a true cooperative), labor relations improved after transition. The cooperative was generally perceived by respondents to have increased the extent of job control by workers. Fifty-four percent of the respondents declared themselves to have become more sympathetic to problems faced by management in the course of their experience in the cooperative, and despite an apparent lack of enthusiasm workers adopted a moderate ideological perception of management's role. Although at the time of our survey only 40 percent were union members, 58 percent were sympathetic to the role of unions in the cooperative. The leading role of the local branch of the CFDT in the cooperative transition was acknowledged. Equally however, the power of the union had since clearly decreased according to respondents. In fact, by the time of the survey, Montesinos had been fired.

Personality conflict

The relationship between Montesinos and Laurent is of interest because it demonstrates the need for a change in the union role for survival in a 'worker-owned' enterprise. It also resembles, in some respects, the struggle between Allister Mackie and Robert Maxwell in the Scottish Daily News (see Chapter 8).

Montesinos and Laurent legitimated their positions by relating to very different developmental stages of the venture. The former achieved prominence in a stage which demanded predominantly protest and struggle against capital. The latter entered at a stage which demanded business expertise and practical management skills:

> The struggle reduced itself to a conflict between Montesinos and myself [Laurent]. Montesinos systematically opposed all managerial decisions. As far as he was concerned everything management did was wrong. He was in an important position as chairman of the board of directors. He had considerable support from the workforce as he was seen to be responsible for saving the jobs of workers. Nobody dared to attack him.[31]

Thus, at the point of Manuest's inception, a militant caucus surrounding Montesinos was in a position of power, and 'conventional' management was in retreat. Laurent, in the unusual position of knowing little of the industry, had been informally set aside by being starved of information: 'At first information was withheld from us, documents hidden and the general functioning of the firm interfered with.'[32]

After two attempts to oust Montesinos had failed, Laurent tried a third time to regain executive control. He called a mass meeting of the workforce and exposed Montesinos' threat to the enterprise's commercial success: 'When the workers were shown evidence of

Montesinos' threat to the company's success the workers overwhelmingly supported management and forced Montesinos to leave.'[33] Evidence suggests that once Laurent had ousted Montesinos and gained control, he proceeded to tighten that control, thus steering the cooperative back to a conventional organisational structure.

At first workers seemed to assume that Manuest was their own personal enterprise and, therefore, they believed they could create their own rules. We quickly realised that individual responsibility and cooperative spirit did not work so we progressively tightened discipline.[34]

Manuest has since weathered financial crisis and fluctuating markets, streamlined its operations and upgraded its products towards high-quality, kitchen fittings. Despite difficulties it continues to operate successfully. Rather like a number of US employee takeovers, the Manuest case is thus far from true worker control. Manuest arose almost entirely because of a need for jobs – should it return to conventional ownership, Chatenois would benefit from an increase in rates, payable by a conventional firm after five years.

8   Intervention and Commercial Failure: The Case of the *Scottish Daily News*

Introduction

On 19 March 1974 Beaverbrook Newspapers announced their intention to move the printing of the *Scottish Daily Express* and the *Scottish Sunday Express* from Glasgow to Manchester. About 1,850 staff out of 1,942 were to be made redundant. The employees occupied the factory, formed an Action Committee to establish a new newspaper and elected Allister Mackie as its chairman. The Action Committee approached various sources for advice and assistance. These carried out feasibility studies: *all* concluded that the chance of success was extremely small. But, on 24 July 1974, Tony Benn, then Secretary of State for Industry, indicated that a 'once and for all' government loan of half the capital costs could be considered, contingent upon the other half being raised from sources aware of the risk of failure.

To warn prospective investors the government insisted that the Scottish Daily News prospectus contain its damning feasibility report. The workers reluctantly agreed, committed their own redundancy money – about £400 apiece – to the enterprise, and coopted Robert Maxwell, millionaire publisher and ex-Labour Party MP, to raise the outstanding sum. Aided by Maxwell's commercial expertise, the purchase of the plant was negotiated and other government conditions met. Maxwell commissioned PA Management Consultants to specify the *minimal* manning level of the proposed *Scottish Daily News*; on the basis of the *same* technology, this was assessed at 500, some 1,450 less than had been employed on Beaverbrook's *Express*. The workers, with skills specific to a declining industry, in a depressed area with a high rate of employment, were determined to make the project a success. They agreed to the manning level and accepted a significant wage cut. On 6 May 1975 the Scottish Daily News (SDN) was launched as a cooperative.

However, crisis soon struck. Sales dropped dramatically: advertising revenue fell far below projected levels. On 8 November, the SDN unceremoniously folded. Only the secured creditors (government, and partly Beaverbrook) recouped any part of their investment. Unsecured creditors and shareholders, notably the workers, lost their entire stake in the project.

The SDN and Private Investors Survey

For methodological reasons the case of the SDN is instructive. A managerial payoff to cooperative conversion might reasonably be expected in the more successful transitions. However, what benefits does the most 'hopeless' case demonstrate? The SDN, therefore, provides a rather rigorous test of any supposed benefits of converting to employee ownership. In the process of investigating the case two postal surveys were conducted: one, of the ex-workers, and another, of the private investors. These were supplemented by interviews and in-depth surveying of key personnel.

From available documents the names and addresses of half the SDN ex-workforce were identified. Since the majority of the SDN workers were ex-Beaverbrook employees – our survey data suggests a figure as high as 99 percent – they were in possession of sufficient redundancy money to cover the employee contribution required by the SDN as a condition of employment. With one follow-up mailing, 179 replies were achieved, 36 percent of the entire workforce, a response rate of 75 percent. Responses were spread fairly evenly over occupations: 41 percent came from more, and 35 percent from less, skilled production and distribution workers; 17 percent from journalists; and 7 percent from those with mainly managerial functions. The response from ex-worker directors was especially high. The objective was a fairly concise and simple questionnaire covering the points relevant to the selection and motivation of workers. Eighty percent of the respondents provided extra comments which were often very helpful.

Feasibility assessments prior to the launch of the SDN were unanimously negative. The Bank of Scotland's advice was 'against investing', and in the judgement of the government and Strathclyde University Business School the project was 'not viable'. How, then, was the project able to raise capital from private individuals? To understand this phenomenon a postal survey of the private investors was carried out: 191 replies were received, a response rate of 60 percent.

Transition to Worker Cooperative and the Process of Iteration

Faced with the daunting task of creating and funding a new enterprise with no managerial expertise, the Action Committee approached the Bank of Scotland, Strathclyde University Business School and the government for support. Feasibility studies were carried out separately by the different bodies, and all concluded that the cooperative would not be viable:

> . . . professional investors are cautious of punters and they do not put a lot of money on outsiders who have not run the course before . . . My financial advice . . . would be against investing . . .'[1]

Similarly, the Strathclyde study suggested that the project was 'not a feasibility' and underlined the fact that:

Potential investors . . . would not only be interested in the arithmetic of the operating budget, but also in the manning and management of the company.[2]

Acting for the government, the Industrial Development Unit (IDU) could 'not accept the Workers' Action Committee's sales predictions'. It suggested that 'success . . . must be regarded as very remote', and concluded that 'the project is not viable'.[3]

Thus, negotiations between the displaced SDN workers and outside bodies, principally the government, had been set in motion. The ex-employees, reasonably certain that no conventional entrepreneur was willing to save them, were therefore forced to take the initiative themselves. This took the form of a proposal for a worker cooperative. After examining its feasibility the government and other bodies concerned judged that it was not viable. The initiative was now firmly back in the court of the workers.

After some deliberations the Action Committee sent a statement to the Department of Industry outlining the points on which it was at issue with the official feasibility study. On the basis of its reassessment of potential sales figures and advertising ratios and revenue, the Committee painted an optimistic trading picture. It was convinced that it could achieve a circulation of 250,000 and break-even while building up this figure.

The onus therefore was back on government. The workers' submission was considered by the Industrial Development Advisory Board (IDAB). The IDAB is an official body set up under section 9 of the Industry Act (1972),[4] and comprised of persons who have 'shown capacity in industry, banking, accounting and finance'. The Board agreed with the official feasibility reports and maintained that the Action Committee's circulation forecast was unrealistic in the highly competitive and contracting newspaper industry. The IDAB was pessimistic about the possibility of obtaining financial subscriptions from commercial sources either to equity or to long-term debt. It also suggested that there were 'risks' in the proposed management structure, and concluded that it could not regard the project as viable.

Thus, initiatives were referred back, in the next phase of the iterative dialogue, to the community of redundant workers for further cost cutting. This enforced responsibility appeared to change workers' attitudes significantly: they realised that the probability of a restart was conditional upon substantial concessions in the areas of manning and wage levels. After a relatively short period, worker leaders abandoned the principle of saving the jobs of all displaced workers and prepared to accept lower wages.

At this point, and despite the wealth of advice against feasibility, Tony Benn, the Secretary of State for Industry indicated that, subject to certain conditions, a 'once and for all' government loan of one-half of the capital costs of the proposal, up to a maximum of £1.75 million, could be considered. However, the government's loan was to be secured on the fixed assets of the company and contingent upon the workers finding '. . . from nongovernment sources funds amounting to 50 percent of the total capital cost of the project'.[5]

To ensure that prospective investors were aware of the financial risk the government insisted that the official money-raising prospectus of the SDN contain the unfavorable report of the Industrial Development Unit. This returned the initiative squarely back to the redundant workers. Reluctantly the Action Committee agreed to the government's conditions, but not without protest. The apparent contradiction in the government's action was pinpointed:

The inclusions insisted upon are so damaging that they make the entire prospectus appear ridiculous and the decision by the government to offer the loan in the first place nonsensical.[6]

The government's stringent loan conditions and its insistence that the main body of the IDU Report be included in the company's money-raising prospectus prompted workers to commit their own savings to the enterprise and to coopt a financier to raise the outstanding sum. Workers therefore invested their redundancy money in the project, and Robert Maxwell, millionaire entrepreneur and publisher, came to be linked with the champion of the Left, Tony Benn.

Rounds of iteration, therefore, steered the redundant workers from a period of resistance, dissent and challenge, to the need to raise funds and prove their commercial viability. They showed initiative and willingness to cut costs and agreed to significant manning and wage reductions, invested relatively large sums in the project and finally agreed to an entrepreneur holding a key position.

With the assistance of Maxwell, the Workers' Action Committee negotiated the sale of the building, plant, and machinery from Beaverbrook. PA Management Consultants were commissioned to assess the minimal manning levels for the proposed newspaper. They concluded that the overall manning level should be 500, which, as was stated earlier, was about 1,450 less than was employed at Beaverbrook's *Express*. This was imposed without recourse to any change in technology. The Action Committee concurred and also accepted wages of between 20 and 30 percent lower than would be prevailing on similar newspapers. On 5 May 1975, the SDN was launched as a worker cooperative.

Originally the Workers' Action Committee believed that financial assistance for the purchase of the company would be forthcoming from the trade unions in return for producing a newspaper sympathetic to their principles.[7] The workers miscalculated. The Committee approached Len Murray, the General Secretary of the TUC, who replied:

we have told delegates visiting Congress House that the initiative continues to lie with the interested unions in this matter, and you will need to pursue this in that setting at the present time.[8]

Employee overtures to the Scottish Trade Union Congress (STUC), however, met with enthusiasm. James Jack, its General Secretary, regretted that the STUC could not invest in the project, but wrote to all affiliated unions urging them to 'assist the redundant workers by taking out shares in accordance with the terms of the Prospectus'.[9] Securing the support of the print unions was thought to be crucial since they were directly involved in the newspaper industry and their attitude towards the SDN was closely monitored by other unions.[10] Despite the backing of the STUC and the enthusiasm of its General Secretary, the Action Committee failed to gain financial support. The majority of unions, lacking a lead from the print unions, and probably influenced more by the official reports on viability of the enterprise than the idea of worker ownership or the enthusiasm of the ex-Beaverbrook employees, dismissed the venture.[11] A typical reply was that of Sir Sidney Greene, the then General Secretary of the National Union of Railwaymen:

our rules are most specific on the matter of investment in shares, laying down that such shares must be in the companies quoted on the Stock Exchange.[12]

Local trade union branches were far more forthcoming with their support but did not have substantial funds. Their support was more moral than monetary. The total union contribution was £36,932 of which £6,432 was contributed by local groups.

The muted trade union response influenced the Action Committee's decision to call on the entrepreneurial abilities of Robert Maxwell. With his assistance the workers were able to put together a financial package and negotiate the sale of the plant from Beaverbrook for the sum of £1.6 million. In addition to the government, the principal sources of capital were: the workers themselves, who contributed £201,000 of the total equity, Robert Maxwell, who provided £114,000 and Beaverbrook who purchased ordinary shares to the value of £141,000 and provided loans of £725,000. Private individuals from the local community invested some £100,000: See Table 8.1.

The worker cooperative structure on the SDN was designed in a two-tier system consisting of a Board of Directors and an Investors' Council. The latter consisted of not more than eight members: the general manager, *ex officio*, two director appointees, and the remainder

Table 8.1   Sources and use of capital in SDN as at 28 March 1975

		£	%
A	*Sources of Capital*		
	Employee Shares	34,000	1.3
	Ordinary Shares:		
	Workers	201,000	7.9
	Public and Unions	125,000	4.9
	R. Maxwell	114,000	4.5
	Beaverbrook Limited	141,000	5.5
	R. Agnew	10,000	0.3
	Department of Industry	1,200,000	47.1
		1,825,000	
	In addition Beaverbrook gave the SDN loans of	725,000	28.4
	TOTAL CAPITAL RAISED	2,550,000	100
B	*Settlement*		
	The purchase price of the building was	1,600,000	
	Leaving a cash balance when the company moved into the Albion Street building of	950,000	

chosen by the holders of ordinary shares. The Investors' Council was a 'watchdog' for the outside shareholders and its principal function was to exercise a power of veto over decisions of the Board in matters relating to dividends and diversification.

The Board of Directors comprised up to ten members. Again the general manager was *ex officio*, as was the editor. In addition there were two appointees of the Investors' Council while the remainder were selected, in general meeting, by holders of employee shares. The Board was vested with the day-to-day control of the company.

Government Intervention, Worker Selection and Internal Efficiency

Selection and motivation of workers.

As described in Chapter 6, the *nature* of this form of government intervention into declining private industry did not arise from conscious policy, but was the result of a three-cornered compromise – inspired by political expediency – between the ideological Benn, the conservative Treasury and a weak Labour government. However, what were the actual consequences? The following two sections investigate the hypothesis that the style of intervention can be functional to the state by selecting employees for the enterprise who (a) see little alternative opportunity, and (b) possess a common distinctive attitude: a belief that *through their own efforts* they can, and will, affect the destiny of their enterprise.

The formal model underlying the analysis is set out in the Annex. Its main points, in relation of the present case, are dealt with briefly here. Collapse of a previous firm is assumed to throw a number of workers onto the job market. To relieve labor market pressure, the government seeks to reduce, or at least to slow down, redundancies and partially to maintain output and employment. From the government's vantage point the most appropriate workers to benefit from intervention are those who will make the greatest contribution to the enterprise, but who have the least alternative employment opportunities. The enterprise is to be financed by a government grant and a uniform employee contribution. Both are considered as government control variables. Workers have three choices:

1. They can volunteer for the enterprise or take their chances elsewhere.
2. If they choose to work on the enterprise they can choose how much 'work effort' to volunteer.
3. If on the enterprise, they can choose what wage level to press for.

Before proceeding further it is important to discuss briefly variables considered to lie in the range of choice of an individual worker. On the SDN, as on other cooperatives, pay was decided jointly and not by individual negotiation. Strictly, therefore, wages are not an individual variable, but the individual choice of pay levels is reflected in the general internal upward and downward pressure on wages. 'Effort' is a complex concept. An individual's actual effort is constrained by many factors, for example, monitoring by management and possibly by fellow workers or, on the demand side, by the work loading of his department. Here effort refers to the voluntary or discretionary component of intended effort above the normal or required effort level. Effort could extend to cooperation and flexibility as well as include more obvious manifestations such as longer hours.

The most difficult task for an essentially new enterprise is to survive long enough to carve out a share of the market. In the present case, a reasonable initial loss-making period might have been a year or so, even had the venture ultimately proved successful. The rewards from participation in the cooperative were highly uncertain, because it was not apparent that it would succeed. We may distinguish three components of reward for the worker joining such an enterprise.

Firstly, a positive component made up of the *possible* future benefits from being a cooperative member if the enterprise survives. This must be contrasted with the alternative level of welfare if thrown onto the job market. Clearly, this incentive will be strongest when a worker sees particular rewards for being a member of a cooperative, rather than an employee in a conventional firm. It will also be powerful when he anticipates few alternative possibilities of employment. The incentive effect may be represented as the difference between two levels of welfare: one if on the enterprise, and the other if not. Ideological and pragmatic motivation therefore both condition the *strength* of the incentive. The motivation to join a cooperative will be high if an individual places great weight on working in an organisation with a cooperative structure, or if he sees little alternative employment opportunities. Particularly strong ideological motivation could therefore induce a worker to volunteer for a cooperative even if his alternative employment opportunities were excellent. However, the benefit of participation is clearly related to a worker's subjective estimate of the probability of enterprise success – if this is thought to be very small, the large, but unlikely, gain would be heavily discounted. As noted in Chapter 6 there is the possibility that less risk-averse individuals will tend to participate, but this is not certain since the alternative of seeking employment is risky also.

The second, probably negative, component reflects the expected loss of the employee contribution. For SDN workers failure meant total loss of employee contributions, but success would reasonably result in their recoupment. Clearly, the more pessimistic is a potential cooperateur, the more heavily will the expected loss of his stake weigh in his computation, and the less attractive will be the cooperative, particularly if worker contributions are large.

The third component of reward for workers joining the enterprise comprises ongoing benefits. Two obvious aspects to this component are (a) absence of 'hard' or undesirable work (leisure), and (b) pay. The harder participants choose to work and the lower the wages, the more assured is the success of the enterprise. An individual constrained to work on the cooperative can, however, be considered as choosing some optimal levels of work effort and wages. This, plus his beliefs about the cooperative's operation, the constraints facing the new enterprise and its potential for growth and improved profitability, will determine an estimate of the probability of it succeeding. Because of the difficulty in obtaining data on attitudes to risk, it is supposed that potential SDN employees were risk-neutral, valuing a risky prospect approximately by its expected outcome. Given the initial state contribution, the maximal welfare level expected by a worker on the cooperative can be compared to the expected level of well-being if he chooses not to volunteer.

Employees actually volunteering will be those for whom the former exceeds the latter.

A potential difficulty faced by government is that, at any level of support sufficient (in its opinion) to permit the project to operate for a reasonable period, the expectations of potential employees might be such to encourage many more than would make the enterprise viable. Some workers who wish to join the project may have ample alternative possibilities of employment. Productive factors would then be withheld from other more advantageous industries, while such cooperative members might care little about the enterprise's success, press for high wages and contribute little effort. An employee contribution may resolve this dilemma. It need not be specified directly by government, which may instead make it difficult to obtain equity from other parties. This will induce a high contribution by a potential member truly in need of work and screen out those who believe the success of the enterprise to be very low. Because the pessimists expect to lose their contribution, only the relatively optimistic among the potential pool of workers remain. Of these, only those for whom expected cooperative welfare exceeds substantially the maximum alternative welfare available actually volunteer for the cooperative. This is particularly likely when the alternative welfare is that provided by the state: unemployment and social security benefits.

What are the causes of such relative optimism and how do these relate to worker motivation? Individuals differ considerably, not only in their expectations of outside influences but in assessments of what actually is controllable. There may well be disagreement over the potential contribution of effort to success. However, given the dismal outlook for cooperative experiments such as the SDN, it is hard to believe that *external* considerations could inspire optimism. The optimistic among the potential workforce could therefore be those who believed that *through their own efforts* it would be possible to relax, or surmount, the constraints to financial viability facing the SDN. We refer to this state of mind as 'voluntaristic'. Voluntarism is related to optimism; any selection mechanism tending to discourage pessimistic employees from joining the cooperative also should leave it with less than its fair share of fatalists.

Voluntarism is also of great importance in motivating work effort. Rewards to employees investing time and money in an attempt to save an enterprise enter mainly through the prospect of success, and it is here that a voluntaristic outlook is needed to convert the *desire* for success into effort. There is little point in participating if a fatalist. Voluntarists, therefore, will select themselves for situations where the subjective probability of success is fairly high, but is conditional on work effort.[13]

The previous discussion refers to the *discretionary* element of effort which must be related to individual motivation. Clearly, work effort is not entirely an individual's decision. Substantial monitoring of performance occurs both by management and by fellow workers. But additionally, the selection of highly motivated individuals will probably lead to increased monitoring of 'slackers' by their fellow workers and greater peer pressure directed towards ensuring the survival of the enterprise.

To sum up, therefore, this argument suggests that a lower level of public sponsorship in the form of loans or loan guarantees raises the premium on employee contribution and leads to a fall in the number of workers willing to work on the cooperatives. Those workers who volunteer have small alternative opportunities of employment, value highly the success of the enterprise and are characterised by voluntarism, which is responsible for a reasonably optimistic view of its prospects. The employee contribution is particularly important for those interventions involving weaker firms where a determined effort and willingness to reorganise are central to success. If high, it will effectively screen out pessimists and also eliminate those pressing for higher wages. The optimists remaining are also probably voluntaristic, believing that by their own efforts they can materially affect the success of the enterprise.

Besides selecting suitable workers, the employee contribution performs two other functions. Firstly, it decentralises some of the burden of financing away from government. Secondly, if government finance is secured and the employee contribution is not secured, risk is shifted onto the latter group and moral hazard effects minimised. Both features may well seem desirable to government. A substantial employee equity contribution does, of course, necessarily link the method of intervention closely to some form of employee ownership, although not to any particular pattern of control.

Testing the theory

Such a framework is undoubtedly oversimplified, and unduly individualistic, omitting many important elements of group interaction. It nevertheless implies a number of hypotheses which may be tested on survey data obtained for the SDN.

Hypothesis 1 Intervention selects workers who would be expected to have little alternative employment opportunity.

Propositions (1) Volunteer workers should have experienced fairly long periods of unemployment prior to the project. (2) Lengthy unemployment should follow collapse of the cooperative, as should: (3) occupational downgrading on re-employment. Volunteers should be less mobile and less able to learn new skills, hence be old.[14] (4) To the vast majority of the volunteer workers the success of the cooperative should be of paramount importance. (5) Pragmatic and ideological motivation are not exclusive, but should be considered as mutually reinforcing. However, for selection to relate to the opportunity cost of labor many workers should be motivated primarily by pragmatic considerations, notably job preservation, rather than support for the cooperative form *per se*.

Evidence (1) Eighty-five percent of respondents had been unemployed for a year or more prior to the launch of the SDN. (2) and (3) In the nineteen months between SDN collapse and the questionnaire, only 38 percent had found new jobs using their skills. Our sample fared worse than workers examined by such other studies as Wedderburn (1965), Martin and Fryer (1973), Daniel (1972), Herron (1975), and Mackay and Reid (1972). This appears to be largely due to its unusual age distribution: only 6 percent were below 30, 20 percent between 30 and 40, 27 percent between 41 and 50 while 47 percent were over 50. This distribution differs very significantly from that of all British newspaper employees, which is roughly uniform across these age categories.[15] As in other studies, older workers fared worse as regards downgrading and re-employment. (4) Only three respondents indicated that success mattered 'a little'. To all 179 other it mattered 'very much'. The three are, indeed, distinctive. They are young and, unusually for young workers, joined the cooperative for employment rather than ideological reasons. On its collapse, two found jobs in one month and the third within three months. That only three such cases appear out of 179 demonstrates the power of the selection procedure as a filter. (5) Workers were asked both for their own major reasons for joining the cooperative, and for their perceptions of other workers' major reasons: see Table 8.2. The pragmatic employment response is very powerful, especially in the perceived responses. It is, in fact, more likely that the proportion of respondents expressing a 'cooperative' motivation exceeds the actual proportion of ideologically motivated workers, than the reverse. Estimates offered by respondents (including committed 'cooperateurs' at director level) put the latter proportion at not more than 20 percent for the workforce as a whole.

Hypothesis 2 The method of intervention screens out pessimists.

Proposition (6) Despite the wealth of evidence against viability, workers actually volunteering should have had a fairly high expectation of the project's success at its start.

Evidence *Ex ante* expectations of success are tabulated in Table 8.3. Only 8 percent rated prospects as less than 'fairly good'. As in Table 8.1 a close identification between own and perceived views is apparent.

Table 8.2 *Major own motivation by major perceived motivation*

| | Major perceived motivation | | | | |
	Employment	Employment/ Worker cooperative	Worker cooperative	No response	
Main own motivation					
Employment	69	3	4	2	78
Employment/Worker cooperative	6	19	1	2	28
Worker cooperative	19	6	43	2	70
No response	2	0	1	0	3
TOTAL	96	28	49	6	179

Chi^2 = 140.8 significant at 0.0001.

Screening by optimism appears to have produced a 'cut off' point below which few workers were willing to participate.

Table 8.3   Own and percieved ex-ante optimism

		Perceived chance of success					
		None	Poor	Fairly good	Good	Very good	
Own	None	0	0	0	0	0	0
	Poor	0	5	4	3	1	13
chance of	Fairly good	0	0	44	15	5	64
success	Good	0	0	5	42	5	52
	Very good	0	0	1	6	41	48
	TOTAL	0	5	54	65	53	177

$Chi^2 = 227.1$ significant at 0.0001

Hypothesis 3   The characteristic distinguishing voluntarists from fatalists is that the former believed that *through their own efforts* it would be possible to relax or surmount the financial constraints on the operation of the SDN. Given the unpromising outlook for the SDN few of the workforce would have been expected to be optimistic purely because of external factors.

Proposition (7) Optimism and voluntarism are closely associated.

Evidence   Workers were asked whether, while on the cooperative, they believed that 'success depended on a special effort by the workforce'. Those answering affirmatively were classified as voluntarists. The voluntarism-optimism relationship is a highly significant one, as shown in Table 8.4.

Table 8.4   Ex-ante optimism by voluntarism/fatalism

	Ex-ante Perceived Chance of Success					
	None	Poor	Fairly good	Good	Very good	
Fatalists	1	6	10	3	0	20
Voluntarists	0	8	54	48	47	157
TOTAL	1	14	64	51	47	177

$Chi^2 = 30.4$ significant at 0.0001

Hypothesis 4 The importance of success suggests that workers should have worked hard. Further, the discretionary effort choice should relate, at the level of the individual, to the importance of success and to his degree of voluntarism.

Proposition (8) Compared to their previous jobs, SDN employees should have worked as hard or harder, if not constrained by lack of demand for their efforts. (9) Individuals working harder should tend towards both a high valuation of the project's success and a voluntaristic, rather than fatalistic, attitude. Such a relationship would provide a further powerful indication of the importance of the selection implications of intervention. It further would suggest that a substantial proportion of any improvement in motivation of its workforce rested, even in the cooperative, with *individual*, rather than group, self-interest. Another implication of a significant relationship would be that individuals possessed considerable discretion over their work intensity.

Evidence Sixty-three percent considered themselves to have worked harder on the SDN than they had previously. Only six percent admitted to having worked less hard. A larger proportion of respondents professing a degree of ideological motivation worked harder (the relationship is significant at the level of 0.3 percent) – this accords with the interpretation of ideology as introducing an additional motivating force through raising an individual's anticipated gains if on a successful cooperative. On the SDN there was less rigid job demarcation than under Beaverbrook, and in its short life there were no industrial disputes. This compares to 54 work stoppages in the last year of Beaverbrook's *Express*, 40 of which disrupted production. (9) Table 8.5 shows the impact of individual work incentive on actual work effort claimed – those working equally or less hard are amalgamated because of the fewness of the latter and the probable constraints on their effort choice. The relationship is, again, as predicted.

As discussed above, motivation-effort relationships may be obscured by organisational constraints which cause actual and intended effort to deviate. The rapid *SDN* circulation decline is known to have left

Table 8.5 Work effort by higher and lower work motivation

		Motivation		
		Higher	Lower	
Work effort compared to	Harder	101	10	111
under previous owner	No harder	54	12	66
	TOTAL	155	22	177

Chi^2 = 2.4 significant at 0.12

certain individuals and departments relatively underloaded. Several respondents indicated that SDN workers were far less tolerant of others not 'pulling their weight' than they were under Beaverbrook; for example, '. . . the (process) department sacked one of its members for drinking too much. He drank less than he did in his Beaverbrook days.'[16] Greater leisure was therefore probably enforced by circumstances. Two attempts to correct for the effects of organisational rigidity were thus attempted: (a) Respondents have indicated that the dispatch department was especially underloaded. Excluding its members from our sample yields a more significant relationship Chi^2= 2.8). (b) Excluding those admitting to have worked 'less hard' yields a still clearer relationship, significant at the 4 percent level.

Hypothesis 5   To generate *internal* low-wage pressure it must be generally believed at the level of initial government funding that extra funds should raise the chances of success.

Proposition (10) Internal pressure for low wages required a belief that extra government funding would have contributed to success, not merely postponed failure. In the absence of such a general consensus, there would have been a natural incentive to raise pay levels, increasing the proportion of costs absorbed by wages.

Evidence   From the start of the project, wage levels were, overall, some 20–30 percent below those then obtaining for similar work in other local firms. Moreover, during its operation, the workforce agreed to reduce further its real wage levels, signing over to the cooperative cost of living adjustments suggested as appropriate by the Labour government. The cooperative's dismal and deteriorating circumstances certainly generated internal low-wage pressure. Correspondingly, no fewer than 89 percent of our respondents believed, *during the project's operation*, that increased state funds would have improved its chances of success, rather than merely have postponed collapse.

In addition to these relationships, data permit a number of crosschecks on variables relating personal, economic and ideological characteristics. These indicate reasonable consistency in the pattern of responses; relationships appearing to be consistent with the theoretical model above or with each other. There is also no evidence of alternative selection mechanisms (for example, deliberate screening by age or opinion) which might have been responsible for such observed response patterns.

Radical Motivation or Pragmatic Acceptance?
Whether cooperatives arise out of pragmatic accommodation or radical responses to cash nexus breaks, participants would still be expected to

be individuals to whom redundancy signalled an abrupt decline in living standards. Living standards *per se* are not the issue. The critical question is rather whether radical attitudes tend to be associated with such declines, or whether they are reflected in economistic, pragmatic responses which result in a movement towards a cooperative solution, as outlined in Chapter 3. What motivated the SDN workers?

The balance between ideology and pragmatism on the SDN relates significantly to age, which itself is correlated with the degree of snapping of the cash nexus. The relationship between age and ideological balance is, however, not in the direction predicted by Westergaard's (1970) cash nexus hypothesis.[17] Approval of the controversial role of Maxwell in the enterprise can be interpreted as implying strong support for a purely managerial approach to the running of the cooperative. Maxwell was far more popular among older workers, who saw less chance of re-employment outside: see Table 8.6.

Table 8.6   *Age by attitude to Maxwell*

Age	Approval	Attitude to Maxwell Non-approval	
Under 50	30	58	88
Over 50	45	31	76
TOTAL	75	89	164

Chi^2 = 10.0 significant at 0.0005

The position of the few younger workers in the sample is especially interesting. Of the eleven under 30, seven were re-employed in less than three months after the SDN collapse. All but one had found employment at the time of answering our survey and eight of the re-employed were able to re-use their skills in their new jobs. Yet this group, for whom the cash nexus can hardly be said to have snapped, appeared to have joined the cooperative more on idealistic than pecuniary grounds. In this sense the group of young workers is more 'radical' than older workers of the sample. In only two cases (out of eleven) was the employment-generating aspect of the cooperative its major appeal for the youngest age group, while for the old this consideration dominated. Radical idealism was clearly a factor in some quarters of the SDN workforce, but not, typically, for those subsets which suffered the largest and most severe cash nexus breaks.

The experience of the SDN provides a number of further indications of this underlying pragmatism. Firstly, support for the Action Committee rose once workers saw that the project offered them a real chance of a job: a few weeks before the launch, attendance at mass meetings sharply increased from 200 to around 400. Secondly, in determining the ideological stance of a newspaper, the choice of editor is clearly a key factor. It is significant that a 'conservative' editor was selected, one with some twenty years of Beaverbrook experience behind him and a career profile similar to those of editors of other national newspapers. According to the editor: 'I doubt if any editor has ever been freer of pressures from noneditorial sources than I was.'[18] Any hypothesis that the workforce attempted to shape editorial policy is thus difficult to sustain.

Thirdly, still unresolved is the important issue of whether the operation of the cooperative itself generated a progressive radicalisation of the mass of the workforce. This bears on the question of whether, in the short term, unconventional forms of organisation resulting from cash nexus breaks are likely to contribute to a change in underlying ideology, as in Moorhouse's (1976) interpretation of the 'cash nexus hypothesis'. Is some level of consciousness a necessary precondition for the development of radicalism, or does action *generate* radical ideology?

Some light is thrown upon this question by the internal dynamics of the cooperative's leadership struggle and the response of its workforce. Its co-chairmen, Mackie and Maxwell, legitimated their positions by relating to totally different developmental stages of the enterprise, the former to a stage which demanded dogged resistance and a commitment towards the cooperative, the latter to a later stage which demanded business expertise and practical management skills. Because the two leaders, with their very different role orientations, shared a joint position at the head of the organisation, conflict was inevitable.

. . . the dichotomy between those who believed in the workers' cooperative as such, and those who saw the cooperative merely as a necessary expedient for preserving 500 jobs, meant that the project had the seeds of conflict in it from the start.[19]

Progressive radicalisation should imply increasing support for the radical caucus at the head of the organisation. Did this, in fact, evolve? The leadership struggle can be considered to have had three distinct stages. Firstly, just before the SDN launch, Maxwell was ousted from the chairmanship by a group surrounding Mackie. It is by no means clear that this was supported by a majority of the workforce. It is better understood in terms of a boardroom power struggle. Thus, at the board meeting which forced Maxwell to resign the worker directors decided that: 'the method of presentation of the facts to the workforce should be decided later'.[20] Maxwell's ousting aroused little obvious reaction from the workforce, largely due to the overwhelming optimism prevailing at the moment of the newspaper's successful launch.[21]

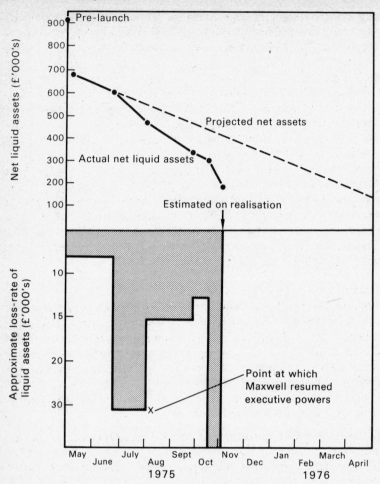

Figure 8.1   Asset erosion and leadership struggle on the SDN
Source: Bradley and Gelb (1980a)

But shortly after the launch optimism became tempered with ever growing doubt as newspaper sales plummeted dramatically and advertising revenues fell short of their targets. Figure 8.1 illustrates the rapid deterioration in SDN profitability. This ushered in the second stage of the leadership struggle. Whether Mackie's inexperience actually contributed to the newspaper's decline is difficult to ascertain. However, Maxwell seized this opportunity to regain control, appealing directly to the economistic and pragmatic attitudes of the workforce, thus bypassing the chairman and the ideologically motivated caucus which surrounded him on the board of directors. On 20 June 1975, he sent a lengthy telex to the SDN workers. This appeared to be designed to expose Mackie's idealism and lack of expertise as being prejudicial to the viability of the enterprise. He outlined the company's serious financial position, and stressed a practical solution to the crisis, suggesting that he had managerial experience which 'may just save the situation'. The telex appealed to the financially motivated workforce. It sidestepped Mackie, outlining the choice between inexperienced worker management and 'experienced' capitalism. Following a mass meeting on July 30, Maxwell was given executive responsibility.

The third and final phase of the leadership battle occurred in September. At a mass meeting the workforce voted 295 to 12 in favor of Maxwell as sole chairman. It is thus difficult to sustain the thesis that the mass of the SDN workers were 'radicalised' by their cooperative response to the cash nexus break. As financial constraints drew tighter, pragmatic responses came to dominate the attitudes of the workforce. The saga of the SDN leadership struggle exhibits interesting parallels with that of Manuest, as described in Chapter 7.

Commercial Failure. Policy Success?

Headlines such as '£2 million lost in collapse of newspaper'[22] did little to dispel the popular view of the SDN venture as a waste of taxpayers' money on a radical project. 'Defunct Workers' Paper Owes £2 million', echoed another national newspaper.[23] But, relative to more conventional means of industrial support, was the method of intervention really so disastrous?

On economic criteria, a strong case for temporary state intervention to support a closing firm may exist, if:

(1) the duration of support is short relative to the delay in factor market adjustment;
(2) intervention does not substantially hinder or slow down factor reallocation to more viable sectors;
(3) factors affected are not unemployed through deliberate government policy.

With regard to (1) and (2), labor reallocation may be so slow that factors appear to be almost specific to a given occupation or region within which demand for their services is deficient. As no labor is intrinsically specific, its apparent specificity largely reflects the weakness of the pressures impelling occupational or geographical reallocation relative to natural preferences for familiar occupations and environments. In Britain reallocation pressures are undoubtedly blunted by available levels of unemployment benefits. Neither is the thrust of industrial policy directed at promoting occupational or regional reallocation.[24] These policy features are taken as given, without wishing to judge their optimality. The net effect on government revenue of intervention to save jobs may, given criteria (1) and (2) above, be positive or negative.

The impact of support on some measure of national 'welfare' also depends most obviously on the social valuation placed on the newly employed workers' loss of leisure. The valuation of unemployment leisure is rather a contentious issue, as noted in Chapters 2 and 6.[25] There seems to be a strong case for assigning it a zero (or perhaps even negative) valuation, given the often-stated 'social' rejection of unemployment leisure as a 'good' and the consequences of unemployment in mortality, crime and social disruption. It might also be argued that even if an individual benefits from his own unemployment leisure, the majority of those employed derive disutility from seeing the enjoyment of such leisure on public money. Such external effects might well dominate in some aggregate sense. For want of a convincing estimate of social value, unemployment leisure is here assigned zero weight.

Criterion (3), invariably neglected in micro-studies of employment creation, must be addressed as it bears on some later discussion. Given the ability of the government to alter the level of economic activity in the short-to-medium run at least, high general unemployment must be seen as a consequence of deliberate policy. As the opportunity cost, in terms of output, of an unemployed worker equals his marginal product, which roughly could be taken as the wage, the marginal social benefit of unemployment as perceived by the government must therefore very approximately equal the wage in policy equilibrium. If this is so, there is no case for employment-creating interventions: to maintain government equilibrium, such projects will merely result in offsetting employment-destroying policies. Here, nevertheless, in analyzing the SDN closure it is assumed that the 'economic' social valuation of SDN employees' unemployment is zero; temporary preservation of their jobs is not assumed to lead to offsetting policy elsewhere. Intervention is thus viewed as a highly selective aid in distributing demand pressures towards high unemployment regions and towards factors with lesser alternative uses, rather than as part of a general job-preserving policy. Given the project's location, the skills of the workforce, and the constraints on the government at the time, this assumption is very plausible, as indeed it would be in most cases described in Chapters 4 and 7.

One advantage of the intervention strategy has already been noted. Support was not open-ended, but explicitly specified as being 'once and for all', and formally accepted as such by the SDN workers. While this assurance did not guarantee that future funding demands would not come forward, it rendered credibility of future demands far harder to maintain. The other advantages relate to the generation of worker commitment and acceptance of lowered pay. Manning cuts and cost reductions permitted the SDN to survive far longer on a given grant than it otherwise would have done. The intervention package also induced self-selection of workers with few alternative job opportunities to work on the SDN. From the point of view of government, another advantage resulted from the securing of government funds by the fixed assets of the enterprise.

Before rather crudely assessing benefits and costs of intervention, it is necessary to estimate a likely *ex ante* date of closure, as plausibly seen before the establishment of the SDN. *Ex post* assessment is clearly not appropriate. On the basis of the Report of the Industrial Development Unit and other submissions on feasibility, a reasonable assumption might have been that the project would run for about one year, which is thus the *ex ante* time horizon assumed here for the project. This period arises from projections of expected losses and the terms of the 1948 Companies Act, under which the project was obliged to register. Section 332 provides for the imprisonment of persons knowingly party to the carrying on of business with intent to defraud creditors. The worker-directors were uncomfortably aware of their personal liability under the Act.[26] This left them with no alternative but to wind up the company once its liquid assets had been eroded to the point where there was a danger that the newspaper would default on its trading liabilities. The government, naturally, would not permit the raising of loans with a lien prior to its own on the fixed assets.

Feasibility estimates were subject to two great imponderables: circulation, and the ratio of sales to advertising revenue, hence their divergent conclusions. Assuming generous, but not unreasonable, figures of 170,000 (midway between IDU 'probable' and workers' guesstimates) and a ratio of 0.8 (the most optimistic IDU figure) yields a projected loss of about £12,000 per week. Actual losses averaged about twice this figure, partly because of circulation averaging only 138,000 but mainly because the advertising/sales revenue ratio averaged only 0.27, well below that envisaged. Figure 8.1 shows the projected erosion of liquid assets compared with the actual erosion as derived from trading statements. The *ex ante* time horizon of about a year is approximately twice the actual lifetime of the project.

It is also necessary to estimate which productive factors employed in the SDN had alternative uses and which were specific to the project. Inputs may be grouped into three categories: (1) newsprint and similar supplies, (2) the buildings and plant, and (3) labor. The extent to which inputs are considered to be specific to the SDN or reallocable to other uses critically affects the argument for temporary support.

The first group of inputs, about 30 percent of running costs, is indeed not specific but for present purposes may simply be viewed as transfers from other newspapers whose output declined approximately

in line with SDN circulation.[27] Newsprint consumption is proportional
to circulation. Other factors in the first group comprise less than 10
percent of running costs: any implied diseconomy of two newspapers
rather than one is therefore small. Whether or not the fixed assets were
considered to have profitable alternative uses is not quite clear, but at
the time no organisation appeared to be interested in purchasing them
other than the Beaverbrook ex-employees. This was largely due to the
plant having been specifically designed for the production of newspapers. The eventual purchasers, George Outram and Co, were indeed
approached, but at the time declined to bid for the premises. These,
therefore, could reasonably be considered to be temporarily unwanted,
and thus available at no opportunity cost. It is clear from the comments
of, among others, the Department of Industry, that the workforce was
considered to have little alternative use because of (a) the worsening
national unemployment position, coupled with a high local unemployment rate (5.4 percent in March 1974), and (b) general overmanning
and contraction of the newspaper industry. The specificity of the actual
workforce during its work on the SDN is further indicated by its
unusual age profile as described previously.

The direct revenue effect of intervention
According to the Public Accounts Committee Report, of the £1.2
million government stake in the initial capital stock of the SDN at least
half could have been expected to have been realised on the collapse of
the project. If, as seemed likely (but not certain), the premises and
plant proved unsaleable as a going concern, an upper limit of £0.72
million was posited. Sale on a going-concern basis would enable the
repayment of the entire government loan. The expected costs thus
depend crucially on p, the probability assigned to sale on a going-
concern basis. Forgone interest has somewhat arbitrarily been imputed
to the government loan at 15 percent p.a. (deliberately a high estimate)
and the average of the upper and lower limits taken as an estimate of
revenue on a 'breakup' sale basis. This yields projected budgetary
intervention costs of £0.72 million if $p = 0.0$, £0.61 million if $p = 0.2$
and £0.50 million if $p = 0.4$, which may be taken as indicating a
plausible range of *ex ante* projections.

   However, what goes out through one account comes in through
another: this is apparently overlooked in the Committee's Report.
After reorganisation, employees of the SDN totalled some 500 with
average earnings of approximately £2,500. For a typical worker,
income tax and national insurance contributions for a year would total
£618. Extra outpayments generated by nonintervention in the event of
unemployment are composed of supplementary benefits plus rents and
rate allowances. Earnings-related allowances are not relevant here, as

these would have been projected to have been paid later – after the project's collapse. Considering therefore only basic scales, non-taxable unemployment benefits total £1,447 for a typical worker. For each worker whose unemployment is delayed by the project, the public purse is therefore saved approximately £2,065. Were all workers in the enterprise projected, *ex ante*, to have otherwise been unemployed, intervention is projected to yield a direct profit to the state of about £0.31 million if $p = 0$, £0.42 million if $p = 0.2$ or £0.53 million if $p = 0.4$. The net direct budgetary cost is, under these assumptions, substantial and negative.

The assumption that all 500 cooperative workers would otherwise have remained unemployed is clearly extreme. There are three ways of arriving at a more reasonable *ex ante* projection of the employment-creating effect of the project. Firstly, we can consider the prior unemployment record of SDN employees. Secondly, we can look at their employment experience after the SDN collapse. Thirdly, we may consider their motivation for joining the SDN.

As described previously, the SDN workforce was unusually old. Over 85 percent had been unemployed since the collapse of the *Express* over one year previously. Given the dismal conditions of the Glasgow job market, entrants would probably, if successful in finding unskilled employment, merely have prevented others from filling the few vacancies available. The same cannot in general be said for workers whose new jobs require their skills – for them, the filling of a vacancy represents more probably a net increase in employment. But in the present case, given the circumstances of the newspaper industry, this also is not an obvious conclusion. A second projection can nevertheless be made by considering the employment record of workers after SDN collapsed, treating re-employment using past skills as an indication of new additions to employment. From survey information, this suggests an employment-creating effect of about 78 percent. A third, informal projection might be obtained by recalling that SDN wage levels were 20–30 percent below those prevailing for similar work in other firms and that the project's success, and consequent return of the employees' contributions, was far from certain. It seems reasonable to suppose that few workers with good alternative employment prospects would have volunteered for the project, had they not been ideologically motivated. The proportion of the workforce motivated purely by ideological factors rather than job preservation thus provides a rough guide to the number who did not feel dependent on the project for a job. Survey results presented earlier suggest that perhaps 40 percent of respondents valued to a degree the 'cooperative' nature of the SDN, but respondents have suggested that the probable proportion with mainly ideological motivation was only 20 percent. This suggests a range of between 60 and 80 percent for the employment-creating effect.

The projected net direct effect on government revenue of SDN support may now be computed, taking into account losses of direct taxes and national insurance from those workers who otherwise would have been net additions to the employed. These may be taken as 20 percent greater than the figure above (to allow for the lower SDN salaries). Also, the taxes which might have been paid by employers on possible profits must be included and may be estimated from the ratio of employers' to employees' taxes which is obtainable from Inland Revenue Statistics for the printing and publishing industry. Estimates of the direct net government revenue effect of SDN support are tabulated in Table 8.7. On most projections intervention emerges as profitable. The rough nature of these estimates is readily acknowledged, but it is not worthwhile, given the unavoidable uncertainty surrounding p and the net employment-creating effect, to go into greater detail. The main objective of this computation is to illustrate that the projected direct state profit (in terms of the narrow revenue criterion) on intervention is possibly substantial given (1) the conditions attached to the government loan and (2) the position of the SDN as a 'residual employer'. The indirect effects below are unlikely to have been large enough to turn a direct profit into a large overall loss. Temporary support of nonviable enterprises need not be a waste of public money if the methods of intervention are appropriate.

Table 8.7   Projected net direct government revenue effect of SDN support (£'000s)

| | Probability of plant sale on 'going concern' basis (p) | | |
	0.0	0.2	0.4
	100	312	422	532
Net employment	85	120	230	340
creating effect (%)	78	30	140	250
	70	−40	70	180

This conclusion about the effect of funding on government revenue has a further important implication for the basis on which the support operation should be judged. As the projected SDN operation cost the state nothing (or less), its funding should not have been seen as inhibiting any other employment-creating scheme through depriving it of public funds. The important criticism that, at a time of high unemployment there are many more worthwhile projects to be undertaken with limited public funds, is therefore not relevant here – the government should have gone ahead and carried them out too![28]

Some indirect effects of SDN support and the welfare impact on 'losers'

The net projected transfers to government, to local SDN suppliers and to the SDN workers must come from elsewhere in the economy, or from the creation of new output. To obtain some idea of the indirect effects of support is important for several reasons. Firstly, indirect effects also affect government revenue. Secondly, it is not appropriate to judge policies only on the basis of their impact on state revenues, since revenue is an instrumental, rather than a 'target', variable. An assessment in terms of national output or, ideally, some measure of 'national welfare' is therefore called for.

Mention of national welfare raises the obvious difficulty of agreeing on the welfare weights appropriate to different individuals and the non-measurability of welfare. While such problems have not prevented the use of explicit welfare-weighted criterion functions in recent cost-benefit studies, formal weighting and aggregation of gains and losses is not necessary here.[29] Certain features peculiar to the SDN funding suggest that the adverse welfare effects of the substantial capital losses following its collapse are more apparent than real.

Transfers received by government, SDN workers and local suppliers stemmed from essentially three sources. Firstly, there was a transfer from Beaverbrook, as sellers of fixed assets, to the cooperative. Secondly, there were the losses suffered by unsecured creditors, here the SDN workers and ordinary public shareholders. Thirdly, there was a loss of circulation revenue to Beaverbrook as proprietors of the rival *Scottish Daily Express*, printed in Manchester. Feasibility studies argued that *SDN* circulation would largely displace that of the *Express*; a possible assumption is therefore that the two papers were close substitutes and that the *SDN* added little to overall newspaper sales.[30] Naturally this assumption biases the analysis against intervention.

To understand better the implications of the losses it is appropriate to split the creditors and losers into two groups; 'voluntary' creditors, and 'creditors under duress'. The first group comprises creditors whose losses arose out of their own free actions in the sense that they were not committed to lend to the enterprise, which was possibly against their better judgment, by the state's decision to fund it. It is reasonable to include amongst them members of the public and Maxwell. Interestingly, their total loss is of a similar magnitude to the projected net direct government profit on intervention. Nevertheless, the circumstances of their involvement make it extremely difficult to infer a large adverse welfare impact from their considerable financial losses. The reason for this is the generally appreciated position of the SDN as a project of very doubtful viability. Few informed investors seeking an investment in the sense usually understood would have chosen to invest in the SDN. Investment opportunities existed which clearly dominated SDN shares both as regards expected return and security. Why did the public decide to lose money – or is the explanation, simply, a lack of information? The survey carried out on private SDN shareholders was designed to answer this question.

Most investors were local. Sixty-five percent were from Glasgow, while 55 percent had relatives or friends on the SDN, who suggested that they invest. A surprising 30 percent of the investors were professionals. Forty-eight percent viewed their contributions as a gift to workers on the SDN rather than as the purchase of shares: fewer than five percent invested mainly for financial return. The dominant motives were: sympathy for the unemployed (31 percent) and the desire for an independent Scottish newspaper (28 percent). Only some 20 percent believed their investment to have been secure – mainly those who had not read the IDU report in the SDN prospectus. Ninety-two percent had bank, building society or similar accounts: of these, 71 percent expected the return on SDN shares to be lower than that on their accounts; only six percent expected a higher return. But the most persuasive evidence that nonpecuniary returns rather than financial gain dominated the motivation of investors is provided by two observations: (1) 87 percent of SDN investors admitted that, had the opportunity to invest in the SDN not arisen, they would not have invested their contributions elsewhere, and (2) 70 percent claimed not to regret having invested money in the SDN – a remarkable number, in view of its failure. Cross-tabulations between the answers to various questions reveal a high degree of internal consistency in answering patterns.

The main conclusion is quite unambiguous. Private investment in the worker cooperative was not 'investment' at all, in the usual sense of the word. With some exceptions, the public's response suggests that they regarded their shares as a *consumption* good, and were not resentful of their losses, despite the paper's failure. Naturally, all the investors would have been happier had the enterprise succeeded – but this does not invalidate the fact that it provided an opportunity to purchase substantial nonpecuniary benefits which were indeed realised.

The only way in which the majority of the shareholders' decisions to lose money can be viewed as a substantial *social* loss is, therefore, if society's valuation of the money in their hands is greater than their own. This implies that society values other uses of SDN investments more than the investors. This has never been suggested. Were it to be seriously advanced, it would involve a wide-ranging debate on society's right to determine individual behavior, which is well beyond the scope of this book. Maxwell has also indicated that his motive in investing lay not necessarily in making a financial return, but in gaining political capital.[31] The losses of the voluntary creditors can be considered to have given rise to negative and probably rather small effects on tax revenues and national output, but these are speculative since their alternative uses of funds are not known.[32]

Turning now to the involuntary creditors, they necessarily incurred losses through the pattern of state support. Most prominent were the SDN employees themselves, and Beaverbrook newspapers. Once again, it is misleading to consider their financial losses as net welfare losses arising out of intervention.

The considerable capital losses of most SDN employee shareholders would have been more than cancelled in one year by the net monetary benefits of participating in the cooperative: post-tax SDN wages would have exceeded welfare payments by about £435, slightly more than the average employee shareholding. Consider now Beaverbrook, who received a cash payment of only £875,000 for the Albion Street plant, accepting the remainder in the form of loans to the cooperative, £225,000 secured and £800,000 unsecured. As proprietors of the *SDN*'s competitor, the *Express*, Beaverbrook would also have lost sales revenues from reduced circulation during the *SDN*'s lifetime, although these would have been partly offset by cost transfers (newsprint, energy costs, etc.) to the SDN. The revenue losses might have reduced, temporarily, Beaverbrook's profits. But to argue that their combined loss exceeded that which would have ensued had the government not intervened is inconsistent with the observation that Beaverbrook were not opposed to intervention. This was apparently because of their difficulties in otherwise disposing of their Scottish operation. Beaverbrook were helpful to the Action Committee:

For their [Beaverbrook's] long-term survival they had to sell Albion Street [the SDN premises]: to sell Albion Street they had to pay off the workforce and to pay off the workforce they had to help to launch a competitor in Scotland . . . The best sequence of events for Beaverbrook would be a sale of Albion Street to the cooperative followed by a quick collapse of the newspaper before it could do irreparable damage to *Express* circulation in Scotland.[33]

An interesting, possible scenario is that Beaverbook were able to take advantage of the threat of a Scottish competitor to reduce manning levels and costs in Manchester to below what they otherwise might have been. Employment would then temporarily be expanded in Glasgow at the apparent cost of unemployment in Manchester. However, this result is highly unlikely to be neutral as regards government revenue, national output or the longer-run criterion of efficient resource allocation. In June 1974 registered unemployment was only 2.4 percent in Manchester, compared with 4.7 percent in Glasgow: per unemployed Mancunian there were 2.5 times as many job vacancies as per unemployed Glaswegian. If 'surplus labor' is to be shaken out of overmanned British industry it surely should be in those regions where it can contribute to increasing the national output. By assuming that *SDN* sales exactly offset the reduction of *Express* sales, any direct increase in national output as a result of the project is ruled out. Alternative uses for some SDN labor suggests an overall negative output effect; but against this must be set the benefit of the SDN in temporarily redistributing the pressure of labor demand more evenly across the economy.

Summary: Some Possible Improvements

The circumstances of the cooperative's funding were responsible for government intervention being proposed as a policy of some permanent and ideological significance, rather than as a temporary employment-maintaining operation. This, no doubt, explains the tendency for the SDN support policy to be judged in this light rather than within our framework, which seems to be far more appropriate given the method by which support was extended.

Despite its origin as the unwanted progeny of a three-way compromise, the unusual method of SDN financing appears to have offered potential savings in government revenues on the basis of reasonable projections. This contrasts with the inevitable losses of public money popularly assumed and condemned in the Sixth Report.

Naturally, the actual outcome of the SDN affair was less favorable, as unexpectedly low advertising revenues and lack of demand cut the life of the project to only six months. Sale of the assets yielded sufficient to repay about half of the government loan, but occurred only two years after the *SDN* was first launched. Imputed interest charges were substantial: a net employment-creating effect of 85 percent yields a direct revenue loss of about £0.54 million; 78 percent a loss of £0.58 million. However, these losses are correctly seen as *ex post*, rather than reasonable *ex ante*, projections.

As noted, the projected effect of support on aggregate national output was less likely to be favorable. The selective intervention had interesting potential in distributing labor demand more equally across regions. The results of our shareholder survey, and an appreciation of the positions of the other substantial losers – Beaverbrook and the SDN workers themselves – brings out the important point that the welfare losses from the government's decision to intervene are not appropriately measured by financial losses relative to what might have resulted had the project succeeded, as is implicit in a conventional judgement involving the totting up of the losses of creditors and shareholders.

The chief benefits obtainable from modelling industrial intervention after the SDN pattern relate to its factor-screening effects and compatibility with necessary incentives to X-efficiency. The self-selecting

SDN workforce was unusually old, slow to obtain alternative employment and, in many cases, unable to re-use its skills. The opportunity cost, in terms of forgone output, of most SDN workers was undoubtedly very low. Successful entrants into an unskilled labor market in the circumstances of Glasgow, 1975, are most likely to have prevented other, similar, workers from becoming employed. Had the SDN not undergone the rigors of the screening process, survey results suggest strongly that the majority of eventual employees would neither have been as strongly motivated nor of equally low opportunity cost. While survey (and other) data should be treated with some caution, results agree with the thrust of theoretical prediction and with each other.

The SDN experience also suggests room for improvement in the method of intervention. Firstly, flexibility in cooperative members' pay levels and differential contributions may be needed across groups of workers if skills are complementary in production but re-employment prospects differ between groups. Otherwise, terms sufficient to screen one group may hinder recruitment from the other. Self-selecting workers could be of lower quality and require some high-quality workers or managers, specialists, or young workers to yield high output. SDN failure was not caused by production shortfalls. No evidence suggests that the age or quality of the nonjournalist workforce hampered the enterprise. However, poor journalism has been cited as a factor which contributed to the rapidity of SDN failure, and rewards were noted by Maxwell to have been insufficient to attract 'named writers'. Re-employment prospects were significantly better for journalists, 87 percent of whom were able to continue their careers after the collapse.

Conventional subsidisation does not obviously induce correct factor selection either, and all methods may require a degree of direct control. But the SDN method case reveals the potential of converting to cooperatives in generating strong pressure for X-efficiency. If the potential contribution of particular individuals or groups is correctly perceived by the mass of workers, and pragmatism dominates over idealism, SDN-type cooperatives evolving out of failed firms should be willing to induce their participation with attractive terms. Respondents suggested the existence of a considerable gulf between SDN journalists and other workers, who appeared not to be fully aware of the difficulties being experienced by their journalist colleagues due to lack of space-filling advertising copy and specialist writers. Initial, clear guidelines on the appropriate skill mix of the workforce could probably do much to overcome this selection problem. Otherwise, restricted X-efficiency, (i.e. efficiency given recruitment patterns) rather than 'full' efficiency will prevail.[34]

Secondly, the 1974 British cooperatives are here seen as alternatives to other forms of reorganisation following bankruptcy. In all cases transitions were lengthy and controversial. Smoother and quicker transitions, as has frequently been the case in the US, might have reduced their difficulties in rebuilding distributive networks and re-establishing themselves in their markets. On the other hand, selection and motivational effects might have been weaker.

Thirdly, pessimism outside the cooperatives made it extremely difficult for them to obtain normal trade credit. This dilemma is a serious one; at sufficiently low levels of initial finance to screen the workforce, few optimists may remain outside the cooperatives. Private and social attitudes to the risk of speedy failure clearly diverge, for, by assumption, the vast majority of the workforce of a failed cooperative would have anyway been unemployed. While not being over-generous, projected financing needs should allow for tighter than usual constraints on normal credit.

Annex. Selection, Motivation and X-Efficiency: A Model of the 'Cooperative' Option

Most, if not all, analyses rest upon a conceptual model, embodying the prejudices, as well as the insights, of the analyst. This book is no exception to the rule, its policy suggestions and interpretation of a number of case studies being heavily influenced by a particular view of the process through which employees, and perhaps communities, come to opt for employee ownership in attempts to preserve their jobs and assure their existence. Such a view is best made as explicit as possible. To this end, a formal model of the self-selection process, and its relationship to efficiency and motivation, is developed in this Annex.

The formal model emphasises decisionmaking at the level of the individual, but could be reinterpreted as expressing communal responses. With such an interpretation, the model deals with the response of *communities*, rather than of individuals, to the conditions set by government in negotiations for assistance. Individual decisions may not, of course, be totally individualistic, and, in the formal treatment below, aspects related to group decisionmaking are suppressed. If the dominant thrust of group decisions is believed to mirror trends in individual decisions then this feature should not prove fatal to the conclusions of the model. Indeed, as noted below, certain group-wide responses are likely to strengthen the conclusions of the individualistic model through mutual reinforcement.

Two other limitations of the formal analysis should also be noted, although, in our view, they are unlikely to seriously limit its applicability. Firstly, the transition from closing to (perhaps partial) employee ownership takes place over a period of time, typically between a few months and two years. The temporal dimension is equally important in any assessment of the record of the new employee-owned enterprise conducted after its establishment. If, for example, such a firm were to survive for ten years, would the experiment be considered a success or a failure? For reasons of analytical necessity the time dimension is suppressed in formal treatment which relies on a comparative-static framework. Associated with the suppression of the time dimension, differential access to information and variations in attitudes to uncertainty are ignored. Individual decisionmaking units are here assumed to be risk-neutral, valuing uncertain outcomes according to their mathematical expectation. The only bias introduced by such an assumption would appear to be to abstract from the unlikely possibility that employee-owned firms would tend to be composed of individuals of a gambling bent. The assumption regarding information is perhaps more contentious.

The experience of the Scottish Daily News might, at first sight, be taken to indicate that only absurdly optimistic workers would attempt to purchase their closing firms. Nevertheless, as a general phenomenon, this is strongly refuted by experience in other countries, most notably in North America. It was also shown in Chapter 8 that the decision of the employees to invest in the Scottish Daily News could not be seen as unjustified on the basis of the survival period reasonably expected on the basis of the IDU feasibility study. Informational asymmetry, real or perceived, should, of course, diminish very considerably with the demise of the previous enterprise. Collapse is certainly one way of 'opening the books'.

Closure of an industrial plant is assumed to result in the redundancy of a large pool of n workers. Of these, a number m are possibly to be reemployed on a streamlined employee-owned enterprise, where typically m is less than n. Here, we abstract from particular occupational requirements and the requisite balance of skills; production-wise, potential workers are relatively homogenous. The community of workers enters into negotiation for public assistance to purchase the firm. The new, employee-owned enterprise is here referred to as a 'cooperative' although it is understood that this need not imply any *specific* pattern of ownership, control or industrial organisation.

Government, the other side in negotiation, is assumed to have three broad objectives. Firstly, whether or not it ultimately proves to be successful, the prospective enterprise should be as efficient as possible. This includes, besides ensuring adequate management, securing agreement to a flexible and broad range of industrial arrangements, the relaxation of artificial demarcation lines, and so forth. In order to do this and generate commitment to the firm, its survival should clearly be of the utmost importance to its workforce. Secondly, the enterprise should employ a high proportion of individuals with limited alternative job prospects in order to be genuinely employment-preserving. Such workers may be constrained by occupational, geographical or ethnic factors, regional attachments or age. There is little point in subsidising highly mobile workers with excellent re-employment prospects. Thirdly, the establishment of the enterprise should require minimal state funding. In reality, a degree of compromise between these objectives will be necessary. For example, a firm composed *entirely* of the otherwise unemployable is likely to lack the organisational expertise and the occupational balance to achieve a reasonable chance of survival.

Less knowledgeable on the industry and production processes, the state cannot, however, directly control the efficiency of the enterprise. Neither can it distinguish individuals easily able to secure re-employment from those perceiving few alternatives. Government, the principal in the problem, therefore attempts to maximise the success of the intervention as judged by its three criteria above, subject to the other agents – members of the redundant workforce – optimising their own objective functions which emphasise pay levels, working conditions, the future availability of permanent employment and, perhaps, ideological preferences for employee ownership. The constraints on the latter agents are established by the conditions set by the state for assistance. Because of the limited information available to the government, formulation is as a classic principal-agent problem.

Worker i (a typical agent) is assumed to have three decisions:

(a) whether to work on the cooperative, or try for a job elsewhere;
(b) if in the cooperative what *voluntary* effort e_i to contribute;
(c) if in the cooperative what total remuneration w (assumed to be independent of hours worked) to press for.

The government, on the other hand, has three controls on the cooperative, at its inception:

(a) its initial level of funding G;
(b) a worker contribution c, set directly or implicitly (for simplicity, c is assumed to be uniform across workers, and could be in cash or in the form of foregone pay and benefits over the establishment period);
(c) an upper bound on w, $\bar{w}$.

These choice variables need further explanation. Strictly speaking, w, the total pay accruing to a cooperative member, is not an individual decision variable. However, the aggregation of individual choices determines the general upward or downward pressure for payment, which here is intended to encompass a range of benefits, overtime premia and so forth, in addition to basic rates. For example, in a voting model of decisionmaking, the choice of the median worker could set the pay level.

The effort variable e_i is also a rather complex concept. Here, e_i refers to the *voluntary* or discretionary component of *intended* effort above some minimal required effort level. 'Effort' encompasses cooperation with management and other employees, agreement to a flexible set of working arrangements and a general willingness to display and use initiative in the interests of the firm as well as longer or harder hours of labor. Effort here is intended as a general efficiency proxy. The actual effort put out by an individual will of course not necessarily equal his intended effort, but is constrained by a number of factors. Monitoring by management or by fellow workers and the workloading of individual departments may set upper or lower bounds to actual effort. Certain restrictive agreements may constrain e_i to be zero, such as when working at 'above-norm' rates is rewarded by social ostracism; but, in general, monitoring constraints may be considered as restricting e_i to be non-negative. Mutual reinforcement is here particularly likely to strengthen the conclusions of analysis based on individual responses. A firm of workers choosing high e_is is likely to also see a high *minimal* effort level, as slacking or obstructionist behavior will be less tolerated.

Notation

S_i^* = maximal welfare of i if he does not join the cooperative or, subsequently, if he does and it fails. S_i^* is closely associated with alternative job prospects, hence the shadow wage. It will be high for younger, highly trained and mobile workers, low for the older, less mobile with redundant skills.

T_i = welfare of i if he joins cooperative.

x = stochastic effect of all combined factors as seen by worker i, except c, G, w and e_i, on the profitability of the cooperative over the unit period of its establishment (see below).

$f_i(x)$ = i's subjective probability distribution on x, assumed to be continuous.

p_{1i} = i's subjective probability of success. $p_{2i} = 1 - p_{1i}$, $0 < p_{1i} < 1$ for all i.

α_i = i's subjective belief in the potential contribution of e_i to success; $\alpha_i \geq 0$ (see below).

u_{1i} = i's anticipated, future, welfare level if on a successful cooperative. For all workers seriously interested in the cooperative option it is only reasonable that $u_{1i} > S_i^*$.

Starred variables denote local certainty-equivalent optima.

Success and failure

The cooperative will be considered as successful if after some 'establishment' period its net liquid assets are still positive. Otherwise it will have failed. This classification reflects the fact that the most difficult task for a new enterprise is to survive an initial period of loss-making before carving out a segment of the market. For convenience this period is designated as a unit. In the subjective judgement of worker i considering whether or not to join such a cooperative, it will succeed if and only if

$$G + mc + \alpha_i e_i - mw + x > 0 \qquad (1)$$

The first three terms represent revenues from government, worker contributions and efficiency improvements. These are offset against wage costs and random events. This implies that the chance of success p_{1i} may be expressed as follows:

$$p_{1i} = \int_{B_i}^{\infty} f_i(x)dx \text{ where } B_i = mw - mc - G - \alpha_i e_i$$

Definitions

Worker i is an *unconditional optimist* relative to j if for all y

$$\int_y^{\infty} f_i(x)dx \geqq \int_y^{\infty} f_j(x)dx$$

Worker i is *optimistic* relative to j if $p_{1i} \geqq p_{1j}$. We term i *fatalistic* if $\alpha_i = 0$. In the absence of a better term for someone who believes that effort matters we term i a *voluntarist* if $\alpha_i > 0$.

Individuals may therefore differ in their assessments of what is likely to prove successful. In particular, they may have different opinions as to what lies outside their control. Some individuals (or communities) may not be willing to adapt, to seek new and innovative solutions because they believe that their best efforts will avail them little; for such units, $\alpha_i = 0$. Optimism depends upon α and upon f, the subjective probability distribution over truly uncontrollable events. Everything else being equal, the wider is the set of phenomena considered to be under control the more optimistic must be the decision maker, as greater α implies a larger choice set. Greater α_i may indeed lead to a translation of f_i by $\alpha_{ij} \sum_{\neq i} e_j$; a voluntaristic worker may feel that the success of the new enterprise is more likely because he values the voluntary efforts of others which he anticipates will be forthcoming. Extra voluntary effort into monitoring also is likely to cause the acceptable minimum effort level to rise through mutual reinforcement, as described previously.

Worker i, in deciding whether to join a cooperative and, if so, what effort to contribute and what wage to press for, seeks to maximise his welfare: to

$$\max W_i = \max [S_i^*, T_i^*] = \max [S_i^*, \max_{w,e_i} T_i(e_i, w, G, c)] \quad (2)$$

where

$$T_i = v(u_{1i}p_{1i} + S_i^* p_{2i}, -cp_{2i}, -e_i, w). \quad (3)$$

v is concave with $v_1, v_2, v_3, v_4 > 0$ and is separable in its last two arguments

$$v_{3j} = v_{4k} = 0 \text{ for } j \neq 3, k \neq 4$$

By risk neutrality, and since u_1 and S^* are in welfare terms, we set

$v_1 = 1, v_2 =$ constant. The first and second arguments of T_i are, respectively, expected future welfare from the cooperative and expected future loss of the employee contribution c.

In this specification, failure of the cooperative is therefore assumed to lead to total loss of c while success simply implies that workers recoup the purchasing power of their contributions at a later date. These assumptions do not restrict the generality of the analysis.

For worker i to decide to join the cooperative at all, $T_i^* > S_i^*$ for T_i^*, the global maximum of T. First order conditions for a local maximum of T_i are:

$$m\{(u_{1i} - S_i^*) + v_2 c\}f_i - v_4 \underset{w}{\overset{\leq}{\underset{<}{}}} \underset{\overline{w}}{0} \Bigg\} \tag{4}$$

$$\alpha_i\{(u_{1i} - S_i^*) + v_2 c\}f_i - v_3 \underset{e_i^*}{\overset{\leq}{\underset{>}{=}}} \underset{0}{0} \Bigg\} \tag{5}$$

and for i to join the cooperative at all, $T_i^* > S_i^*$ where T_i^* is again the global rather than the local maximum.

Even with smooth single-peaked f, multiple local optima $\mu, \nu, \ldots$ generally exist and may be ranked in descending order by their associated probabilities of success, $p_{1i}^\mu > p_{1i}^\nu \ldots$. A local optimum with high associated p_1 is termed a *high level local optimum*. By (4), (5), given $\alpha_i, e_i^{*\mu} \geq - e_i^{*\nu}$ and $w^{*\mu} \leq w^{*\nu}$, worker i will in general work harder *and* accept lower pay at a high level local optimum if it represents also his global optimum, to contribute to a higher probability of success. Figure A.1 shows possible local optima in the (e, w) plane. Comparative statics analyses must be supplemented by noting probable 'switches' between them.

Empirical evidence on all four worker characteristics u_1, S^*, f and α cannot easily be obtained. Assume $f_i = f$ for all i, and characterise workers by $u_1 - S^*$ and α. Potential cooperative employees are then distributed over a region in $(\alpha, u_1 - S^*)$ space. Considering any local optimum of T_i we note the important results:

$$\frac{dT_i^*}{dG} = \frac{\partial T_i^*}{\partial w}\frac{dw}{dG} + \frac{\partial T_i^*}{\partial e_i}\frac{de_i}{dG} + \frac{\partial T_i^*}{\partial G} = \frac{\partial T_i^*}{\partial G} > 0 \tag{6}$$

$$\text{Similarly,} \quad \frac{dT_i^*}{dc}\bigg/_{mc+G} = \frac{\partial T_i^*}{\partial c}\bigg/_{mc+G} = -v_2 p_{2i} < 0 \tag{7}$$

$$\frac{dT_i^*}{du_{1i}} = p_{1i} > 0, \quad \frac{dT_i^*}{dS_i} = p_{2i} > 0 \tag{8}$$

$$\frac{d}{dS_i^*}(T_i^* - S_i^*) < 0 \tag{9}$$

$$\frac{d}{d\alpha_i}T_i^* = [(u_{1i} - S_i^*) + v_2 c]f_i(B_i^*)e_i^* \tag{10}$$

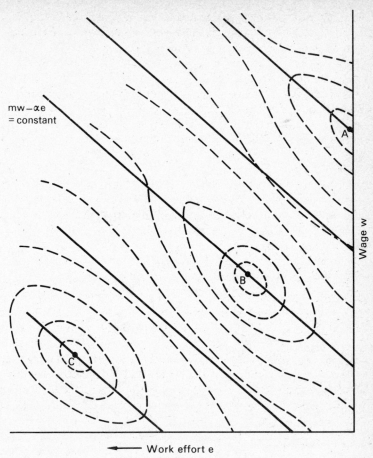

Figure A.1   *Effort–wage local optima*
Notes: Here A, B, C are local optima.
          C is highest-level optimum.
Source: *Review of Economic Studies* (Bradley and Gelb, 1980)

Assuming an interior maximum, let δ represent a shift in expectations towards pessimism: $f(x)$ becomes $f(x - \delta)$. Total differentiation of (4) and (5), yields:

$$de^* = \frac{k_1}{j}\,(\alpha f'v_4'')\,d\delta \qquad (11)$$

$$dw^* = \frac{-k_2}{j}\,(f'v_3'')d\delta \qquad (12)$$

$$de^* = \frac{-k_3}{j} f v_4'' \, du_i \qquad (13)$$

$$dw^* = \frac{k_4}{j} f v_3'' \, du_1 \qquad (14)$$

where $k_1, k_2, k_3, k_4 > 0$ and j is positive by second order conditions.

Equations (4) through (14) indicate the characteristics of workers most likely to volunteer for an employee-owned firm. They also offer some behavioral predictions. By (5), only voluntarists will contribute voluntary effort (since fatalists believe their efforts are useless anyway). This reduces B^*, so increasing the subjective probability of success and the attraction of the cooperative solution at *any* optimal set of points e_i^* w_i^*. By (10) and (5) high-level equilibria have their attraction especially increased by voluntarism since such equilibria typically require a large effort input; increased voluntarism tends to induce switches to high-level optima. This strengthens the link between voluntarism and optimism. Voluntarists generally favor high-level equilibria and are more optimistic. If $\alpha > 0$ also implies a translation of f by $x_i \sum_{j \neq i} e_j^*$, the project's attraction is further increased but this alone may not induce i to work harder.

Screening out pessimists therefore leaves the enterprise with a harder-working and more dedicated workforce. By (7) this screening is the function of the employee contribution c which has differential effects on T^* at high- and low-level equilibria. By requiring a proportion of initial risk capital to come from workers, the government can reduce welfare at low-level equilibria to below the alternative level of welfare S^*. Raising c screens out low-level optimum workers with progressively less attractive prospects elsewhere, holding u_1 constant. It may be necessary to bound the possible cooperative wage above by $\bar{w}$, so that high c cannot simply be recovered rapidly through high w, holding p_1 near zero. Such a strategy may be attractive if payments can eat into other sources of capital besides c.

Although, by (8) it is better to have good alternative prospects in case the project fails, by (6), (8), (9) the attraction of the cooperative rises with G and u_1 and declines as alternative employment prospects improve. U_1 includes both pragmatic (monetary) and ideological incentives which reinforce each other in increasing the attraction of a successful cooperative. By (13) and (14) higher u_1 increases effort and leads to a fall in desired payments; by (8) higher u_1 is also likely to switch a worker to a higher-level equilibrium. Clearly, for the project to be highly attractive, both u_1-S^* and p_1 should be fairly large – the latter condition is, we argue, closely related to the degree of voluntarism.

The conclusions of this part of the model may be summarised diagrammatically. An individual worker is characterised by (a) the

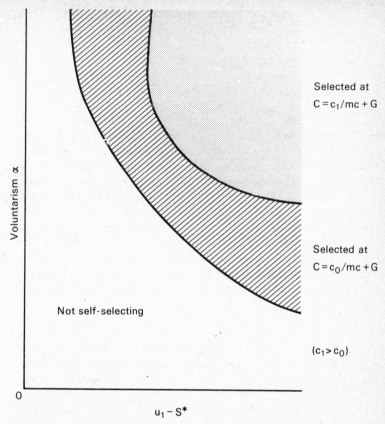

Selected at
$C = c_1/mc + G$

Selected at
$C = c_0/mc + G$

Not self-selecting

$(c_1 > c_0)$

Voluntarism α

0

$u_1 - S^*$

Figure A.2   Self-selecting SDN workers in characteristic space
Notes: Here $mc + G$ is held constant while c is raised from c_0 to c_1. The set of
self-selecting workers contracts.
Source: As Figure A.1

extent to which being a member of a successful cooperative is likely to
be preferred to alternative prospects on the labor market, and (b) his
degree of voluntarism. These characteristics are represented on the
horizontal and vertical axes of Figure A.2 respectively. Volunteers tend
to be both voluntarist and either ideologically committed to cooperativism (high u_1) or with few alternative possibilities of employment (low
S^*).

Total initial financing $mc + G$ affects the probability that the enterprise will succeed, but its distribution between the worker and government contributions determines a crucial breakdown of the financing
burden between the community of workers and central government.
The more stringent is the set of conditions established by government,

the less attractive will the venture appear to the workers, fewer of whom will volunteer. Figure A.2. shows the contraction in the set of self-selecting workers as the required worker contribution increases. It can also be interpreted as showing the self-selection of *communities*, those with easier options (and perhaps less interest in social cohesion) voting with their feet against the requirements laid down by government to secure its assistance. The employee or community contribution does more than simply shift the financing burden from the shoulders of central government; it represents a significant decentralisation of equity and opens the way for similar devolution of decisionmaking power, with reduced danger of moral hazard.

Under the assumption that f is single-peaked, it is also possible to distinguish low level equilibria from those at high levels. As previously described, workers at the highest level equilibrium consider the likelihood of the cooperative experiment succeeding to be high, relative to those at lower-level equilibria. Additionally, by (11) and (12) and the concavity of v, deterioration of the cooperative's prospects (an increase in σ) leads to greater effort and lower wages at the highest level optimum (f', v''_4 and v''_3 negative) but reversed responses at lower-level equilibria (where f' is necessarily positive). To interpret this result, high-level equilibria are those in which benefits from the cooperative project enter essentially as future rather than immediate payoffs, and in which the survival of the firm is of the utmost importance. At lower-level equilibria, on the other hand, a greater proportion of overall reward accrues near the start of the project, in the form of higher payments or more favorable working conditions. The priority placed on the viability of the enterprise at high-level equilibria leads members of its workforce to accept even more difficult conditions in the hope of securing its survival. As described in Chapter 8, this was exactly the form of response to the deteriorating situation of the Scottish Daily News worker cooperative.

References and Notes

Chapter 2

1. *Congressional Record*, vol. 125, no. 17, Feb. 15, 1979: Testimony of Congressman P. Kostmayer.
2. See Pagoulatos and Sorensen (1980).
3. See, for example, *Report of the Secretaries of State for Industry, Scotland and Wales on Operations Under the Industry Act 1972*, London, HMSO July 1976, and, in contrast, Golt (1980).
4. See Balassa (1978).
5. See Maddison (1980), and Nelson (1980) for descriptions of these trends.
6. How productivity increase would affect industrial employment in the UK is not entirely clear. On the one hand, labor-saving productivity may reduce jobs, on the other, more competitive industry could mean more rapid expansion. Bacon and Eltis (1976) ascribe the decline of British manufacturing to 'crowding-out' by government on the labor market, but this has been disputed. For an analysis, see Blackaby (1979).
7. These trends and their implications for old established communities in the northeast US are described in Stern, Wood and Hammer (1979).
8. 'Reindustialisation' is the subject of a number of US articles although the concept is still imperfectly defined. The most extensive treatment is perhaps that in *Business Week* (1980). Another clear statement of the problem associated with the impending loss of the manufacturing base of the Northeast is due to Rohatyn (1980) who also puts forward suggestions to rebuild industry. For a more radical statement – and prescription, see Rifkin and Barber (1978). This subject is addressed in the British context by Blackaby (1979).
9. British industrial policy is discussed in Golt (1980) and its failure in key areas documented in Blackaby (1979). The Employment Protection (Consolidation) Act (1978) combines much previous legislation in one comprehensive piece of legislation. For a comprehensive review of British legislation relating to plant closures and redundancy, see Gennard (1978).
10. The estimate is due to Gennard (1978).
11. Packer (1980), p. 16.
12. For example, the proposed National Employment Priorities Act (1979) would have required up to two years advance notice of plant closings, provided assistance and benefits to affected employees and used criminal and civil penalties as well as economic incentives to ensure compliance.
13. Cited in Dreze (1979).
14. In this connection it is interesting to note the comments of the 1972 Committee of Public Expenditure regarding the selective help given to Rolls Royce and Concorde: see *Public Money in Private Industry* (1972), paras. 70 and 91. In each case, as with shipbuilding, it concluded that parliamentary control of the use of funds had been inadequately monitored and that the information provided to the public funding bodies had not been efficient or adequate.

15. Young and Lowe (1975).
16. Allocative efficiency concerns the appropriate choice of techniques and productive factors given the structure of incentives (prices). The theory of X-efficiency, on the other hand, recognises that given techniques may be operated with different levels of efficiency (ratio of output to an index of inputs). See Leibenstein (1966) for a discussion of X-efficiency.
17. See, for instance, Stout, D. (1979), p. 179, and Jones (1977). For a comparative analysis of the British automotive industry, see Thatcher (1979).
18. OECD (1975); also see Cassing (1980).
19. Nelson (1980), pp. 92–3.
20. Ohlin (1978), 'Subsidies and Other Industrial Aids', as cited in Golt (1980), pp. 336–7.
21. See footnote 8; also Bluestone and Harrison (1980).
22. See *Business Week* (1980).
23. Stern *et al* (1979), pp. 17–18.
24. See Rothschild-Witt (1981), p. 21.
25. There appears to be a high degree of inertia, both occupationally and geographically on the part of redundant workers, particularly those over 40. For the UK, redundancy is twice as frequent for workers over 55 as it is for young workers. Only 5 percent of all workers affected by major redundancy even think about retraining, and even fewer take and complete any courses to this end: see Gennard (1980). US studies suggest that only 7 percent of workers over 45 moved, on becoming redundant: see Bartel (1979). Only 2 percent of recipients of trade adjustment assistance underwent retraining. UK studies suggest that older workers experience appreciable job downgrading on reemployment after redundancy: see Wedderburn (1965) and Martin and Fryer (1973). The financial losses incurred on plant closure may extend beyond income foregone due to unemployment, to include lower pay levels on re-employment, and loss of pension rights.
26. See Stern *et al* (1979) and Select Committee on Small Business (1979).
27. *Business Week* (1980).
28. *Ibid.*
29. Swift (1975) analyzes this phenomenon and describes regulations dealing with associated closure.
30. The best known example is perhaps that of the *Times*, whose future has been threatened, despite its status as a major quality newspaper, by persistent labor disputes and stoppages. In a less dramatic way, the inability to resolve industrial conflict has almost certainly played a part in the demise of much industry, not only in the UK (see Blackaby (1979)), but also in other major industrial countries.
31. Dynamic conservatism is described by Toffler, A. (1970).
32. Michels (1915); also Passfield (1911).
33. Sainsbury (1981) attributes the prevalence of short-term managerial horizons in the UK to pressures exerted by equity holders more concerned for short-term capital gains than for longer-run prospects. Such a myopic perspective may inhibit research and innovation. In a similar discussion for the US, *Business Week* (1980) attributes myopia to the mobility of management and executive rewards system. However, it is interesting to

note that such major institutional investors as US pension funds, which also have mainly longer-term liabilities, commonly judge the performance of their portfolio management by fairly short-term criteria over horizons of less than three years. Inflation and a more troubled economic picture have tended to shorten their horizons further over the 1970s. Who then, are the farsighted equity holders?

34. The Scottish Daily News and Tembec experiences described in Chapters 7 and 8 bring out the problem of informational assymetry clearly. The role of trust relationship in an industrial setting is discussed by Fox (1974).
35. See Jacobson (1976), Glenday and Jenkins (1980).
36. Brenner (1976), p. 53.
37. Wilcock and Franke (1963), p. 85.
38. Glazer and Rice (1959), Komarovsky (1971).
39. Daniel (1974).

Chapter 3

1. Consider the case of Vermont Asbestos in the US.; for the UK, see the Ferranti case described in Sainsbury (1981).
2. The closer a supported enterprise comes to viability, the longer will a small increase in profitability extend its lifetime. For a given grant, the lifetime is inversely proportional to the rate of loss.
3. The modern corporation, for example, evolved to reconcile the production requirements of large scale and advance planning with the need on the part of asset holders for diversified portfolios and limited liability.
4. Worker ownership is, nevertheless, viewed positively in the US. A poll conducted by Hart Associates asked citizens in which type of economic enterprise they would choose to work. Only 8 percent opted for a government agency, 20 percent chose private investor ownership and 66 percent opted for employee owned and run companies. See Rifkin (1977), pp. 45-57.
5. For a nontechnical survey of the interlinking literature, see Bardhan (1981).
6. Stiglitz (1974) and Salop and Salop (1976) discuss the relationship between the labor market internal to the firm and the external market.

Chapter 4

1. For an overview of Rath see Chapter 7. Byers Transport is described in Long (1979).
2. Pioneer Chain Saw has been documented in the Guardian, October 31, 1978; Tembec is described in more detail in Chapter 7.
3. See, for example, Thompson and Hart (1972).
4. The 'Benn' cooperatives are documented in Coates (1976), McKay and Barr (1976), and Eccles (1981): see Chapter 8.
5. The case of Youngstown is described, along with a number of other US examples, in Frieden (1979). For a detailed study and assessment, see also Policy and Management Associates, Inc. (1978). The Ford case is discussed in *The Financial Times* 23 October 1981 and *The Wall Street Journal*, 9, 22, 24 and 30 November 1981. For a discussion of the UK cases see Co-operative Development Agency, *Annual Report*, (1981) Appendix 2. pp. 23-4.

6. Lip is described by de Virien (1975), Maine and Piaget (1973).
7. See Laurent and Gautier (1978), also Chapter 7.
8. See Chapter 5: this feature of US labor ideology is noted also by Stern and Hammer (1978). As described in Chapter 2, however, there are indications that the unfettered rights of capital in this regard may come to be challenged in the US also.
9. See Greenwood (1977).
10. See Gurdon (1979).
11. Long (1979).
12. Policy and Management Associates, Inc. (1978).
13. Such was the experience of the Scottish Daily News. Responses to a survey of its workforce were especially critical of a BBC documentary which, they claimed, prejudiced its commercial prospects by '. . . making us look like a bunch of communists'. Jack Spriggs of Kirkby admitted that he had wanted a private takeover to enable unions to continue their traditional role but that Benn would only provide support through a cooperative: see Eccles (1981) p. 95.
14. *The Guardian*, November 1, 1974. Despite the rhetoric, Kirkby workers were reluctant to abandon systems of target setting and demarcation which undoubtedly hindered the further expansion of output: Eccles (1981).
15. *The Times*, January 12, 1975.
16. See Chapter 8, and Policy and Management Associates, Inc. (1978).
17. To cite one US example: although decline of the Jamestown manufacturing base was undoubtedly being accelerated by poor labor relations (see Chapter 5), union representatives attributed it to the attempts of manufacturers to hold wages low by keeping out new business.
18. Rothschild-Whitt (1981) cites one example here of Colonial Press, a publisher in Clinton, Massachusetts, which was acquired by Sheller-Globe (a maker of auto parts and school buses) in 1974 and closed three years later. Colonial was charged $900,000 per year in return for a management who knew little of publishing. Although Colonial had no known problem with theft, Sheller, as part of corporate policy, required it also to construct a security fence and hire 22 guards to search workers.
19. *Guardian op cit.*
20. Estimates are due to the Canadian Paperworkers Union.
21. Ross (1980). For an update on Roth, see *Wall Street Journal*, 2 December 1981.
22. For a general overview of the potential impact of employee ownership on productivity, see Frieden (1978) and the studies cited in Chapter 6.
23. Rothschild-Whitt (1981), p. 11.
24. The case of S.W. Hart is described in the *West Australian*, 18 August 1975, *Canberra Times*, 30 August 1975, and *Rydges Magazine*, July 1979.
25. *Financial Times*, January 11, 1977. Eccles (1981) suggests however, that restrictive practices persisted in Kirkby, and that skilled (as opposed to semi-skilled) workers were loath to perform lower-status tasks.
26. *Sunday Times*, June 4, 1978.
27. See Long (1979), p. 114.
28. Responses to surveys; see Chapter 8. A similar phenomenon is noted in accounts of Tembec cited in Chapter 7.
29. Data on the distribution of shareholding and its relationship to control in

employee-owned firms may be found in Conte and Tannenbaum (1978).

30. Select Committee on Small Business (1979), Section VII.
31. Stern, Wood and Hammer (1979), p. 70.
32. Select Committee on Small Business (1979), p. iv.
33. Kester (1980), Tables 3.1, 2 and 3. The present discussion of Malta is based on this excellent work.
34. Ibid, Ch. 9.
35. Ibid, p. 350.
36. Ibid, p. 350.

Chapter 5

1. This interpretation is supported by the eagerness of US banks to lend internationally to countries of *all* political complexions – provided borrowers are considered to be creditworthy.
2. Trade union perspectives are discussed further in Chapters 4 and 6.
3. See for instance, Antoni (1978), Oakeshott (1978) and Thornley (1981).
4. This section benefited from discussions with Tim Morris.
5. Hartz (1955), pp. 5–6.
6. Mann (1970).
7. The 'Oxford School' refers to the liberal pluralist tradition pursued by a group of industrial relations specialists in the 1960s. It includes such scholars as Hugh Clegg and Alan Fox, although Fox's work developed away from this tradition in the early 1970s.
8. Grob, G. (1961), p. 177.
9. These were contained in a 11-point program which was ratified in 1893 and rejected in 1895.
10. Clegg (1976), p. 103.
11. Gompers, S. (1941).
12. Commons (1921), pp. 522–34.
13. Ibid, p. 527.
14. Perlman (1928), p. 154.
15. Ibid, pp. 161–2.
16. Ibid, p. 168.
17. Hawkins (1972), p. 43.
18. Hofstatder (1954) p. 254.
19. See, e.g. Latta (1978).
20. Blasi, J. and Whyte, W. (1981), 'Worker Ownership and Public Policy', paper delivered at the International Conference on Producer Cooperatives, Institute of Economic and Social Studies, Copenhagen, Denmark. *Broadening the Ownership of New Capital: ESOPs and Other Alternatives*, Joint Economic Committee, Congress of the US, Government Printing Office, Washington, D.C., Nadal, M. (1976), *Corporations and Public Accountability*, Heath, Lexington, *Personal Wealth*, IRS. 1976.
21. *Congressional Record*, vol. 127, no. 507, April 7, 1981.
22. *Congressional Record*, vol. 127, no. 50, March 27, 1981. Allowance for productive wealth held through intermediaries might, however, show a less concentrated profile.
23. *Congressional Record* (1978).
24. *Congressional Record* (1979).
25. Ibid.

26. There are potentially four sources of public funds for employees wishing to buy their business: EDA's title IX program, program 7a of the Small Business Administration, Farmer's Home Business and Industrial Loans and Loans to Producer Cooperatives from the Cooperative Bank. The actual involvement of these sources in worker purchases has been small: for an evaluation, see Select Committee on Small Business: US Senate (1979) pp. 16–19.

27. US Senate Small Business Committee (1980), Small Business Development Act 1980. Report no. 96–1087, Washington, D.C., Government Printing Office 1980.

28. *Chrysler Corporation Loan Guarantee Act* (1979), HR-5860.

29. *Congressional Record*, vol. 125, no. 183, Dec. 19, 1979, SI-9186.

30. Adlai Stevenson, Nov. 15, 1979, *Press Release*.

31. See, for example, Parkin (1973), Jessop (1973), McKensie and Silver (1968).

32. Westergaard (1970).

33. Ibid, p. 120.

34. *Bankruptcy: General Annual Report* (1977), HMSO, London.

35. *The Daily Telegraph*, 26 July 1974; see also, *The Financial Times*, 8 November 1974, and *The Times*, 23 December 1976.

36. *The Daily Telegraph*, op. cit.

37. *Sixth Report of the Committee on Public Accounts*, (1976).

38. See, *Industrial Democracy* (1968): a statement by the National Executive Committee to the Annual Conference of the Labour Party, London; *Industrial Democracy* (1972), Labour Party Research Department Information Paper no. 27, London; *Industrial Democracy* (1974): a statement of policy by the Trade Union Congress, London; *The Community and the Company* (1974), Labour Party Green Paper, London.

39. The ample documentation setting out official Labour policy *vis a vis* industrial democracy includes: *Industrial Democracy* (1968), *Industrial Democracy* (1972), *Industrial Democracy* (1974). *The Inland Revenue Press Release* Dep. of Trade, London, 2 February 1978, which favors profit sharing, is correctly seen as Liberal Party policy. Worker participation has been advanced within an explicitly managerial framework by Flanders (1964), and Daniel and McIntosh (1972), although its managerial potential is not lost on those espousing it primarily for ideological reasons.

40. Mandel, Institute of Workers Control, Pamphlet No. 10.

41. *International Socialist* (1974).

42. Coates and Topham (1974).

43. Coates (1971), p. 12.

44. See McKay and Barr (1976), Coates (1976) and Eccles (1981).

45. Mackie (1976), p. 109.

46. Benn, T.I.W.C. Pamphlet no. 45, p. 5.

47. We have managed to obtain detailed perspectives from three British government ministers, and from prominent individuals involved in the funding.

48. This was certainly the case of Upper Clyde Shipbuilders in Britain, and Lip in France, see Thompson and Hart (1972) and Maine and Piaget (1973).

49. Benn (1976), p. 76.

50. Private communication between government minister and the authors,

June 1977. For Benn's views on industrial democracy and on the co-operatives see Bodington (1974), Benn (1975 and 1976).

51. Benn (1975), p. 7.
52. Private communication between government minister and authors, June 1977.
53. Ibid.
54. See, *The Times*, 5 March 1974, and *Labour Party Manifesto*, February 1974, pp. 2–4.
55. See, *The Times*, 4 March 1974: 'The Fund is likely to ask the British government to commit itself to a "convincing policy" to reduce the risk of wage-led inflation, particularly if most of the miners' demands are conceded.'
56. *Conservative Party Manifesto*, February 1974, p. 41.
57. Because of the miners' strike, power stations were deprived of their fuel, which led to a power shortage. As a result, British industry went on a three-day working week. It was this which prompted Heath, then the Prime Minister, to call a general election fought under the banner: 'Who governs Britain, the government or a trade union?'
58. The 'social contract' amounted to an agreement between the Labour Party and the trade unions under which the trade unions were to be consulted on economic policy in return for accepting voluntary constraints on collective bargaining.
59. See Lipsey (1977).
60. Between 1970 and February 1974 the Scottish National Party had gained six seats, four from the Conservatives and two from Labour.
61. Private communication from Benn to the authors, August 1977.
62. Private communication from government minister to the authors, June 1972.
63. See Edwards, S. (1971); Antoni, A. (1970); Thornley (1981).
64. SCOP and its associated cooperatives are described by Antoni (1978), Demoustier (1981) and Oakeshott (1978).
65. See, for instance, Bradley and Gelb (1981).
66. *Community at Work* (1977), and Meek and Whyte (1980).
67. The work of the CDA is described in its *Annual Report* (1981) 31 March HMSO, London. The experience of Kirkby Manufacturing suggests that such an organisation might have played an important role in helping the firm to realise its cooperative potential.

Chapter 6

1. Stern, Wood and Hammer (1979), Policy and Management Associates, Inc. (1978).
2. See Cole (1979) for a discussion of quality circles in the context of comparing US and Japanese industry. Numerous examples of successful contributions emanating from such groups could be cited. One case investigated in 1980 by an author involved the corrosion of a small washer which persistently led to the adulteration and rejection of product batches at a chemical plant. A simple suggestion to change the washer material was made, reducing wastage considerably at negligible cost.
3. How prolonged closure would affect the attitudes of workers is not clear.

On the one hand, a survival struggle might develop ideological commitment along the lines suggested by Moorhouse (1976) and Lane and Roberts (1971). Alternatively collapse might condition employees to accept conventional management more readily for job security. Depending on ideological predisposition, different individuals could conceivably follow divergent paths in the course of a transition, the radicals becoming more radical and the conservatives more conservative.

4. More specifically, the 'once-and-for-all' condition provides a useful shelter to government in the event of repeated requests for funding, see Eccles (1981), pp. 129–30, for the example of Kirkby.

5. See Chapter 8, also the General Motors case described in *Forbes* 23 November 1981, pp. 41–2.

6. See Select Committee on Small Business (1979), pp. 15–16.

7. See the results of the 1975 Hart Poll, cited in Rifkin (1977).

8. See Ellerman (1979), Ellermann and Mackin (1980) and Long (1979) for discussion of the union role in worker-owned enterprises. The case of Manuest in Chapter 7 also illustrates the weakening of union power due to a failure to adapt to its new role. Whyte notes that surveys show a large majority of employee-owners in previously unionised plants still to perceive a need for union representation, but qualifies this by the caveat concerning the change of union role: Whyte, W.F. (1978), 'Statement in Support of the Voluntary Job Preservation and Community Stabilisation Act', *Congressional Record*, June 19, PE 3327.

9. See Shirom (1972).

10. Welsh TUC interest led to their sponsoring a study of Mondragon in 1980. Attitudes of the Mondragon workforce to unions are discussed in Bradley and Gelb (1982). More ominously for the union position, workers in the control group of local capitalist firms surveyed for that study expressed more enthusiasm for a cooperative route to labor relations than for a strong union role. Stern, Wood and Hammer (1979), p. 189, note the reluctance of US unions to support the Voluntary Job Preservation Act, and the tension between locals and national (or international) headquarters raised by the issue of employee ownership. American unions did not, however, actually oppose the Act as had been feared by its sponsors. See, also, Select Committee on Small Business (1979), p. 12. Moves by the United Auto Workers to permit local variations from nationally negotiated positions are discussed in *The Wall Street Journal* 10 December 1981.

11. For information on the plywood cooperatives, see Berman (1967). These as well as other case studies are also reported in Zwerdling (1978).

12. Select Committee on Small Business (1979), p. 14.

13. Ibid, p. 19.

14. *Congressional Record*, 25 August, 1978, PE 3328.

15. See Thomas and Logan (1981) for an assessment of Mondragon relative to its environment: also Bradley and Gelb (1981a), (1982), (1982a). A most readable description of Mondragon may be found in Oakeshott (1978).

16. *Congressional Record*, 19 June, 1978, p. E 3326: testimony of William Foote Whyte. See, also, Aldrich and Stern (1978).

17. *Congressional Record*, 19 June, 1978, p. E 3326.

18. This was discussed in Chapter 4: see especially Zwerdling (1980).

19. *Wall Street Journal*, 2 December, 1981.

Chapter 7

1. 'No loans are to be authorised except when a feasibility study indicates that there is a reasonable chance that the company can become viable.' *Congressional Record*, vol. 125, no. 17, 15 February 1979.

2. See Aldrich and Stern (1978); Long (1977), (1978), (1979); Meek and Whyte (1980); Stern and O'Brien (1977); Stern and Comstock (1978); Stern and Hammer (1979), (1980); Stern *et al* (1979); Whyte (1976), (1980); Gurdon (1979), Zwerdling (1978), (1980), Frieden (1979), Ross (1980). For the recent cases involving General Motors and Ford see Sloan (1981), *Financial Times* 23 October 1981 and *Wall Street Journal* 9, 22 and 30 November 1981.

3. Jimm Zarello Channis of Clark UAW local. *Forbes*, 23 November 1981, p. 41.

4. See, e.g., *Congressional Record*, vol. 125, no. 17, 15 February 1979.

5. Ibid.

6. See, for example, Zwerdling (1978, 1980).

7. The mine's property tax constituted 50 percent of the total tax income for the town of Lowell. It also straddled two counties, contributing to them $100,000 in taxes. The unemployment rate in the area at the time of collapse was 12 percent.

8. See *Congressional Record*, vol. 124, no. 94, 19 June 1978; and Long (1979).

9. GAF's asking price was a low $650,000, but it eventually sold the company for $450,000.

10. Despite the 100 percent loan guarantee, there always existed a high degree of skepticism on the part of the banks. Their loan was technically granted to the Community Development Corporation and not to workers themselves. The company was purchased by workers on 13 March 1975.

11. See Zwerdling (1978).

12. See, *Congressional Record*, vol. 124, no. 94, 19 June 1978.

13. Gurdon (1979) suggests that this might have been because of another attempt on the part of the workers to unionise the plant.

14. See Zwerdling (1978), p. 69.

15. Only 18 percent of the local population was involved in manufacturing and this was steadily decreasing. In 1976, the town's unemployment rate was 10 percent, comparable with that for New York State as a whole.

16. Quoted in Gurdon (1979), p. 39.

17. Through a local banker, Peter Waite, Cox arranged a meeting with the New York Business Development Corporation, a semi-public concern owned by the state banks and designed to handle applications which do not qualify for standard commercial loans.

18. Gurdon, op. cit., p. 39.

19. Ninety percent guaranteed by the Small Business Association, 4.66 percent by two individually named managers, and the unlimited guarantees of the company president and his wife. The loan from the N.Y. Business Development Corporation was guaranteed by the company president and his wife.

20. For a discussion of Rath see Sklar (1982), Whyte and Blasi (1981), Blasi (1981), and *The Wall Street Journal*, 2 December 1981.

21. This account of Tembec Forest Products draws on Shiller (1978), Brassard (1974), Challenge for Change (1977), and benefits from interviews with

Serge Lord, Director of Education, Canadian Paperworkers Union, December 1980.

22. House sales may not have been encouraged deliberately because of any long-standing plan to close the mill. However, it is significant that CIP's refusal to modernise its Temiscaming plant had led to the departure of Jack Stevens and Jim Chantler, later to become founders of Tembec.

23. The capital-intensive nature of pulp milling (about $100,000 per job in 1978) meant, of course, that workers' saving could never finance more than a small fraction of the equipment. It also weakens the case for support of such plants on general employment grounds, as the cost per job is likely to be high. This criticism applies equally to attempts, particularly in the US, to save steel and similar heavy industrial plants as opposed to lighter, more labor intensive industry. On the other hand, low mobility may reduce leakages of subsidisation and minimise distortions.

24. Quoted in Shiller (1978), p. 29.

25. These estimates are due to the Canadian Paperworkers' Union.

26. Ibid.

27. Charlie Carpenter, President of Local 233.

28. This account of Manuest draws on Laurent and Gautier (1978), a survey carried out by the authors in July 1979 and interviews with key management and union personnel.

29. Even in 1979, company officials claimed to have been receiving bills for payments on television rentals, etc, which had been contracted by the previous owners.

30. Private communications with Georges Laurent and authors, April 1979.

31. Ibid.

32. Ibid.

33. Ibid.

34. Ibid.

Chapter 8

1. Letter from F.D. Campbell, manager, Bank of Scotland Finance Co. Ltd, to SDN Action Committee, 22 April 1974.

2. University of Strathclyde, (1974).

3. See *Scottish News Enterprises* (1975), p. 24.

4. Section 9 of the *Industry Act* (1972) provides for the setting up of the IDAB to advise the Secretary of State in respect to all provisions of selective financial assistance to certain industries.

5. Letter from Benn, Secretary of State for Industry, to Mackie, chairman of the SDN Workers' Action Committee, 24 July 1974.

6. Letter from Mackie to Benn, 11 December 1974.

7. In a letter to the General Secretary of the STUC, Mackie suggests: 'The need for a newspaper of the Left such as we agreed ours would be, has shifted from one of urgency in the creating of employment in a trade that now has surplus labor, to one of fulfilling a political need,' 18 October 1974. To Benn he wrote: 'We have committed our newspaper to aligning itself to the Left and in support generally of the Labour movement,' 11 October 1974.

8. Letter from Len Murray, General Secretary, TUC, to E. Hooper. SDN Workers' Action Committee, 17 July 1974.

9. Letter from James Jack to all affiliated unions, September 1974.

10. '. . . the majority of the unions stated that they would not show a financial interest unless and until the print unions had first declared their support'. Mackie (1976), p. 120.

11. The Associate Society of Locomotive Engineers and Foremen (ASLEF) was an exception. Within a few weeks of receiving the Action Committee's appeal, Ray Buckton, The General Secretary, invested £5,000 on behalf of his union.

12. Letter from Sir Sidney Greene to Dennis Magee, SDN Workers' Action Committee.

13. Given the declining position of the newspaper industry, the evidence against the project and the almost unique position among national newspapers of the SDN as not being part of a large diversified commercial group, few of the workforce would have been optimistic purely because of external factors.

14. See Wedderburn (1965), Herron (1975), Mackay and Reid (1972), and Martin and Fryer (1973).

15. Department of Employment (1974) and (1975).

16. Ex-SDN In-depth Worker Survey (1977).

17. See Chapter 5.

18. Ex-SDN In-depth Worker Survey (1977).

19. McKay and Barr (1976), p. 85.

20. Board minutes, 13 April 1975, p. 3.

21. As described previously, our ex-SDN Worker Survey (1977) indicated that *initially* virtually the entire workforce believed the cooperative's chances of success to be high.

22. *The Times*, 22 March 1977.

23. *The Guardian*, 22 March 1977.

24. As in the case of some countries, notably Sweden prior to the economic slowdown of the mid-1970s: see, Whiting (1976), p. 50. Survey evidence revealed that the SDN workforce displayed marked reluctance to work outside the newspaper industry.

25. The impact of different leisure valuation on cost-benefit criteria is illustrated by Sen (1972). Our procedure, of analysing government options subject to constraints on changing *overall* policy, accords with the spirit of Sen's approach.

26. See minutes of the SDN Board, 1 September 1975: '. . . (The Department of Industry) will under no circumstances take the legal onus off the Directors of the company.' See also Eccles (1981) pp. 129–30 for the Act as applied to Kirkby.

27. *Scottish Daily Express* sales fell by a reported 150,000 following its move to Manchester, but only temporarily.

28. This conclusion assumes that the other projects did not need to employ the particular factors (labor, capital) employed by the SDN. However, this seems a very reasonable assumption: no such alternative uses for SDN factors were ever proposed to our knowledge. There were, after all, many other British unemployed, particularly in Glasgow. Further, the assumption that SDN workers successful in obtaining other (probably unskilled) employment would largely displace other unemployed Glaswegians implies that their actual work histories after SDN collapse are not important

determinants of the overall cost to the government. Had there been demand for newspaper workers following an initial 'clogging' of local markets on SDN collapse, the phasing of redundancy implied by the SDN intervention would have been advantageous.

29. For cost-benefit studies using distribution-weighted criteria, see Little and Scott (1976).
30. This assumption is suggested by the *Scottish Daily News Feasibility Study* (1974), section 8.1.
31. See for example, McKay and Barr (1976), p. 9.
32. The negative revenue effect depends on the extent to which SDN capital losses could be offset against capital gains. As the majority of shareholders did not possess other shares, the scope of such offsetting would probably have been limited to the few larger shareholders, notably Maxwell.
33. McKay and Barr (1976), pp. 32–3.
34. The difficulty relates to the observation by Williamson (1975), p. 44, that peer group organisation is likely to be more successful within an integrated-task group (production activities) than across individuals or groups carrying out essentially task-unrelated activities. The natural channels for communication in journalism are 'vertical' – product is attributable to individuals and carries the stamp of personality. Thus, it may not be a fertile field for cooperative organisation.

Bibliography

Akerlof, G. and Main, B. (1980), 'Unemployment Spells and Unemployment Experiences', *American Economic Review*, **70**, Dec.

Aldrich, H. and Stern, R.M. (1978), 'Social Structures and the Creation of Producers' Cooperatives', Paper presented at the IX World Congress of Sociology.

Antoni, A. (1970), *La Coopérative Ouvrière de Production*, Confederation Générale des Sociétés Ouvrières de Production, Paris.

Antoni, A. (1978), *La vie dans une Scop*, Confédération Générale des Sociétés Cooperative Ouvrières de Production, Paris.

Arrow, K. (1965), *Aspects of the Theory of Risk-Bearing*, Yrjo Jahnsson Foundation, Helsinki.

Bacon, R. and Eltis, W. (1976), *Britain's Economic Problem: Too Few Producers*, Macmillan, London.

Balassa, B. (1978), 'The New Protectionism and the International Economy', *Journal of Law and Economics*, **12**, Sept./Oct.

Bardhan, P. (1981), 'Interlinking Factor Markets and Agrarian Development: A Review of Issues', *Oxford Economic Papers*, vol. 32, no. 1.

Bartel, A.P. (1979), 'The Migration Decision: What Role Does Job Mobility Play?' *American Economic Review*, Dec. **69**, no. 5.

Bell, D. (1962), *The End of Ideology*, The Free Press, New York.

Benn, T., Pamphlet no. 45, Institute for Workers' Control, Nottingham.

Benn, T. (1975), 'Tony Benn Speaks at the IWC Rally', *Workers Control Bulletin* XXIII, Institute for Workers' Control, Nottingham.

Benn, T. (1976), 'The Industrial Context', in Coates, K. (ed.) (1976), *The New Worker Cooperatives*, Spokesman, Nottingham.

Berman, K. (1967), *Worker-Owned Plywood Cooperatives*, Pullmann, Washington State University Press.

Birch, D. (1979), 'The Job Generation Process', MIT (mimeo), Cambridge, Massachusetts.

Blackaby, F. (ed.) (1979), *De-Industrialization*, Heinemann Educational Books, London.

Blackburn, R. and Mann, M., (1979) *The Working Class in the Labor Market*, Cambridge University Press.

Blasi, J. (1981), 'Employee Ownership and Self-Management in Legislation and Social Policy', paper presented to the American Sociological Association Conference, 24 August 1981, Toronto, Canada.

Blasi, J. and Whyte, W.F. (1981), 'Worker Ownership and Public Policy', paper prepared for the International Conference on Producer Cooperatives (mimeo), Denmark.

Bluestone, B. and Harrison, B. (1980), 'Why Corporations Close Profitable Plants', *Working Papers for a New Society*, pp. 15–23, May-June, Cambridge, Massachusetts.

Bodington, J. (ed.) (1974), *Speeches of Tony Benn*, Spokesman, Nottingham.

Bradley, K. and Gelb, A. (1979), 'The Political Economy of "Radical" Policy: An Analysis of the Scottish Daily News Worker Cooperative', *British Journal of Political Science*, **9**.

Bradley, K. and Gelb, A. (1980), 'Worker Cooperatives as Industrial Policy: The Case of the "Scottish Daily News" ', *Review of Economic Studies*, vol. XLVII.

Bradley, K. and Gelb, A. (1980a), 'The Radical Potential of Cash Nexus Breaks', *British Journal of Sociology*, vol. XXXI, no. 2, June.

Bradley, K. and Gelb, A. (1981), 'Motivation and Control in the Mondragon Experiment', *British Journal of Industrial Relations*, vol. XIX, no. 2. July.

Bradley, K. and Gelb, A. (1982), 'The Replication and Sustainability of the Mondragon Experiment', *British Journal of Industrial Relations*, vol. XX, no. 1.

Bradley, K. and Gelb, A. (1982a), 'The Mondragon Cooperatives: Guidelines for a Cooperative Economy?' in Jones, D. and Svejnar, J., *Participatory and Self-Managed Firms: Evaluating Economic Performance*, Lexington.

Brassard, C. (1974), 'Les Nouvelles Formes d'Interessement Dans l'Entreprise: Les Cas de Dupan-Sogefor, Cabano et Tembec', mimeo, April.

Brenner, H. (1976), *Estimating the Social Costs of National Economic Policy Implications for Mental and Physical Health, and Criminal Aggression*, paper prepared for the Joint Economic Committee, United States Congress, Washington, D.C. Oct. 26.

Bruno, M. (1981), 'Raw Materials, Profits and the Productivity Slowdown', (mimeo), Jerusalem.

Business Week (1980), June.

Cassing, M. (1980), 'Alternatives to Protectionism' in Leveson and Wheeler (eds.) (1980).

Challenge for Change (1977), *Temiscaming, Quebec*, National Film Board, Ottawa, Canada.

Chrysler Corporation Loan Guarantee Act, 1979, 96th Congress, 1st Session, HR-5860.

CIR. (1974), *Worker Participation and Collective Bargaining in Europe*, HMSO, London.

Clark, K.B. and Summers, L.H. (1979), 'Labor Market Dynamics and Unemployment: A Reconsideration', Brookings Papers on Economic Activity.

Clegg, H. (1976), *Trade Unionism Under Collective Bargaining*, Blackwell, Oxford.

Coates, K. (1971), *Industrial Democracy*, Spokesman, Nottingham.

Coates, K. and Topham, T. (1974), *The New Unionism*, Penguin Books, London.

Cole, R. (1979), *Work, Mobility and Participation*, University of California Press.

Commons (1921), *History of Labor in the United States*, Macmillan, New York.

Community and the Company, The (1974), Labour Party Green Paper, London.

Community at Work (1977), The Five Year Report of the Jamestown Area Labor-Management Committee, Jamestown.

Congressional Record (1978), vol. 124, no. 94, June 19.

Congressional Record (1979), vol. 125, no. 17, Feb. 15.

Conte, M. and Tannenbaum, A.B. (1978), 'Employee-Owned Companies: Is the Difference Measurable?' *Monthly Labor Review*, July.

Cordon, W.M. (1974), *Trade Policies and Economic Welfare*, Oxford University Press.

Corden, W.M. and Fels, G. (eds.) (1976), *Public Assistance to Industry: Protection and Subsidies in Britain and Germany*, Macmillan, London.

Co-operative Development Agency (1981), *Annual Report*, HMSO, March 31.

Crosland, C.A.R. (1956), *The Future of Socialism*, Jonathan Cape, London.

Dahrendorf, R. (1961), *Class and Class Conflict in Industrial Society*, Routledge and Kegan Paul, London.

Daniel, W.W. (1972), 'Whatever Happened to the Workers of Woolwich: a Survey of Redundancy in South East London', *Political and Economic Planning*, 38, Broadsheet 537, London.

Daniel, W.W. (1974), *A National Survey of the Unemployed*, PEP, vol. XL, Broadsheet no. 546, London.

Daniel, W.W., and McIntosh, N. (1972), *The Right to Manage*, PEP, London.

Demoustier, Daniele (1981), *Entre L'Efficacité et la Democratie*, Editions Entente, Paris.

Department of Employment (1974, 1975), *New Earnings Survey*, HMSO, London.

de Virien, F.H. (1975), *100,000 Montres sans patron*, Editions Calmann-Levy, Paris.

Dreze, J.H. (1979), *Human Capital and Risk Bearing*, Geneva paper on Risk and Accident Insurance, Association Internationale pour l'Etude de l'Economie de l'Assurance Génève, no. 12 June.

Eccles, T. (1981), *Under New Management*, Pan, London.

Economist (1977), 'Let's Go Where the Unions Aren't', July 4.

Edwards, R. (1979), *Contested Terrain: The Transformation of the Workplace in the Twentieth Century*, Basic Books, New York.

Edwards, S. (1971), *The Paris Commune 1871*, Eyre and Spottiswoode, London.

Ellerman, D. (1979), 'The Union as the Legitimate Opposition in an Industrial Democracy', (mimeo), ICA, Somerville, Mass., Dec.

Ellerman, D. and Mackin, C. (1980), 'Unions and Industrial Cooperatives: Past History and Future Prospects', (mimeo), ICA, Somerville, Mass., March.

Flanders, A. (1964), *Collective Bargaining: Perspective for Change*, Faber, London.

Flanders, A. (1964), *The Fawley Productivity Agreement*, Faber, London.

Fox, A. (1974), *Beyond Contract: Work, Power and Trust Relations*, Faber, London.

Frank, R.H. and Freeman, R. (1976), 'The Distributional Consequences of Direct Foreign Investment', paper prepared for the Bureau of Internal Labor Affairs, Cornell University, (mimeo), Dec.

Frieden, K. (1979), *Productivity and Worker Participation*, National Center for Economic Alternatives, Washington, D.C.

Gennard, J. (1978), 'The Protection of Workers in Great Britain in the Case of Reductions of the Workforce in the Undertaking', report prepared for the International Labor Office, LSE, London.

Gilman, H. (1978), 'The Economic Costs of Worker Dislocation: An Overview', International Labor Office, U.S. Department of Labor, Washington, D.C.

Glazer, D. and Rice, K. (1980), 'Crime, Age and Employment', *American Sociological Review*, **24**, Oct.

Glenday, G. and Jenkins, G.P. (1980), 'Industrial Dislocation and the Cost of Labor Adjustment', York University, (mimeo), May.

Goldthorpe, J., Lockwood, D., Blechhofer, F. and Platt, J. (1968) and (1969), *The Affluent Worker Study*, 3 Volumes, Cambridge University Press.

Golt, S. (1980), 'The New Protectionism', in Leveson and Wheeler (eds.).

Gompers, S. (1941), *The American Labor Movement*, American Federation of Labor, Washington DC.

Greenwood, J. (1977), *Worker Sit-ins and Job Protection*, Gower Press.

Gretton, J. (1972), 'To Sit or Not to Sit?' *New Society*, vol. 20, no. 501.

Grob, G.N. (1961), *Workers and Utipia*, Evanston, Illinois.

Gunn, C. (1980), 'Towards Worker Control', *Working Papers for a New Society*, May-June, Cambridge, Massachusetts.

Gurdon, M.A. (1979), *The Structure of Ownership: The Implications for Employee Influence and Organisation Design*, unpublished Ph.D. thesis, Cornell University.

Harrison, B. and Kanter, S. (1976), 'The Great State Robbery', *Working Papers for a New Society*, Spring.

Hartz, L. (1955), *The Liberal Tradition in America*, Harcourt, Brace and World, Inc., New York, NY.

Hawkins, K. (1972), *Conflict and Change: Aspects of Industrial Relations*, HRW, London Management Books.

Herron, F. (1975), *Labor Markets in Crisis*, Macmillan, London.

Hofstatder, R. (1954), *The American Political Tradition and the Man Who Made It*, Vintage Books, New York.

Hoxie, P.F. (1966), *Trade Unionism in the United States*, Russell and Russell, New York.

Industrial Democracy (1968): A statement by the National Executive Committee to the Annual Conference of the Labour Party, Labour Party, London.

Industrial Democracy (1972): Labour Party Research Department, Information Paper no. 27, London, Feb.

Industrial Democracy (1974): A statement of the Policy by the Trade Union Congress, TUC, London.

Jacobson, L.S. (1976), *Earnings Losses of Workers Displaced from Manufacturing Industries*, Public Research Institute Professional Paper 167, Washington, D.C., Nov.

Jenkins, G., Glenday, G., Evans, J. and Montmarquette, C. (1978), 'Trade Adjustment Assistance: The Costs of Adjustment and Policy Proposals', paper prepared for the Department of Industry, Trade and Commerce, June.

Jessop, B. (1973), *Traditionalism, Conservatism and the British Political Culture*, Allen and Unwin.

Joint Report of the Committee on Environment and Public Work and the Committees on Banking, Housing and Urban Affairs, US Senate (1979), US Printing Office, Washington, D.C., July 27.

Jones, D. (1977), 'Output Employment and Labor Productivity in Europe Since 1955', *National Institute Economic Review*, August.

Jones, D.C. (1979), 'Producer Cooperatives in Industrialised Western Economies', Feb. 12, (mimeo), Hamilton College, Clinton, New York.

Kester, G. (1980), *Transition to Workers' Self-Management: Its Dynamics in the Decolonising Economy of Malta*, Institute of Social Studies, The Hague.

Kochan, T. (1979), 'The Federal Role in Private Dislocations: Towards a Better Mix of Public and Private Efforts', (mimeo), US Department of Labor, Washington, D.C.

Komarovsky, M. (1971), *The Unemployed Man and His Family. The Effect of Unemployment Upon the Status of the Man in fifty-nine Families*, Octagon Books, New York.

Lane, T. and Roberts, K. (1971), *Strike at Pilkington*, Fontana.

Latta, G. (1979), *Profit Sharing, Employee Stock Ownership, Savings and Asset Formation in the Western World*, IRU, University of Pennsylvania.

Laurent, G. and Gautier, J. (1978), 'Reprise en société coopérative ouvrière de production SCOP d'une entreprise en liquidation dans le secteur de meuble: Manuest', Centre de coopérative, Ecole des hautes études commerciales, Montreal, Canada.

Leibenstein, H. (1966), 'Allocative Efficiency versus X-Efficiency', *American Economic Review*, June.

Let Us Work Together: Labor's Way Out of the Crisis (1974), Labour Party Manifesto, Oct., London.

Leveson, I. and Wheeler, J. (eds.) (1980), *Western Economies in Transition: Structural Change and Adjustment Policies in Industrial Countries*, Westview Press, Colorado and Croom Helm, London.

Lipsey, R.C. (1977), 'Wage Price Controls: How To Do A Lot Of Harm by Trying To Do A Little Good', in Walker, M. (ed.), *Which Way Ahead?*, Frazer Institute, Vancouver.

Little, I.M.D. and Scott, M.Fg. (1976), *Using Shadow Prices*, Heinemann Educational Books, London.

Long, R.J. (1977), *The Effects of Employee Ownership on Organisational Identification, Job Attitudes and Organisational Performance: An Exploratory Study*, unpublished Ph.D. thesis, Cornell University.

Long, R.J. (1978), 'The Effects of Employee Ownership on Organisational Identification, Employee Job Attitudes and Organisational Performance: A Tentative Framework and Empirical Findings', *Human Relations*, vol. 31, no. 1.

Long, R.J. (1979), 'Employee Ownership and Attitudes Towards the Union', *Industrial Relations Industrielles*, vol. 33, no. 2.

Mackay, O.I. and Reid, G.L. (1972), 'Redundancy, Unemployment and Manpower Policy', *Economic Journal*, 82.

Mackie, A. (1976), 'The Scottish Daily News', in Coates, K. (ed.) (1976), *The New Worker Co-ops*, Spokesman, Nottingham.

Mackin, C. (1981), 'The Social Psychology of Ownership: Moral Atmosphere in a Cooperatively Owned Workforce', Harvard Graduate School of Education, March.

Maddison, A.C. (1980), 'Economic Growth and Structural Change in the Advanced Countries', in Leveson, J. and Wheeler, I. (eds.) (1980), *Western Economies in Transition*, Westview Press.

Maine, E. and Piaget, C. (1973), *Lip 73*, Editions du Sunil, Paris.

Mandel, E., *A Socialist Strategy for Western Europe*, Pamphlet no. 10, Institute of Workers Control, Nottingham.

Mann, M. (1970), 'The Social Cohesion of Social Democracy', *American*

Sociological Review, no. 35.

Mann, M. (1973), *Consciousness and Action in the Western Working Class*, Macmillan, London.

Martin, J.P. (1978), 'X-Inefficiency, Managerial Effort and Production', *Economica*, **43**, Aug.

Martin, M. and Fryer, R.H. (1973), *Redundancy and Paternalist Capitalism*, Allen and Unwin, London.

McKay, R. and Barr, B. (1976), *The Scottish Daily News*, Canongate, Edinburgh.

McKensie, R. and Silver, A. (1968), *Angels in Marble: Working Class Conservatism in Urban England*, Heinemann Educational Books, London.

Meek, C. and Whyte, W.F. (1980), 'The Jamestown Model of Cooperative Problem Solving', Cornell University, (mimeo).

Michels, R. (1915), *Political Parties: a Sociological Study of the Oligarchical Tendencies of Modern Democracy*, Hearst's International Library Company, New York.

Miliband, R. (1969), *The State in Capitalist Society*, Merlin, London.

Moorhouse, H.F. (1976), 'Attitudes to Class and Class Relationships in Britain', *Sociology*.

Nelson, R. (1980), 'Technical Advance and Productivity Growth: Retrospect, Prospect, and Policy Issues', in Leveson and Wheeler (eds.) (1980).

Nightingale, D. (1977), 'The Concept and Application of Employee Participation in Canada', *Labor Gazette*, April.

Oakeshott, R. (1978), *The Case for Worker Co-ops*, Routledge and Kegan Paul, London.

OECD (1975), *Adjustment for Trade: Studies on Industrial Adjustment Problems and Policies*, Paris.

Ohlin, G. (1978), 'Subsidies and Other Industrial Aids', in Warnecke, S.J. *et al*, *International Trade and Industrial Policies*, Macmillan, London.

Packer, A.H. (1980), Statement before the Oversight Subcommittee, Committee on Ways and Means, US House of Representatives, Feb. 21.

Pagoulatos, E. and Sorensen, R. (1980), 'Industrial Policy and Firm Behavior in an International Context', in Leveson and Wheeler (eds.) (1980).

Parkin, F. (1973), *Class Inequality and Political Order*, Paladin, London.

Passfield, Sidney James Webb (1911), *History of Trade Unionism*, Longman Green and Company, London and New York.

Perlman, S. (1928), *Theory of Labor Movements*, Augustus M. Kelly, New York.

Piaget, C. (1973), *Lip*, Editions Stock, Paris.

Policy and Management Associates, Inc. (1978), *Socioeconomic Costs and Benefits of the Community-Worker Ownership Plan to the Youngton-Warren SMSA*.

Public Money in Private Industry (1972), HMSO, London.

Reum, W.R. and Reum, S.M. (1978), 'Employee Stock Ownership Plans: Pluses and Minuses', *Harvard Business Review*, July-Aug.

Rifkin, J. (1977), *Own Your Own Job*, Bantam Books, New York.

Rifkin, J. and Barber, R. (1978), *The North Will Rise Again: Pensions, Politics and Power in the 1980s*, Beacon Press, Boston.

Rohan, T. (1977), 'Requiem for a Factory', *Industry Week*, Jan.

Rohatyn, F. (1980), 'The State of the Nation's Industry – All Talk and No

Action', *Washington Post*, July 20.

Ross, I. (1980), 'What Happens When the Employees Buy the Company', *Fortune*, June 2.

Rothschild-Whitt, J. (1979), 'The Collectivist Organisation: An Alternative to Rational-Bureaucratic Models', *American Sociological Review*, **44**, Aug.

Rothschild-Whitt, J. (1981), 'The Social and Economic Context of Worker-Ownership in the US.: Varieties of Ownership and Control', paper prepared for the International Conference on Producer Cooperatives, Denmark, (mimeo), Yale University.

Sainsbury, D. (1981), *Government and Industry: A New Partnership*, Fabian Research Series, no. 347, London, Jan.

Salop, J. and Salop, S. (1976), 'Self-Selective Turnover in the Labor Market', *Quarterly Journal of Economics*, **90**.

Schoof, M. (1977), *Cooperatives*, National Center for Economic Alternatives, Washington, D.C.

Scottish News Enterprises (1975), Glasgow, 17 March.

Select Committee on Small Business: US Senate (1979), *The Role of the Federal Government and Employee Ownership of Business*, U.S. Government Printing Office, Washington, D.C., March 20.

Sen. A.K. (1972), 'Control Areas and Accounting Prices: An Approach to Economic Evaluation', *Economic Journal* LXXXII

Sheffrin, S. (1977), *The Costs of Continued Unemployment*, National Center for Economic Alternatives, Washington, D.C.

Shiller, K. (1978), 'Worker Participation in Management Decision Making: Tembec Forest Products, Ltd.', University of Montreal (mimeo), April 10.

Shirom, A. (1972), 'The Industrial Relations History of Industrial Cooperatives in the United States, 1880–1935', *Labor History*, Fall.

Sixth Report of the Committee on Public Accounts (1976), HMSO, HC 584.

Sklar, S., (1982), 'An Experiment in Worker Ownership', *Dissent*, Winter.

Sloan, A. (1981), 'Go Forth and Compete!', *Forbes*, November 23.

Smith, D. and McGuigan, P. (1979), *Towards a Public Balance Sheet*, National Center for Economic Alternatives, Washington, D.C.

Stern, R.N. and Comstock, P. (1978) 'Employee Stock Ownership Plans (ESOP's): Benefits For Whom?' New York State School of Industrial and Labor Relations Key Issue Series No. 23, Cornell University, New York.

Stern, R.M. and Hammer, T.H. (1978), 'Buying Your Job: Factors Affecting the Success or Failure of Employee Acquisition Attempts', *Human Relations* **31**, no. 12.

Stern, R.M. and Hammer, T.H. (1980), 'Employee Ownership: Implications for the Organisational Distribution of Power', *Academy of Management Journal*, vol. 23, no. 1.

Stern, R.M. and O'Brien, R.A. (1977), 'National Unions and Employee Ownership', Cornell University, (mimeo).

Stern, R.M., Wood, K.H. and Hammer, T.H. (1979), *Employee Ownership in Plant Shutdowns*, Upjohn Institute for Employment Research, Kalamazoo, Michigan.

Stern, R.M. (1978), 'The Union Under Employee Ownership', paper presented at the 1978 Meeting of the American Psychological Association, Toronto, Canada.

Stiglitz, J. (1974), 'Alternative Theories of Wage Determination and Unemployment in LDCs: The Labor Turnover Model', *Quarterly Journal of Economics*, **88**, May.

Stillman, D. (1978), 'The Devastating Impact of Plant Relocations', *Working Papers for a New Society*, July-Aug.

Stout, D. (1979), 'De-Industrialisation and Industrial Policy', in Blackaby, F. (ed.), *De-Industrialisation*, Heinemann Educational Books, London.

Swift, R.A. (1975), *The NLRB and Management Decision Making*, IRU, University of Pennsylvania.

Thatcher, A. (1979), 'Labor Supply and Employment Trends', in Blackaby, F. (ed.) (1979), *De-Industrialisation*, Heinemann Educational Books, London.

Thomas, H. and Logan, C. (1981), *Mondragon: An Economic Analysis*, Allen and Unwin.

Thompson, W. and Hart, F. (1972), *The UCS Work-In*, Lawrence and Wishart, London.

Thornley, J. (1981), *Worker Cooperatives: Jobs and Dreams*, Heinemann.

Toffler, A. (1970), *Future Shock*, Bodley Head, London.

UK Department of Employment (1978), 'Age and Redundancy', *Department of Employment Gazette*, Sept.

United States Comptroller General (1978a), *Report to the Congress of the United States*, HRD 77–152, Jan. 11.

United States Comptroller General (1978b), *Report to the Congress of the United States*, HRD 78–153, May 8.

University of Strathclyde (1974), *Scottish Daily News Feasibility Study*, University of Strathclyde, Glasgow.

Vanek, J. (ed.), (1975), *Self-Management: The Economic Liberation of Man*, Penguin Books, London.

Wedderburn, D. (1965), 'Redundancy and the Railwaymen', University of Cambridge, Department of Applied Economics, Occasional Paper no. 1, Cambridge University Press.

Westergaard, J. (1970), 'The Re-discovery of the Cash Nexus', in Miliband, R. and Saville, J. (eds.), *The Socialist Register*, Merlin.

Whiting, A. (ed.), (1976), *The Economics of Industrial Subsidies*, HMSO, London.

Wilcock, R.C. and Franke, W.H. (1963), *Unwanted Workers – Permanent Layoffs and Long-Term Unemployment*, The Free Press, Glencoe, New York.

Williamson, O. (1975), *Markets and Hierarchies: Analysis and Antitrust Implications*, The Free Press, New York.

Whyte, W.F. (1976), 'From Private to Employee Ownership: Notes for Transforming the Shut-Down Plant' (mimeo), Cornell University, Nov.

Whyte, W.F. (1980), 'Progress Report on United Transportation Union', Cornell University, Aug. 21.

Whyte, W.F., and Blasi J., (1981), 'Recent Developments in Worker Ownership and the Unions', discussion paper presented to a Conference on Worker Ownership and Unions, 26 June, 1982. Mimeo, Cornell University.

Young, S. and Lowe, A. (1975), *Intervention in a Mixed Economy*, Croom Helm.

Zwerdling, D. (1978). *Democracy at Work*, Association for Self-Management, Washington, D.C.

Zwerdling, D. (1980), 'Workers Turned Owners Find They're Still Just Workers', *The Washington Post*, May 11.

Index

This is designed chiefly as a subject index. Authors of references cited in the text are not included.